Palgrave Studies in Economic History is designed to illuminate and enrich our understanding of economies and economic phenomena of the past. The series covers a vast range of topics including financial history, labour history, development economics, commercialisation, urbanisation, industrialisation, modernisation, globalisation, and changes in world economic orders.

Palgrave Studies in Economic History

Series Editor
Kent Deng, London School of Economics, London, UK

Shan Shanne Huang

The Political Economy of Reforms and the Remaking of the Proletarian Class in China, 1980s–2010s

Demystifying China's Society and Social Classes in the Post-Mao Era

palgrave
macmillan

Shan Shanne Huang
United Nations Development
Programme
New York, NY, USA

ISSN 2662-6497 ISSN 2662-6500 (electronic)
Palgrave Studies in Economic History
ISBN 978-3-031-20454-8 ISBN 978-3-031-20455-5 (eBook)
https://doi.org/10.1007/978-3-031-20455-5

Cover credit: @ dowell/gettyimages

This Palgrave Macmillan imprint is published by the registered company Springer Nature Switzerland AG
The registered company address is: Gewerbestrasse 11, 6330 Cham, Switzerland

Dedicated to my grandfather- Li Qidong 李启东

Acknowledgements

I would like to thank my parents who have been consistently supporting me throughout my research and writing. I missed many major events with family. Thanks to their tolerance and love.

I would like to thank Professor Kent Deng's kind invitation on publishing this book. Many thanks to my three referees, Dr. Jeff Hass, Professor Shouhui Zhao and Professor Jinghan Zeng, for their recognition of my research and their valuable support for this book's proposal and comments on the draft. The same thanks also go to my Ph.D. supervisors, Professor Kerry Brown and Dr. Jan Knoerich. This book's manuscript is based on my Ph.D. dissertation. Thanks for their guidance during my Ph.D. research.

I also want to thank all the respondents of this research for sharing with me their history, life and work experiences, and to help and support me during the fieldwork research. This empirical study relies on their histories and memories to analyse the changes and differences of this specific state-owned enterprise before and after the Reform and Opening Up, and to tease out their varying sense of status.

I was born in Sichuan Province. In order to get higher education, I moved to Beijing and then relocated to Bristol and London. This book is for my hometown, my family and me. Almost a decade of living abroad let me have a deeply emotional connection with where I grew up and the people there. Wherever I will be in the future, this book will remind me of where I come from and who I am.

New York, USA
September 2022

Shan Shanne Huang

Contents

About the Author

Shan Shanne Huang is currently a fellow in management consultancy at United Nations Development Programme (Headquarters in New York, the USA). She is expecting to be awarded a Ph.D. in Chinese Studies Research and Sociology from King's College London. She completed her M.Sc. degree in Sociology at the University of Bristol. She is an experienced researcher with expertise in sociology, methodology and Chinese political economy. She has been invited to present her research at over ten international conferences in the UK, the USA, Japan, Norway and China. She is also the President of the British Postgraduate Network for Chinese Studies from 2019 to 2020.

Abbreviations

*ST Stock	Special Treatment Stock
CCP	Chinese Communist Party
CHMI	China Heavy Machinery Industry Association
EGC	E Group Corporation (Pseudonym for the fieldwork site)
GDP	Gross Domestic Product
HDI	Human Development Index
HR	Human Resources
IPO	Initial Public Offerings
PRC	People's Republic of China
RMB	Renmin Bi (Chinese currency, Yuan)
SASAC	State-Owned Assets Supervision and Administration Commission of the State Council
SINOMACH	China National Machinery Industry Corporation
SOEs	State-Owned Enterprises

List of Figures

List of Tables

CHAPTER 1

Introduction

On 1 July 2021, Xi Jinping stated in his speech at the conference of celebration of the one-hundredth anniversary of the founding of the Chinese Communist Party (CCP) that the Reform and Opening Up and socialist modernisation is one of the greatest achievements of the CCP.[1] In the speech, he said the People's Republic of China (PRC) "achieved the implementation from the highly centralised planned economic system to the dynamic system of a socialist market economy" (*shixian le cong gaodu jizhong de jihua jingji tizhi dao chongman huoli de shehui zhuyi shichang jingji tizhi*). Raised up in 1978, the Reform and Opening Up (*gaige kaifang*) has lasted for 44 years now, as has the state's reform of the economic system. As Xi mentioned in his speech, due to the reform of the economic system, China has become the second-largest economy in the world.

In the past four decades, China transferred from a planned economy which is copied the industrial development model from the Soviet Union. The characteristics of the Soviet Union model are the state-controlled economy and set the plans for market supply and demand (Bian et al., 2002; Walder, 2015; Whyte & Parish, 1985), an open market where

[1] *Xinhua* News. (2021). *Xi jinping: zai qingzhu zhongguo gongchandang chengli 100 zhounian dahui shang de jianghua*. 15th July, 2021. Available on 12th September, 2022, *vide*: http://www.xinhuanet.com/politics/leaders/2021-07/15/c_1127658385.htm.

S. S. Huang, *The Political Economy of Reforms and the Remaking of the Proletarian Class in China, 1980s–2010s*, Palgrave Studies in Economic History, https://doi.org/10.1007/978-3-031-20455-5_1

competitiveness and marketisation are introduced and the government monopoly is not as strong as it was before economic reforms. Many previous studies have researched this economic reform process and have found that due to the introduction of marketisation, state-owned enterprises (SOEs) in China faced the need for reform and restructuring to meet the updated market and emerging private and foreign-capital enterprises (Hong, 2004, pp. 23–42; Hurst, 2009; Lee, 2006, 2007; Wright, 2010). Many SOEs' monopolies in their own industry have weakened (Lardy, 1998). The focus of social life also changed from class conflict and struggle to economic development and benefits along this economic reform process (Lin, 2015, pp. 24–53; Yan, 2012). The working class, who were gloried and honoured by the state and the Communist Party for a long time since the establishment of the PRC, have now experienced great changes in their social status (Chen Feng, 2006, pp. 42–60; Chen Zhouwang, 2015, pp. 142–147; Gold et al., 2009, p. 6; Hurst & O'Brien, 2002, pp. 345–360; Lu, 2003; Pang & Qiu, 1989; Qiu, 2001, p. 23; Wright, 2010; Zhang Yi, 2004, p. 79; Zheng, 2002).

By evaluating factors that have influenced both SOEs and their workers during the economic reform era, dating from 1978 till today, this research argues for a re-emergence of the proletariat class in society despite what the government says. Moreover, the mapping of changes experienced by SOE workers allows this research to engage with the debate on how and why a Marxian class society has returned to China. The centrality of this study is that China's reforms have generated economic growth and efficiency at expense of ordinary workers' social standing and rights.

This research will prove that SOE was a utopian socialist idea created by the national state for the purpose of meeting the standard for the socialist enterprise. However, this idea did not meet the natural development of the market and economy and has led to improper operation and the enterprise's improper development. When the reform was put forward and applied to SOEs, it condemned the experiences learnt from the Soviet Union and the practices in China experienced the same failures. Meanwhile, SOEs' old traditions, for example the caring of its workers, can still be observed in today's China. In fact, it is an attempt to provide its employees with good welfare as it was before the SOE reform. However, the SOE reform made the workers' life more miserable than before. From both the enterprise's and the workers' side, they contradict the target of improving people's economic benefits and the main aim of SOE reform: to separate social responsibility from SOEs.

Under such circumstances, SOE workers are no longer a privileged group dubbed "the masters of socialist society". Rather, they have fallen back to the proletarian status of their pre-1949 counterparts. This means that SOE workers now sell their labour to factory owners for a wage and lose their previous "socialist welfare" from their enterprises who are now full-blooded capitalists in nature. Workers have dropped to the bottom of the factory hierarchy. If such once privileged workers from the privileged enterprises can be examined, a broader picture of the working class in society can be established. These points will be elaborated in the following chapters.

This study takes the advantage of information and opinions from the existing literature on SOEs, their workers and social changes in China under reforms, and provides first-hand fieldwork which was conducted in 2018 regarding an SOE in Sichuan. The findings show the interplay between SOEs, factory workers and society which challenges the conventional wisdom. The insight is micro-level with societal implications.

1.1 Research Background

Chinese State-Owned Enterprises

Chinese SOEs were adopted from the Soviet Union, and this can be reflected in the primary characteristics of SOEs in China, which concentrated investments on the expansion of heavy industry, simplified production and supply plans, fixed salaries according to the rank of workers and the welfare system (Bian et al., 2002; Shirk, 1993; Walder, 2015; Whyte & Parish, 1985; Xu Congwen, 2010).

Guided by experts from the Soviet Union, China had its 1st Five-Year Plan for developing the national economy (*diyige wunian jihua*) in 1953. This is also the beginning of the national industrialisation plan (Ye Shuzong, 2010, pp. 29–37). During the planning period (1953–1957), China followed the development path of socialist countries, prioritising the development of heavy industries (Chen Guoqing, 2000, pp. 7–10). Based on state ownership and relying on the highly centralised state power, China centralised and unified a plan for human resources, financial funding, property, industry and production, supply and marketing (Wang Huasheng, 1989, pp. 49–50). Shirk (1993, pp. 107–108) stated that the CCP set up China's National Economic Bureaucracy in 1953 to reflect their development priorities, which were industry over agriculture and heavy industry over light industry. This strategy for extensive growth was adopted from the Soviet Union, which concentrated investment on the expansion of the heavy industry. The bureaucratic structure favoured heavy industry over light. According to Shirk, Chinese leaders established an administrative structure that would give heavy industry the strongest voice and thereby produce policies favouring this industry. While there were approximately 15 industrial ministries, only a few were concerned with agriculture. Between 1949 and 1978, the value of heavy industrial output multiplied 90.6 times, while the agriculture and light industry only grew 2.4 times and 19.8 times, respectively (Dong Furen, 1982, pp. 5–7).

The financial support for heavy industry not only relates to factories, but also to essential construction and services that work with production. For instance, to support production, SOEs developed meal halls, food stalls, and shower and bath facilities for employees and their family members. Retail shops, grocery stores, barber shops, hair salons and even auditoriums and gymnasiums were built by SOEs for their employees. Some SOEs provided transportation for commuters who did not live on-site, while others organised and paid for periodic vacations for employees and family members (Walder, 1988). Walder's later studies (2015) showed that SOEs became integrated communities with employees living together on-site throughout their adult lives, raising their families together in housing complexes and staying after retirement. According to Walder's studies, SOEs acted as the housing provider for their employees.

In fact, the preference for the heavy industry had placed potential challenges for SOEs within the heavy industry sector. Having support from the policy and finance, these SOEs can make good use of these resources to develop the infrastructure, set up factories and workshops, purchase complete sets of equipment and improve the construction of production lines at the initial stage of establishment. Huang (2003) noted that SOEs held a large part of the investment, with better assets and privileged access to financing, market opportunities and quality personnel. Besides the advantages in production and construction, these SOEs can also use the funding to meet the needs of the workers to improve their life, which is what Walder mentioned above, where integrated communities were formed. However, once this preference no longer exists, these SOEs could not operate efficiently due to the financial burden and the lack of production capacity. For instance, these SOEs were required to generate their welfare funds from their profits. However, Lardy (1998) pointed out the fact that the average SOE's sum of bank debt, unpaid taxes, unfunded pension liabilities and net indebtedness to non-state firms far exceeded the value of its assets. Walder's research (1992, pp. 524–539) in Tianjin city strengthened this point by pointing out that over 85% of work units (*gongzuo danwei*) had meal services,[2] medical clinics and shower facilities; 66% had infant day care centres and libraries; 50% of units had auditoriums; more than 33% had organised sports teams; 25% had barber shops and on-site sports facilities; and 20% offered bus services for commuters.

The older the enterprise, the heavier the pension burden on the enterprise's budget and the less profitable the enterprise therefore became. Besides pensions for retirees, some SOEs provided health clinics and in-patient hospital services, kindergartens for pre-school children of employees, and sometimes even primary schools on-site. Therefore, the demand for reforms in SOEs is predictable according to policy changes.

The transformation from a planned economy to a market one is praised as a great achievement by socialism in China (Xi, 2021). The drama has been associated with SOEs which were a product of Mao's era when central planning was crude and simple. Such an industry-planned economy means buyers and their annual quotas of products for this enterprise are listed in the production plan; and supplies and factories that are permitted to purchase products are listed in the supply plan. From the two plans, it is not difficult to see that the entire industrial system was essentially an interlocking network of production and supply plans that created elaborate connections among enterprises and state purchasing agencies. This seems like the perfect match for each other's requests, while gaps between the production and supply plans were always there. Under these

[2] What is unit (*danwei*) and what is the function of unit system in China? Summarised from existing research, administrative units, public institutions and SOEs are at the centre of the redistribution system in cities as typical units, while rural grassroots organisations have some unit's characteristics, non-state sector does not belong to the category of unit. Unit is a special form of organisation and social regulation in China's urban society. It is the basic unit of social regulation and resource allocation. Unit has the meaning of the social structure, which means it is also a kind of social stratification system. The main characteristics of unit system are as follows: (1) The labourers' overall attachment to the workplace is essentially the individual's attachment to the state. Unit is incorporated into the state's administrative organisation structure, so it is the organisation means of the state's direct administrative management to the society and (2) it is the main place for members of society to participate in the political process (Li Meng et al., 1996; Li Lulu, 2002, pp. 23–32; Li Lulu et al., 1991, pp. 65–76; Liu Jianjun 2000; Lu Feng, 1989, pp. 71–88; Wang Huning, 1990; Zhang Yuqin, 2011, pp. 92–94).

circumstances, planners encouraged efficiency in the use of resources by devising tight plans rather than using price mechanisms. Not all supplies needed for production quotas were specified in purchasing plans. Planners assumed that managers stockpiled inputs in their storerooms or, if not, they would have to find ways to economise the use of materials: reducing scrap and waste in the production process or economising on fuel and energy (Walder, 2015).

The characteristics of SOEs' industry-planned economy changed radically when encountering the economic reforms with the introduction of marketisation. For instance, in September 1985, the National Party Congress passed the Central Committee of the Communist Party Advice on the 7th Five-Year Plan of the Development of the National Economy and Society (1986–1990) (*Zhonggong zhongyang guanyu zhiding guomin jingji he shehui fazhan diqige wunian jihua de jianyi*). This document aimed to revitalise state enterprises, especially large and medium-sized ones in what was considered to be public ownership, and to make them relatively independent producers and operators as a socialist commodity. It also aimed at further developing the socialist planned commodity market, gradually aiming to improve all aspects of the market in this system. Lastly, it supported the management of enterprises gradually moving from direct control to indirect control by the government (Wu Jinglian, 2018, pp. 18–22). It was not until 2005 that the Minister of the National Development and Reform Commission, Ma Kai, announced the task of replacing state planning with a "socialist market economy" was completed (People's Daily, 2005).[3]

Some Chinese researchers believed that under specific historical background after the World War II (1939–1945), newly established socialist countries successively established their model by imitating the Soviet Union. However, the industrialisation of the country had left the agriculture and light industry alone. Meanwhile, the opposition between the socialist and the capitalist camp at that time made PRC's socialism

[3] A brief discussion of the term, socialist market economy, will be discussed later because it supplies the ideological and political backdrop to the changes SOEs experienced in the reform period. However, this term is not the focus of my research. This research believes that "socialism with Chinese characteristics" provides ideological rationality for reform and marketisation of SOEs. However, many socialist countries have made this attempt. The essence is to accept the logic of the capital market and admit the inefficiency of the conceived socialist enterprises.

development and establishment isolate itself in the initial stage and separate itself from the globalisation trend and the process of modernisation (Song & Li, 2001). Therefore, reforming the borrowed socialism was the requirement of the development of the times for all these socialist countries (Ye, 2010; Zhang Yu, 2016). Then, what is the Chinese socialist characteristics (*zhongguo tese shehui zhuyi)*? Especially, how do these characteristics reflect on the economy?

"To construct socialism with Chinese characteristics" was officially proposed by Deng Xiaoping in 1982 at the opening ceremony of the CCP 12th National Congress.[4] Quoted from Chinese scholars, the Chinese socialist characteristics are theory and practice that result from the interaction between socialism and globalisation process. In the comparative interaction and combination of history and reality with the practices of Marxist theory in China and in contemporary socialist, Deng examined and refined the goals and approaches of Chinese socialist development in the background of globalisation development to consider China's pathway and design the country's future (Song & Li, 2001; Xu Juezai, 2008; Ye, 2010). The term provides Chinese socialist pathway in economic, political, cultural and social system (Xu, 2011, p. 41) as well as defining ideological justification. The Chinese socialist characteristics also reflect the government's initiative in Sinicising the dominant ideologies: Marxism and Leninism (Lu Zhenxiang, 2006b, pp. 5–17). Mun Young Cho (2013) discussed, socialism is an ideology of revolution and an ideology of national modernisation that have deep roots in the history of Chinese socialism. Since the economic reform, the regime has promoted only the latter one, which means the main purpose of proposing this ideology is at economy.

The socialist market economy allows controlled marketisation, where the state still plays an important role, though the role of the market increased a lot after the Reform and Opening Up Era (Wang Feiling,

[4] Deng Xiaoping was the main leader of the CCP, the Chinese People's Liberation Army and PRC. He was then Chairman of the Chinese People's Political Consultative Conference National Committee, Party Vice-Chairman, Vice-Premier and Vice-Chairman of the Central Military Commission; he is regarded as the chief architect of the reform and opening up by the CCP.

The CCP 12th National Congress: A major proposition *"To construct socialism with Chinese characteristics"* (*Zhonggong shier da: tichu "jianshe you zhongguo tese de shehui zhuyi" zhongda mingti*). (2021). Baomi Gongzuo, (08): 2.

2010). Wu Jinglian (2018, pp. 18–22) discussed that after the publication of the 7th Five-Year Plan, Chinese economists suggested that the socialist commodity economy is an organic whole made up of multiple elements, such as what was referred to as independently self-financing (financial autonomy) enterprises, a competitive market system that was allowed in some areas, like the selling of grain and other consumer goods, and government involvement through indirect macro regulation. These three aspects were to be rebuilt at the same time to construct the socialist commodity economy. Their suggestions were accepted and were reflected upon later in the policies focusing on SOEs.

Any apparent contradiction between being socialist and having a market economy had already been dismissed by Deng Xiaoping. Deng held the opinion that both the planned economy and the market economy are economic means to be used by capitalist and socialist states to attain different goals. The rationality of the socialist market economy was proved in Deng's South Inspection Speech (*Nanxun Jianghua*) in 1992 (Duan, 2019). He defined the Chinese socialism by stating that "Socialism has many tasks, but the fundamental one is to develop the productive forces", "The characteristic of socialism is not poverty but wealth, but the common prosperity of the people", "Socialist countries should develop their economy relatively fast and gradually improve the people's living standards".[5] In October 1993, the Chinese economy was redefined as a socialist market economy (*shehui zhuyi shichang jingji*) which was officially regarded as an achievement of socialism with Chinese characteristics (Wang Dongjing, 2018).

Back to the third characteristic of SOEs: the set pay system. Zheng Jinghui (2016) concluded that at the early 1950s, the pay system in PRC was modelled after the Soviet Union. It can be inferred from the translation work of a series of Soviet Union's documents relating to pay issues

[5] The original Chinese text: *Shehui zhuyi de renwu henduo, dan genben yitiao shi fazhan shengchanli.* Selected literature since the 16th National Congress (2008). Beijing: Central Party Literature Press.

Shehui zhuyi de tedian bushi qiong, ershi fu, dan zhezhong fu shi renmin gongtong fuyu. Xing Fensi (1996). Adhere to Marxism unswervingly, draws a clear line between Marxism and anti-Marxism. People Daily, June 6th, 1996 (*Jianchi Marxism budongyao - huaqing Marxism he anti-Marxismi de jiexian. Shehui zhuyi guojia yinggai shi jingji fazhan de bijiao kuai, renmin shenghuo zujian hao qilai.* Zhao Zhikui (ed.). (2008). 30 years of ideological history of Reform and Opening Up (*Gaige kaifang 30 nian sixiangshi*). Beijing: Renmin Press.

and pay setting process, which was organised by special translation departments of state sector and academic research institutes. The set pay system means the uniform wage scale was applied nationwide in China according to the ranks of workers. To apply this system, there was a very refined division of administrative personnel, technical personnel and works into different levels and the country avoiding regional wage differentials to the maximum extent. Huang Xinyuan (2005, p. 49) summarised that since the state implemented pay system in July 1955, the enterprise's workers were divided into 8 technical levels (some types of work had seven technical levels) and cadres were divided into 30 administrative levels. The geographical differences were taken into consideration, for instance, natural conditions, commodity and living expenses, and transportation in different regions. There were 11 "pay zones" nationwide and those that were in areas of difficulty had an advantage in receiving a higher pay. Wang Li (2021) said wages reflect fundamental theoretical issues such as the basic social structure with ownership as the core and the principle of justice regulating it. For PRC, the pay system embodied the socialist pursuit of fairness and justice of a rigid practice. At the same time, it also left a foreshadowing for contradictions such as the widening of the gap between the rich and the poor and the insufficient wages to meet workers' needs after reforms.

The welfare that was provided by SOEs has been mentioned previously. Central or municipal government managed SOEs, generally the manufacturing, processing industry or in the field of production, according to Zhou, Tuma and Moen's research (2002), these enterprises provided favourable conditions to their workers, such as housing, health care and welfare allowances. The state's financial funding addressed the advantaged position of SOEs in heavy industries as well as people within these enterprises. When the general wages were low and the differences in income were modest, SOEs had better resources at their disposal and in a more profitable situation could provide a better standard of living to their workers (Walder, 2015). In the Era of material scarcity, people working for these SOEs received benefits from the barter trade between firms. Large SOEs provided benefits to their workers either free or at a nominal charge. For example, procuring agents would obtain a large number of scarce consumer items like radios, wristwatches, famous-brand bicycles and black-and-white television sets. These items would be distributed to favoured employees and their families. Some work units had long-standing relationships with collective farms, replacing scarce foodstuffs with manufactured items (Lv & Perry, 1997).

SOEs' "parenting-style care" welfare is more than that. When the household registration system (*hukou)* was applied,[6] permanent SOE workers were guaranteed urban-registered permanent residence by the SOEs they worked for. In Chinese cities, if the person does not hold an urban residence permit, they cannot access compulsory education, free medical service or pensions. The residence is a deciding factor for a person's social class, pay, pension, food supply and housing security (Solinger, 2009). When the central government decided to establish the public healthcare plan to serve city dwellers who had urban household registration permits, regular SOE employees had access to this, but the migrant workers, if they still had rural status, were excluded from the medical care services, nor could they rely on the government to enforce the laws and regulations that obliged employers to arrange medical treatment for work-related health problems (Biao, 2003, pp. 1–40; Solinger, 1999; Yip, 2010, pp. 147–165). Meanwhile, this "parenting-style care" feature made the lifelong job security as the workers' iron rice bowl (*tie fanwan*) highly significant, which must be mentioned when studying SOEs. Goodman (2014) sees Chinese SOEs as an essential part of the socio-economic structure of state socialism. Learnt from the Soviet Union, SOE was created as an ideal socialist enterprise by the state. As discussed by Yang (2017, p. 65), unemployment was viewed as a typical product of capitalist societies, and in a communist society, it was not something that occurs. Therefore, when SOEs workers were signed onto the labour contracts, rather than guaranteed a job by a social contract (Lee, 2007), the permanent employment of the "classical" socialism had disappeared.

According to the policies and documents issued later, the reforming of SOEs was aimed at the welfare system. By shifting the burden of social insurance and home ownership from SOEs to a combination of state, enterprises and individuals, the state helped SOEs separate from their social welfare role according to market principles (Zweig, 2001). For instance, the State Council's (1986a and 1986b) publications: *Provisional Regulations on the Institution of the Labour Contract*

[6] The household registration system was created in the 1950s to designate people's residential status.

System in State-Owned Enterprises and *Provisional Regulations on State-owned Enterprises Recruiting Workers*,[7] aimed to dismantle the "iron rice bowl" and "communal pot" (*daguo fan*) to recruit workers through open recruitment and a uniformly implemented labour contract system.[8] The State Council repeatedly noted that SOEs should separate their social functions in 2015, 2016 and 2017.[9] September 2015, *Guiding Opinions of the Central Committee of the Communist Party of China (the CCP Central Committee) and the State Council on Deepening the Reform of State-owned Enterprises* (*State Council*, 2015)[10]; 2016, the State Council issued a *Notice on Speeding Up the Divestment of State-owned Enterprises' Social Functions and Resolving Problems Left Over from History* (*State Council*, 2016a)[11]; *Guidelines on the Socialised Management of Retirees in State-owned Enterprises (draft for comments)* (*State Council*, 2016b)[12]; in June 2017, the State-owned Assets Supervision and Administration Commission (SASAC) and the Ministry of Finance announced the *Guiding Opinions on the Separation and Transfer of the Workers' Family Dependency Areas in State-owned Enterprise*,[13] which aims at the separation of the supply of water, electricity, gas and property management in enterprises' residential areas; *Guidelines on the Separation and Transfer of Functions such as Municipal Community Management by State-owned Enterprises*[14]; and, in July 2017, *Guidance on the Deepening Reform of Educational and Medical Institutions Run by State-owned*

[7] The original Chinese text: *Guoying qiye zhaoyong gongren zanxing guiding*; *Guoying qiye shixing laodong hetongzhi zanxing guiding*.

[8] *Daguo fan* refers to the characteristics of a public-owned economy. People eating from the same big pot means that people share the outcomes of their labour. In other words, it refers to the equalitarianism in wage distribution.

[9] Available on 12th September, 2022, *vide*: http://www.gov.cn/zhengce/content/2016-06/22/content_5084288.htm.

[10] The original Chinese text: *Zhonggong zhongyang*、*Guowuyuan guanyu shenhua guoyou qiye gaige de zhidao yijian*.

[11] The original Chinese text: *Guowuyuan guanyu yinfa jiakuai boli guoyou qiye ban shehui zhineng he jiejue lishi yiliu wenti gongzuo fangan de tongzhi*.

[12] The original Chinese text: *Guanyu guoyou qiye tuixiu renyuan shehuihua guanli de zhidao yijian (zhengqiu yijian gao)*.

[13] The original Chinese text: *Guowuyuan guoyou zichan jiandu guanli weiyuanhui. Guanyu guoyou qiye zhigong jiashuqu "sangongyiye" fenli yijiao gongzuo de zhidao yijian*.

[14] The original Chinese text: *Guanyu guoyou qiye ban shizheng*、 *shequ guanli deng zhineng fenli yijiao de zhidao yijian*.

Enterprises (SASAC and the Ministry of Finance, 2017a, 2017b and 2017c).[15] These plot an erosion of the extent and privileges of SOEs.

These characteristics of SOEs reflect how China, like other socialist countries, learned from the Soviet Union's socialist model in the early stage of establishment. However, also like other socialist countries, inconsistencies of these characteristics were found by China in the process of development. Therefore, these four features analysed in this section: the bias towards heavy industry, the rigid plans for production and supply, the unified pay system and the advantaged welfare system, are required to be rebuilt when facing the economic reforms in China. SOEs found themselves in a new context where their privileges were different or simply ceased to exist. These changes led to a change in the rights of SOE workers.

This section made a descriptive summary of economic reforms in China. Further analytical discussion will be made on what the existing research was found regarding SOEs and economic reforms later.

1.2 The Working Class in China

The Chinese working class is a key factor for my research and my observations and arguments about society will be derived from it. By observing changes in workers' status over time, the mechanisms between SOE reforms and the remaking of a class society can be established. In this section, I will overview the changes of the Chinese working class in different historical periods. Before that, this section will make a summary of the concept of class and class structure. The view of class is quite controversial. Some sociologists assert the death of rank (Clark & Lipset, 1991), while others hope to revise the traditional class theory through careful empirical research to revitalise it in sociological research (Wright, 1985). This section will not discuss this complex problem too much but put forward the concept of class, how the Marxism and Leninism class theory apply in China and specifically, point out Mao Zedong's understanding of class.

The generation of class concept is closely related to the cognitive ability and desire of human beings. It originated in Ancient Rome "the Roman census takers introduced the term 'classis' when they differentiated the

[15] The original Chinese text: *Guanyu guoyou qiye ban jiaoyu yiliao jigou shehui gaige de zhidao yijian.*

population based on property status for the purpose of compulsory military service" (Mann, 1989). In modern times, this concept has been widely used in sociology and plays a decisive role in Marxist theory. Karl Marx's understanding of class is not in the static social structure. He summarised his new findings about "class" by three points in one of the letters to friend: (1) class related to a certain historical stage of production development, (2) class struggle inevitably leads to the dictatorship of the proletariat and (3) the dictatorship is just a transition to the elimination of all classes and to a classless society (Marx, 1995). As a Marxist orthodox, Lenin defined "class" from the social and economic structure perspective. "A class is a big group. These groups' positions in a certain historical stage of social production system, relations with production (most of the relations are written in the law), roles in social labour organisation are different. Therefore, the way and the amount of social wealth at their disposal are different. Classes are these groups, owing to their different positions in a given socio-economic structure, one group is able to occupy the labour of another" (Lenin, 1995). Marx and Lenin's definitions contributed to the political reality in China after 1949 and therefore constructed the reality of class. Beyond an academic concept or a peripheral theory, Marxism impacted on what China became and how people in China saw their social lives.

The application of Marxism's class in modern Chinese society, as Shang Qingfei and Han Bujiang (2007) discussed revolution is the theme of the national political life. Marxist theory is a revolutionary theory which showed that real power was accepted by Chinese society quickly and became the guiding ideology of the CCP, supporting the clearance of the mission of proletarian revolution and the aim of socialist society. The CCP represented by Mao Zedong emphasised the viewpoint of proletarian revolution when Sinicising Marxism and in the initial stage of Sinicisation of Marxism, placed the logical foothold on the concept of class. Mao realised the class consciousness would allow the proletariat to consciously organise economic and political struggle from the theoretical and practical aspects. He stated, "The struggle of the proletariat and the revolutionary people to transform the world includes the following tasks: to transform the objective world, to transform their own subjective world- their cognitive capacity, and to transform the relationship between the subjective and the objective world"[16] (Mao, 1991, p. 296).

The process of Sinicising Marxism did not really promote as supposed due to the misunderstanding of the concept of class struggle by Mao Zedong. According to orthodox Marxism, class is an economic category. The basic symbol of class differences is its position in social production (their relationship to the means of production) (Lenin, 1959, p. 233). Thus, class division can only be based in terms of economic relationships between people. However, Mao's interpretation deviated from Marxism's fundamental principles because of the confusion of class attributes with class origins. He saw class as categories of both an economic and political thought. For instance, there was a contradictory duality in the standard of dividing intellectual's class attribute according to Mao's thought. On the one hand, intellectuals belonged to the working class; on the other hand, they were part of an exploiting class (bourgeoisie) (Sun Jihu, 1998). In 1957, Mao put forward two kinds of social contradictions in the article *On Correctly Handling Contradictions among the People* (*Guanyu zhengque chuli renmin neibu maodun de wenti*). One is the contradictions between the people and the enemy; the other is the contradictions among the people. However, in practice, the class struggle was exaggerated and a lot of internal contradictions among people had been managed as contradictions with the enemy. The theme of class struggle was strengthened, and the concept of class struggle was generalised in China. Moreover, at the 10th Plenary Session of the 8th CCP Central Committee in 1962, Mao wrote "taking class struggle as the first force" (*yi jieji douzheng wei gang*) as the basic line in the communique (Shang & Han, 2007; Yan Yongqi, 2002). This ideological framework based on class struggle changed the direction of Mao Zedong's exploration on Sinicising Marxism, turning his focus from exploring a suitable Chinese pathway of socialist construction to the revolution under the dictatorship of the proletariat. As mentioned above, from Marx's idea, the next step of the dictatorship of proletariat is the classless society. However, the continued revolution under the dictatorship of the proletariat did not proceed in accordance with the basic principles of Marxism. Instead,

[16] The original Chinese text: *Wuchan jieji he geming renmin gaizao shijie de douzheng, baokuo shixian xiasu de renwu: gaizao keguan shijie, ye gaozao ziji de zhuguan shijie—gaizao ziji de renshi nengli, gaizao zhuguan shijie tong keguan shijie de guanxi.*

China took the Cultural Revolution in 1966 as an important opportunity to conduct the political revolution by using one class to overthrow another (Xu, 2010, p. 139). Rather than calling the Cultural Revolution a success of the proletarians' rise to power, it caused a decade of chaos in China.

After a summary of 'class' concept, I want to discuss the concept of social structure and the class structure of society. Social structure is a stable relationship model between different social groups, which is the basic factor determining the behaviour and attitude of social members (Li Lulu, 2019). According to Max Weber and other sociologists, the so-called social structure is not a social fact but an abstract and speculative without empirical basis (Johnson, 1988, p. 267). Weber believes that social reality is based on individual social actions and social structure is only a possibility, which cannot exist independently without people's behaviours. On the contrary, other sociologists believe that social structure is entities that play a huge role for everyone in society and exist independent of behaviour. Émile Durkheim regarded social structure as an objective reality that transcends the individual and influences and restricts everyone's behaviour. He believes that society over the individual (Ye Qizheng, 1992). Marx agrees with this. He also believes that social structure is an objective reality which is independent of people's will (Li Qiang, 2005, p. 68). There are a variety of dimensions to analyse social structure, such as relationship structure between social groups or groups formed based on regions, functions and organisations. Among these, taking class stratum as the dimension is the most special.[17] The class structure is the core part of social structure, and the change of social structure can be regarded as the change of class structure to a substantial extent. For a long time, people believed that class status is the most basic social status, class interests are the most fundamental interests, class relations are the most important social relations and class contradictions are the most important social contradictions. Class structure is one of most important structural foundations of social relations, interests, incentives resources and opportunities distribution, contradictions and conflicts

[17] 'Social class' and 'social stratum' will be regarded as a unified concept in this section because these two terms can be used interchangeably in many situations. Sociologists like Max Weber and Peter Michael Blau use the two terms as one concept, and according to the *Concise Encyclopaedia Britannica*, the explanation of social class is actually the explanation of the social stratum (Blau, 1991; Weber, 1997; Wu Zhongmin, 2004, p. 87).

(Li Lulu, 2019, p. 169). From sociology perspective, the transformation of class structure is one of the core processes of the whole social transformation (Clark & Lipset, 1991).

China's social structure is based on the "identity hierarchy" society formed by the basic socialist system, with sub-systems such as household registration, ownership, job management and work unit system, constructing a corresponding identity hierarchy in the society (Li Lulu, 1992; Li Hanlin, 1993; Lu Feng, 1989). In different historical periods, the social structure is not fixed.

Under Mao's China, especially during the Cultural Revolution (1966–1976), the main purposes that social structure (class structure) served were social engineering and regime consolidation.[18] It granted CCP a level of control. People endowed with proletarian categories were in an advantaged position to join the party (Li Bobai and Walder, 2001, pp. 1371–1408), receive promotions at work and enter higher educational institutes to remedy their loss of opportunity before the PRC was established. The CCP classified Chinese citizens based on their class "composition" (*chengfen*). According to the regulations issued in 1950, a person's class composition was assigned based on the source of their economic support in the three years preceding 1949 (White, 1976). Although this kind of class structure was regarded as an expression of officially dismissed traditional "feudalism" by the CCP, it created a "new privileged class" in the late 1950s (Stacey, 1983). People complained of the growing gap between a dictatorial party and the people (Goldman, 1962, pp. 138–153). Furthermore, the classification of households (the entire family) was linked to an individual's political status, which could be passed down through generations (Fitzpatrick, 1993, pp. 745–770) and controlled by the personnel department (enforced by bureaucratic rules). This kind of management became the foundation of a new ruling class (Doolin, 1964). Yan (2012, p. 84) summarised the previous studies on the dominant form of socialism. The authority of the party and the state is based on a monopoly of resources and opportunities. The newly privileged class maintained and consolidated this monopoly (Djilas, 1959; Szelenyi, 1978, pp. 63–87). This monopoly led citizens to have organised dependence on the officials due to their material needs and lack of social

[18] This means people were born into their class status and so either experienced privileges or discrimination as a result. So, the class under Mao has a genetic or biological nature.

Table 1.1 Social structure in China under Mao

Label	*Identity*
Red	Worker
	Poor and lower-middle peasant
	Revolutionary cadre
	Revolutionary soldier
	Families of revolutionary martyrs
Ordinary	Intellectual
	Freelancer
	Petty dealer
Black	Landlord
	Rich Peasant
	Counterrevolutionary
	Rightist
	Evildoer

Data Source Li Qiang (1997, pp. 34–43), Huang (1995, pp. 126–127), Tong and Zhang (2005, pp. 68–80), and Walder (2015)

mobility (Lee, 1999, p. 45; Walder, 1983, pp. 51–76; Walder, 1988). Based on the previous studies, this research developed the Table 1.1 to present the social structure in Mao's China.

Mao Zedong's opinions on class (social) structure and class identity strengthened the consciousness of the workers and peasants as the masters of the new hierarchy, guiding them to actively participate in various social affairs and had a strong role in mobilisation force and internal cohesion. He advocated fierce class struggle, which was highly practised in a specific period (Wu Zhongmin, 2004, pp. 77–79). In rural areas, Mao emphasised the important status and role of the peasant class. He believed that the peasants were the greatest driving force of the Chinese Revolution,[19] the natural and most dependable ally of the proletariat and the main force of the Chinese revolutionary team (Mao, 1991, p. 643). In cities, Mao classified the various classes such as revolutionary cadres, revolutionary soldiers, workers, shop assistants, bourgeoisie, industrial and commercial landlords, small business owners, handicraftsmen, employees, freelancers, senior staffs, urban poor and street vendors into the proletariat, semi-proletariat, little bourgeois and big bourgeoisie in his article "Analysis of

[19] Peasants without land or have insufficient land. According to Mao, they are the semi-proletariat in the rural areas.

Table 1.2 Social structure in 2000

Class from low to high	*Proportion (%)*	*ISEI points*
Peasants	64.7	23
Labour workers	9.1	29–31
Service staff in the transportation industry, commercial service and technical workers	10.3	33–38
White-collar workers	2.3	43–45
Professional and technical personnel	2.6	68–69
The leading members of the CCP and government, senior professional and technical personnel and enterprise managers	0.5	85–88

Data Source Li Qiang (2005, pp. 55–73)

Various Classes in Chinese Society" (*Zhongguo shehui ge jieji fenxi*). In fact, the political and class structure of Chinese urban and rural societies was formed on this basis (Sun Liping et al., 1994).

In some studies, on post-Mao's social structure, scholars put forward discussions on the shape of Chinese social structure. For instance, by taking the International Occupational Socio-economic Status Index (ISEI) to analyse the population census in 2000,[20] Li Qiang (2005, pp. 55–73) uses an inverted T-shaped social structure to describe the overall social structure of China.[21] He took 641,547 people aged between 16 and 64 years old as the sample. Li's research is summarised in Table 1.2.

Li Qiang (2017, pp. 1–11) further concluded that the significant differences between groups show this structure is worse than the general pyramid structure due to the obvious lack of a middle class. Li argued that the reverse '丁' (*ding*) shape of social structure existed before the economic reforms in China after analysing the population census in 1982, 1990 and 2010. With the Reform and Opening Up and economic development, the middle-class group has continued to grow. The social class structure has thus transformed from a reverse '丁' (*ding*) shape to '土' (*tu*) shape. Li's model (2005) reflected the division between urban and

[20] ISEI ranges from 16 to 90 points, while 16 points indicate the lowest possible socio-economic level and 90 points present the highest. The points are weighting calculated according to profession's average education and income.

[21] Li also uses the reversed Chinese character '丁' (*ding*) to describe this shape.

rural areas in China. The horizontal of the T-shaped structure represents the huge rural social classes, while the vertical represents the urban social classes. The social structure in the urban area is characterised by a relatively high proportion of the lower-middle class, while in the rural area, the proportion of the real lower-class group is not high but the proportion of the group between the lower and the middle class is relatively high. There are obvious middle-class groups in the city, and the boundary between the middle and upper classes is not noticeably clear but overlaps in many aspects. The division of social structure between urban and rural areas is supported by Pang and Qiu (1989, pp. 63–75). Their findings could be presented visually in Table 1.3.

Lu Xueyi (2006a, pp. 28–35; 2010, pp. 1–12) described Chinese social stratification as an 'onion dome', which means the middle and bottom class account for a larger number of people. Lu Xueyi (2003, pp. 1–9) divided China's contemporary society into ten social strata from top to bottom: (1) state and society management class; (2) manager class; (3) private business owners; (4) professional and technical personnel; (5) clerical personnel; (6) individual industrial and commercial households; (7) commercial service personnel; (8) industrial working class; (9) the agricultural labourer; (10) the unemployed and partly employed class in urban and rural areas. He argued (2002) that compared to the pre-reform era, the current social structure is more modern, but a mature social structure should be an "olive" shape, in which the middle class comprises the major group in society.

Table 1.3 Difference between rural and urban areas in China

Area	*Inclusion*
Rural society	Peasants Household non-farm operators The working class Technicians
Urban society	The working class Service staff Managers Professional and technical personnel The private businesspeople Retirees

Data Source Pang and Qiu (1989, pp. 63–75)

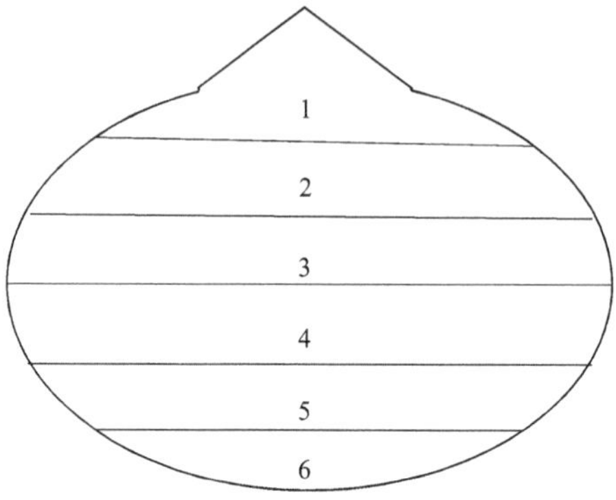

- 1. Owners of medium and large private enterprises
- 2. Professionals such as lawyers, medical doctors, accountants and engineers
- 3. Rank-and-file state sector workers
- 4. Self-employed small-scale entrepreneurs
- 5. Migrates from rural areas to cities (non-professional private sector workers and street- side sales and services)
- 6. Farmers

Fig. 1.1 The onion dome of Chinese Social Stratification (*Data Source* Lu, 2002, 2003, 2006a, 2006b)

This research generated Fig. 1.1 based on Lu's studies to show China's onion dome social stratification.

Another scholar Zhang (2008) used 'pyramid' and 'diamond' shapes to describe the stratification system. Like Lu Xueyi, he believed that the contemporary Chinese social stratification is not healthy due to the large populations belonging to the lower and mid-levels, though the middle-class group has constantly driven and influenced the economic reforms in contemporary Chinese society.

Meanwhile, the existing research uses profession, work unit and resource allocation and possession to outline the social structure in China. In a quantitative research, Zhou et al. (2002) defined the social structure in the early 1990s vertically regarding profession and work unit. The stronger its relationship with the state, the higher rank it occupies (Tables 1.4 and 1.5).

Lu et al. (1992, pp. 137–151) stated that, based on profession, the usage of same means of production and having the same power over production materials should be considered when outlining the social stratification. They divided rural residents into 13 strata from bottom to top: agricultural labourer, peasant workers, hiring workers, intellectual agent class, individual businesses and individual worker class, private business

Table 1.4 Profession rank in the national socialist redistribution system

Rank	*Profession*
1	Cadres (cadres in enterprises and the CCP)
2	Professionals (such as professors at the university, teachers and researchers)
3	Workers (including service and transportation department)
4	Peasants and educated youth back to the city from rural areas

Data Source Zhou et al. (2002)

Table 1.5 Work unit rank

Rank	*Type of work unit*
1	The party and government institutions
2	Public institutions
3	SOEs
4	The collective enterprises
5	Rural villages and people's communes

Data Source Zhou et al. (2002)

owners, managers at a collective enterprise and the rural society management class.[22] Qiu (2001, p. 23) used the professionals' reputations to outline the social stratification in urban areas. There are five profession groups in this: cadres, clerks and staff, professionals and technical personnel, businesspeople, and workers and peasants. Zhang Yi (2004, p. 79) divided the society into seven classes according to the level of their profession: fruit and vegetable farmers, rural professionals, manual

[22] Notes on the collective firms. The so-called collective ownership (*da jiti suoyouzhi*) refers to the ownership of emerged large numbers of cooperative factories that basically completed the socialist transformation of handicraft industry. The nature of the collective ownership is a local SOE owned by the whole people (Wu Jiapei et al., 1978). There are not too many differences between the collective firms and SOEs in terms of the nature of ownership, the plans for production and marketing, and the remuneration of labour wages is also determined by the state authorities. Unlike SOEs, the formation of collective firms' fixed assets does not come from the state direct allocation investment, but from its own accumulation and surplus products created by their workers (including profits after paid the state tax). The management power of collective firms is concentrated in the local authorities (for instance, municipal authorities or as subsidiary units of SOEs) (Xiao Liang et al., 1980).

Table 1.6 Social strata according to resource allocation and possession

Rank	*Profession*
1	Management
2	Professional and technical personnel
3	Clerk class
4	Working class
5	Self-employed class
6	Private business owners' class
7	Other classes (class)

Data Source Zheng (2002, pp. 5–9)

workers, commercial service workers, office clerks, professional technicians, officials, managers of state-owned enterprises and private owners. Zheng (2002, pp. 5–9) suggested that class is the relationship between resource allocation and possession in a society. His analytical framework includes the relationship between possession and distribution of multiple resources. He argued the social strata in Table 1.6:

Yan (2012, p. 33) argued there are three aspects that decide the social stratification in China: economic status, political power and social status. For instance, after the economic reform, the rising status of emerging private entrepreneurs contributed to the change of social structure. Unger and Chan's research (1999, pp. 45–74) showed that many private businesses registered as a local government-controlled collective enterprise gain a more reputable status and take advantage of the tax breaks granted to new collectives. Wright (2010) stated that before the early 1990s, private entrepreneurs constituted less than 1% of China's population; but now the concept of "bourgeoisie" has been transformed into people who live by their own labour, repealing the notion that private businesspeople engage in exploitation and are part of the 'tail of capitalism'. With the acceleration and expansion of state-led economic privatisation and marketisation, the CCP leadership moved from tolerating the private sector to embracing it (Dickson, 2008). The leadership even invited private businesspeople to join the party from 2002 onwards. The economic reforms in China gave economic freedom to private businesses. Permitting private businesspeople to join the party led to a larger population who could share the related privileges. Wright further stated that this connection with the party-state enabled private businesspeople to profit from the partially state-controlled and partially privatised economy; their prosperity depended on the ruling regime. Hong (2004, pp. 23–42) noted that private entrepreneurs have relied on tech-intensive and creative projects to benefit from the privatisation of China's domestic economy and its opening up to the global capitalist system by attracting venture capital. They sit within the upper echelons of China's socio-economic hierarchy, while their employees are at the bottom.

To overview the changes of Chinese social structure, Li Lulu (2019, p. 168) concluded that since the Reform and Opening Up, the social structure "has gradually evolved from a highly centralised and relative homogenous structural system to a relatively dispersed and independent structural system with respect to resources, status, opportunities and interests" and "the most important manifestation of this differentiation" can be reflected on the gradually diverging class society, which means "a simple two classes and one stratum framework or a 'status hierarchy' society constructed by the state" has evolved to a complex class society.

From above, the social status of the working class had changed from a "master" position in the society to the lower-middle class in the city and their privileged possession of certain resources was no longer a monopoly. In China, the working class was a broad class concept to refer to the class attribute that distinguishes people between revolutionary groups or class enemies. For instance, at the national conference on intellectual issues held in January 1956, Premier of the State Council Zhou Enlai, on behalf of the Party Central Committee, declared that the vast majority of Chinese intellectuals are already part of the working class. Developed by the CCP, the working class includes production workers, commercial service personnel, enterprise managers, state cadres and intellectuals (Xu & Shi, 2006). Zhang Wei (2009) summarised that the definition of working class has three extensions. The first extension included the cadres (management class) and service staffs to the working class after the competition of the socialist transformation of private ownership, though the working class in this period was divided into two political identities: cadres and workers.[23] The second extension included intellectuals to the working-class group. Due to the emerging of the migrant workers, the third extension had led to the concept of working-class generalisation and could be divided into four levels: Managers are the upper

[23] Sun et al. (1994) discussed that among the employees in urban area, there were two identities: cadres and workers.

level, composed of party and government cadres, senior management managers and senior professionals; professional and technical personnel are the upper and middle level, composed of high-tech personnel and workers in the state monopoly industries; industrial workers are middle level, including employees of SOEs, collective enterprises and other enterprises under ownership; special workers, such as unemployed laid-off workers, unemployed workers and urban migrant workers, are the lower class. However, the working class in previously mentioned research of social structure does not include the managers nor technicians but just workers, especially focusing on industrial workers.

Shen Yuan (2006, pp. 30–31) discussed that the largest industrial working class in the world was formed in China; furthermore, the dualistic structure of urban and rural division in China caused the Chinese working class dividing into two parts. One is the old workers: the original SOE workers; the other is the new workers: migrant workers. Different from the new workers who face typical labour relations in the market society and form the working class,[24] the old workers were cared by a variety of national welfare. In the reconstruction of the relationship with the state, SOE workers lost their master status. Especially in the process of marketisation, such as lay-offs (*xiagang*), they gradually developed a sense of class identity (consciousness).

Shen's argument on the division of the working class is supported by many scholars. Within the same class, subgroups exist (Lin & Li, 2007, pp. 63–68) and the differences do not only occur after economic reforms. Chen Xi (2019, p. 63) discussed that the distinction between permanent and temporary workers has led to severe confrontations between these two groups ever since the workers' protests in 1957. SOE workers distinguish themselves from workers in the non-state sector within the working class (Wright, 2010). Chen Zhouwang (2015, pp. 142–147) argued that SOE workers comprise of a group of professionals, rather than comrades in terms of class identity. Among SOE workers, permanent SOE workers have a distinctly higher status than other types of urban workers in urban areas (Wu Qingjun, 2008, pp. 58–79) and this may be reflected in the next generation's job positions and education (Li Peilin, 2004). Elizabeth J. Perry (1993) agreed that the growing divide between permanent

[24] This labour relation matches the original model of capitalism industrial production of Marx: the strict control of labour process, the strict management of workers' production behaviour and the sweat wage system (Xu & Shi, 2006).

and temporary workers led to severe confrontations between these two groups.

Lee (2007) and Tong (2002) agreed that government policy leads to division among workers. After the Reform and Opening Up, the emergence of large numbers of contract workers (*hetong gong*), casual workers (*linshi gong*) and rural migrant workers (*nongmin gong*) caused a clearer classification between regular workers (*zhengshi zhigong*) and the others. In the state sector, the economic status of collective workers (*dajiti gongren*) was lower than that of regular SOE employees. SOE workers developed substantially different interests from employees in collective enterprises, and therefore, the two groups had no incentive to cooperate with each other (Cai, 2011, pp. 71–93). Depending on whether they were on work duty, SOE workers can be divided into three subgroups: employed workers (*zaigang zhigong*), pensioners (*tuixiu zhigong*) and laid-off workers (*xiagang zhigong*). The last group did not exist during the Mao Era (Stockman, 2013).

The largest number of SOE workers is rank-and-file workers, which fit Marx's definition of the working class. As the work of Andrew G. Walder (1988) and Teresa Wright (2010) shows, rank-and-file state sector workers are economically dependent on the state and hold a privileged position relative to other unskilled workers. In China, rank-and-file state sector workers can be divided according to their skills, contributions and how intensive their struggles are. The core workers are those who hold special skills, who make a greater contribution to profits and whose collective protests are more aggressive. The rest are fringe workers. Managers adopt an autonomous strategy towards core workers, while they directly control the fringe workers. During a recession, the core worker's job position will be protected, but the fringe workers are easy to lay-off (Friedman, 1977; You, 2006, p. 9).

However, from the 1980s, SOE workers no longer had a monopoly on privilege and status. Skilled and more entrepreneurial SOE workers began to change their careers to enter the private sector where there was more money to be made. Non-state actors appeared, creating their own class structure, competing with the space the SOE workers occupied and eroding their privileges. SOE workers were forced to compete with unskilled rural migrants (whom most city dwellers view as social inferiors or second-class citizens) (Lee, 2007) for jobs with low and often delayed pay, extremely long hours, and draconian working conditions due to the expanding production's demand for labour and the aim of reducing labour costs. A 1996–1997 survey shows that SOE workers were experiencing a sense of loss in status, as the "master" status they enjoyed during the Mao period vanished and they were degenerating into an "underclass" in the new market (Mok & He, 1999, pp. 67–82). Due to the deteriorating financial situation of SOE workers in the late 1980s, workers became increasingly dissatisfied with their political status (Wright, 2018). SOE workers who experienced the Maoist planned economy developed certain reservations about the post-Mao economic reforms. Even though they were aware of the inefficiencies and general limitations on the economic opportunities of the planned economy and the higher material standard of living brought about the economic reform, they were frustrated by the restructuring campaign. This was partly because, as the working class that had been rhetorically glorified under Mao, they felt betrayed and abandoned by the socialist state (Chen Feng, 2006, pp. 42–60; Hurst & O'Brien, 2002, pp. 345–360). SOE workers still hold some privileges and are regarded as ideologically important, but they have become China's new urban poor (Wu Qingjun, 2008, p. 64). In later chapters, I will further summarise the findings and conclusions of existing research into SOE workers in more detail, indicating the innovation points of this study.

1.3 Research Question

This research interrogates the remaking of classes in China's SOEs in post-Mao era with the following questions: (1) How has the status of the working class in post-reform China been affected by SOE reforms? and (2) how does their current situation reflect the class structure of society? This research holds the hypothesis that after economic reforms, the working class (including SOE workers) has fallen back to Marx's classical capitalist class structure in which they have returned to the bottom of society. In addition, economic reforms-cum-SOE reforms have worked as an initial shock which let the new proletarians dwelt on a nostalgia of rights including decision-making and management-sharing prior to the reforms. Consequently, they have taken actions to claim their entitlements due to newly emerged class consciousness. The division of interest groups and the conflicts they have reflect the recreation of a class society as well. More detailed explanations are given below.

After the founding of the PRC, the CCP overthrew the old class society and claimed to have established a classless society. Mao Zedong's series of cleansing campaigns, for instance, '*Sanfan*' '*Wufan*' *Yundong* (the Movement against Three Evils, Five Evils), *Siqing Yundong* (Four Clean-ups) and Cultural Revolution were all aimed at establishing and strengthening a classless society.[25] During the Cultural Revolution, ordinary workers did participate in decision-marking and management. It gave the illusion of classlessness within the enterprise.

During Mao's period, workers in SOEs, especially in military and heavy industry SOEs, enjoyed higher social and economic status in society than others in the working class. Their welfare benefits and employment security were advanced. They were in aristocratic status in the social structure. However, the insurmountable inefficiency of the Maoist economy led to Deng Xiaoping's reforms.

[25] "*Sanfan*" movement refers to the anti-corruption, anti-waste and anti-bureaucracy (*fandui tanwu, fandui langfei, fandui guanliao zhuyi*) movement that started within the party and state agencies in December 1951. "*Wufan*" movement refers to: on January 26th 1952, Central Committee of the CCP issued the "Instructions on first launching the '*wufan*' struggle in large and medium cities" (*guanyu shouxian zai da zhong chengshi kaizhan "wufan" douzheng de zhishi*). It emphasised that relying on the working class, uniting with the law-abiding bourgeoisie and other citizens in large and medium-sized cities, to launch a large-scale and resolute and thorough opposition to bribery, tax evasion, theft of national property, cut corners and steal national economic information (*fandui xinghui, fandui toushui loushui, fandui daopian guojia chaichan, fandui tougong jianliao, fandui daoqie guojia jingji qingbao*) (Tong Hua & Ding Xiaoli, 2009, pp. 25–30; Wang Shanzhong, 1993, pp. 70–76; Zhang Junguo, 2008, pp. 75–80).

"*Siqing*" movement also known as the urban and rural socialist education movement is a political movement launched in the vast urban and rural areas in China from 1963 to 1966 with the purpose of 'combat and prevent revisionism' (*fanxiu fangxiu*). Urban socialist education includes: oppose corruption and theft, oppose speculation, oppose extravagance and waste, oppose decentralism and oppose bureaucracy (*fandui tanwu daoqie, fandui touji daoba, fandui puzhang langfei, fandui fensan zhuyi, fandui guanliao* zhuyi); rural socialist education includes: clear accounts, clear warehouses, clear work points and clear finances (*qing zhangmu, qing cangku, qing gongfen, qing caiwu*). The content of the socialist education movement in urban and rural areas developed into four aspects: clear politics, clear economy, clear ideology and clear organisation (*qing zhengzhi, qing jingji, qing sixiang, qing zuzhi*), collectively referred to as the '*Siqing Yundong*'.

Many scholars believe that the "*Siqing Yundong*" prepared for the Cultural Revolution. This movement pointed to the cadres who were "four unclear" (*si bu qing*) politically and organisationally. These cadres were described as: have no distinction between enemy and people, lose their positions, exclude the poor and middle peasants, conceal their class attributions and falsify their history (*diwo bufen, sangshi lichang, paichi pingxia zhongnong, yinman chengfen, weizao lishi*) (Lin Xiaobo, 2003, pp. 48–56; 2005, pp. 4–10; Wang Yonghua, 2007, pp. 72–76; Wang Yuqiang, 2006, pp. 46–52; Zhou Huahu et al., 1993, pp. 335–339).

Deng's reform measures were to sacrifice fairness to gain efficiency. In the process, labour relations were rebuilt, workers' rights were deprived, and contradictions appeared. In the post-reform period, managers cannot be included in the working class and workers and managers were mutually exclusive. Managers became de facto business owners. The aristocratic workers who enjoyed the privileges in SOEs became victims of the economic reforms and their original privileges were systematically deprived. This can be told from: (1) They cannot participate in the management of the factory, (2) the declined income and (3) the declined welfare. These are material reasons that caused workers to have nostalgia for past-entitlements and made them feel the loss of the original fairness (which is workers' privilege).

It is commonly recognised that in the hands of the ordinary workers nostalgia has become an open and important weapon for defending their rights. Chinese workers' resistance and protests are similar to the union movements of the Western proletariat, which are organised as collective activism and targeted at better pay. My research will include the observations of Chinese workers' nostalgia as part of labour activism whereby workers' class consciousness transforms the group from the *class-in-itself* to *class-for-itself*.[26] Furthermore, this research will disprove the Marxian linear development in China[27]: Marx's capitalist relations and social classes have both now returned to China after economic reforms.

Empirical research and analysis can prove: (1) SOE workers have formed a class; (2) SOE workers have reached the *class-for-itself* level. Compared to the *class-in-itself* stage, which matches an objective awareness stage, *class-for-itself* commands a clear understanding of one's class belonging both objectively and subjectively; and (3) China's society has returned to a class one.

References

Bian, Y. J., Lu, H. L., & Sun, L. P. (Eds.). (2002). *Shichang Zhuanxing Yu Shehui Fencing: Meiguo Shehuixuezhe Fenxi Zhongguo* [Market Transformation

[26] See Marx's definitions of *class-in-itself* and *class-for-itself* in *The Poverty of Philosophy* ([1847]1920), p. 195.

[27] See Marx and Engels's *Communist Manifesto* (1848). The nostalgia (back to Mao's socialism) is contrary to Marx's theory of the linear development of society.

and Social Stratification: An Analysis of China by American Sociologists]. Joint Publishing.

Biao, X. (2003). *Migration and Health in China: Problems, Obstacles and Solutions* (pp. 1–40). Asian Metacentre for Population and Sustainable Development Analysis.

Blau, M. P. (1991). *Bu Pingdeng Yu Yizhixing* [Inequality and Heterogeneity: A Primitive Theory of Social Structure (1977)] (Wang, C.G. & Xie, S. Z., Trans.). China Social Science Press.

Cai, Y. S. (2011). Distinguishing Between Losers: Institutionalizing Inequality in China's Corporate Restructuring. *Going Private in China: The Politics of Corporate Restructuring and System Reform* (pp. 71–93). Walter H. Shorenstein Asia-Pacific Research Center Books.

Committee of the CCP. (2021). *Zhonggong Shier Da: Tichu "Jianshe You Zhongguo Tese De Shehui Zhuyi" Zhongda Mingti* [CCP 12th National Congress: A Major Proposition "To Construct Socialism with Chinese Characteristics"]. *Baomi gongzuo* [Confidential Work], (08), 2.

Central Party Literature Press. (Ed.). (2008). *Shiliu Da Yilai Zhongyao Wenxian Xuanbian* [Selected Important Documents Since the Sixteenth National Congress].

Chen, G. Q. (2000). *Qianxi Gongheguo Dizaozhe Jianguo Chuqi Guanyu Zhongguo Xiandaihua De Ruogan Sixiang* [An Analysis of PRC Founders' Ideas on China's Industrial Modernisation in The Early Years]. *Journal of Wuhan University of Water Resources and Electricity: Social Science Edition, 20*(1), 7–10.

Chen, F. (2006). Privatization and Its Discontents in Chinese Factories. *The China Quarterly, 185*, 42–60.

Chen, Z. W. (2015). State, Worker, and Identity Struggle: Look Back on Marx. *Fudan Journal (Social Sciences), 2*, 142–147.

Chen, X. (2019). The Logic of Fragmented Activism Among Chinese State-Owned Enterprise Workers. *The China Journal, 81*(1), 58–80.

Cho, M. Y. (2013). *The Specter of "the People": Urban Poverty in Northeast China*. Cornell University Press.

Clark, T. N., & Lipset, S. M. (1991). Are Social Classes Dying? *International Sociology, 6*(4), 397–410.

Dickson, B. J. (2008). *Wealth into Power: The Communist Party's Embrace of China's Private Sector* (pp. 32–66). Cambridge University Press.

Djilas, M. (1959). *The New Class: An Analysis of the Communist System*. Praeger.

Dong, F. R. (1982). Further Develop the Study of China's Economic Development Strategy. *Economic Digest*, (4), 5–7.

Doolin, D. J. (1964). *Communist China: The Politics of Student Opposition*. Stanford University Press.

Duan, H. M. (2019, 23 September). *Shehui Zhuyi Shichang Jingji Rang Zhongguo Zhenzheng Huo Le Qilai* [Socialist Market Economy Makes China Truly Come Alive]. *Southern Daily*. Available on 12th September, 2022, *vide*: https://theory.southcn.com/node_4274ee5d35/cea83d9467.shtml

Fitzpatrick, S. (1993). Ascribing Class: The Construction of Social Identity in Soviet Russia. *The Journal of Modern History, 65*(4), 745–770.

Friedman, A. L. (1977). *Industry and Labour: Class Struggle at Work and Monopoly Capitalism* (Vol. 82). Macmillan.

Gold, T., Hurst, W., Won, J., & Li, Q. (2009). *Laid-Off Workers in a Workers' State: Unemployment with Chinese Characteristics*. Springer.

Goldman, R. (1962). The Rectification Campaign at Peking University: May—June 1957. *The China Quarterly, 12*, 138–153.

Goodman, D. S. (2014). *Class in Contemporary China*. John Wiley & Sons.

Hong, Z. (2004). Mapping the Evolution and Transformation of the New Private Entrepreneurs in China. *Journal of Chinese Political Science, 9*(1), 23–42.

Huang, P. C. (1995). Rural Class Struggle in the Chinese Revolution: Representational and Objective Realities from the Land Reform to the Cultural Revolution. *Modern China, 21*(1), 105–143.

Huang, Y. S. (2003). *Selling China: Foreign Direct Investment During the Reform Era*. Cambridge University Press.

Huang, X. Y. (2005). 1956 Nian de Gongzi Dingji Neimu (Wage grading in 1956). *Party Construction*, (11), 49.

Hurst, W. (2009). The Power of the Past: Nostalgia and Popular Discontent in Contemporary China. In T. Gold, W. Hurst, J. Won, & Q. Li (Eds.), *Laid-Off Workers in a Workers' State* (pp. 115–132). Palgrave Macmillan.

Hurst, W., & O'Brien, K. J. (2002). China's Contentious Pensioners. *The China Quarterly, 170*, 345–360.

Johnson, D. (1988). *Shehuixue Lilun* [Sociology Theory] (Sociology Department, Nankai University, Trans.). China International Culture Press.

Lardy, N. R. (1998). *China's Unfinished Economic Revolution*. Brookings Institution.

Lee, C. K. (1999). From Organized Dependence to Disorganized Despotism: Changing Labour Regimes in Chinese Factories. *The China Quarterly, 157*, 44–71.

———. (2006). *Working in China: Ethnographies of Labour and Workplace Transformation*. Routledge.

———. (2007). *Against the Law: Labour Protests in China's Rustbelt and Sunbelt*. University of California Press.

Lenin, V. (1959). *Lenin Quanji* [The Complete Collections of Lenin] (1959 ed., Vol. 21, p. 233). People's Publishing House.

———. (1995). *Liening Xuanji* [Selected Collections of Lenin] (Vol. 3 and 4). People's Publishing House.

Li, L. L. (1992). *Shehui Jiegou De Zhuanxing: Jiegou Zhuti He Jiegou Guize De Biange* [The Transformation of Social Structure: Changes in Structural Subjects and Structural Rules]. *Sociological Research,* 5, 16–30.
Li, H. L. (1993). *Zhongguo Danwei Xianxiang Yu Chengshi Shequ De Zhenghe Jizhi* [The Integration Mechanisms of Work Unit and Urban Communities]. *Sociological Research, 5*(9), 23–32.
Li, Q. (1997). *Zhengzhi Fenceng Yu Jingji Fenceng* [Political Stratification and Economic Stratification]. *Sociology Research,* (4), 34–43.
Li, L. L. (2002). *Lun "Danwei" Yanjiu* [Studies on "Work Unit"]. *Sociological Research,* 5, 23–32.
Li, P. L. (2004). *Huashuo Shehui Fenceng* [Talking About Social Stratification]. China Social Science Literature Press.
Li, Q. (2005). *"Dingzi Xing" Shehui Jiegou Yu Jiegou Jinzhang* ["T-Shaped" Social Structure and Structural Tension]. *Sociological Research, 2,* 55–73.
———. (2017). *Zhongchan Guoduceng Yu Zhongchan Bianyuanceng* [The Transitional and Marginal Strata of the Middle-Class]. *Jiangsu Shehui kexue* [Jiangsu Social Science], *2,* 1–11.
Li, L. L. (2019). Evolution of the Structure of Social Stratification Over 40 Years of Reform and Opening Up in China. *Social Science Digest,* 4, 5–7.
Li, B., & Walder, A. G. (2001). Career Advancement as Party Patronage: Sponsored Mobility into the Chinese Administrative Elite, 1949–1996 1. *American Journal of Sociology, 106*(5), 1371–1408.
Li, L. L., Yu, X. Y., & Wang, F. Y. (1991). Xiandaihua Guocheng Zhong De Shehui Jiegou Jiqi Biange [Social Structure and Change in The Modernisation Process]. *Sociological Research,* (1), 68–79.
Li, M., Zhou, F., & Li, K. (1996). The Unit: The Internal Mechanism of Institutionalized Organizations. *Chinese Social Science Quarterly (Hong Kong),* 16(5), 135–167.
Lin, X. B. (2003). *'Siqin' Yundong Yanjiu Shuping* [Review of the 'Four Clean-Ups' Movement]. *Party History Research and Teaching,* 3, 48–56.
Lin, X. B. (2005). *Siqin Yundong Shimo* [The history of the Four Clean-ups Movement]. *Dangshi Tiandi* [Party History], (6), 42–46.
Lin, C. (2015). The Language of Class in China. *Socialist Register, 51,* 24–53.
Lin, K. L., & Li, Q. S. (2007). *Guangyi Ziben He Shehui Fenceng—Bourdieu De Ziben Lilun Jiedu* [Capital and Social Stratification—Bourdieu's Capital Theory]. *Journal of Yantai University, Social Science Edition, 20*(4), 63–68.
Liu, J. J. (2000). *Danwei Zhongguo- Shehui Tiaokong Tixi Zhong De Geren Zuzhi Yu Guojia* [Unit China—Individuals, Organizations and the State in the Social Control System]. Tianjin People's Publishing House.
Lu, F. (1989). *Danwei: Yizhong Teshu De Shehui Zuzhi Xingshi* [The Unit: A Special Form of Social Organization]. *Chinese Social Sciences,* (1), 71–88.

Lu, X. Y. (2002). *Dangdai Zhongguo Shehui Jieceng Yanjiu Baogao* [Contemporary Chinese Social Class Research Report]. Social Science Literature Press.

———. (2003). *Dangdai Zhongguo Shehui Jieceng De Fenhua Yu Liudong* [The Division and Mobility of Social Classes in Contemporary China]. *Jiangsu Shehui Kexue* [Jiangsu Social Science], *4*, 1–9.

———. (2006a). Zhongguo Shehui Jiegou De Bianhua Ji Fazhan Qushi [The Changes and Development Tread of Chinese Social Structure]. *Journal of Yunnan University for Nationalities, Philosophy and Social Sciences Edition, 23*(5), 28–35.

Lu, Z. X. (2006b). *"Marxism Zhongguohua" Jiedu Shizhong Ruogan Wenti Kaocha* (An Examination of the Interpretation of Sinicization of Marxism). *Studies in Socialism with Chinese Characteristics,* 01, 5–17.

Lu, X. Y. (2010). *Zhongguo Shehui Jieceng Jiegou Bianqian 60 Nian* [The Changes of China's Social Class Structure in 60 Years]. *Journal of Beijing University of Technology: Social Science Edition, 3*, 1–12.

Lu, X. Y., Zhang, H. Y., & Zhang, Q. Z. (1992). *Zhuanxing Shiqi Nongmin De Jieceng Fenhua-Dui Dazai, Liuzhuang, Huaxi Deng 13 Ge Cunzhuang De Shizheng Yanjiu* [The Stratification of Farmers in the Transition Period: An Empirical Study of 13 Villages Including *Dazhai*, *Liuzhuang*, and West China]. *Chinese Social Sciences,* (4), 137–151.

Lv, X. B., & Perry, E. J. (1997). The Changing Chinese Workplace in Historical and Comparative Perspective. In X. B. Lv & E. J. Perry (Eds.), *Danwei: The Changing Chinese Working Place in a Comparative Perspective.* ME Sharpe Inc.

Mann, M. (1989). *Guoji Shehuixue Baike Quanshu* [The International Encyclopedia of Sociology] (Y. Y. Yuan, Trans., 1989 ed., p. 79). Sichuan People's Publishing Houses.

Mao, Z. D. (1991). *Mao Zedong Xuanji* [Selected Works of Mao Zedong] (1991 ed., Vol. 1, pp. 296, 643). People's Publishing House.

Marx, K. ([1847]1920). *The Poverty of Philosophy* (pp. 194–195). Foreign Language Publishing House.

Marx, K., & Engels. F. ([1848]2009). Gongchandang Xuanyan [The Communist Manifesto]. In *Marx and Engels Collection Vol. 2 1848–1859* (Bureau for the Compilation and Translation of the Works of Marx and Engels, Lenin and Stalin, Central Committee of the CCP, Trans., pp. 3–67). People's Publishing House.

———. (1995). *Marx Engels Xuanji* [The Selected Works of Marx and Engels] (Bureau for the Compilation and Translation of the Works of Marx and Engels, Lenin and Stalin, Central Committee of the CCP, Trans., Vol. 1). People's Publishing House.

Mok, K., & He, C. (1999). Beyond Organized Dependence: A Study of Workers' Actual and Perceived Living Standards in Guangzhou. *Work, Employment and Society, 13*(1), 67–82.

National Party Congress. (1985). *Zhonggong Zhongyang Guanyu Zhiding Guomin Jingji He Shehui Fazhan Diqige Wunian Jihua De Jianyi* [The Central Committee of the Communist Party Advice on the 7th Five-Year Plan of the Development of the National Economy and Society (1986–1990)]. Available on 12th September, 2022, *vide*: https://www.ndrc.gov.cn/fggz/fzzlgh/gjfzgh/200709/P020191029595672223126.pdf

Pang, S. Q., & Qiu, L. P. (1989). *Woguo Shehui Xianjieduan Jieji Jieceng Jiegou Yanjiu Chutan* [A Preliminary Study of the Class Structure of Current China]. *Sociological Research,* (3), 63–75.

People's Daily Online. (2005, July 13). *China Has Socialist Market Economy in Place.* Available on 12th September, 2022, *vide*: http://english.peopledaily.com.cn/200507/13/eng20050713_195876.html

Perry, E. J. (1993). *Shanghai on Strike: The Politics of Chinese Labor.* Stanford University Press.

Qiu, L. P. (2001). *Zhiye Diwei: Shehui Fenceng De Zhishiqi* [Professional Status: An Indicator of Social Stratification]. *Sociological Research, 3*(24), 23.

Shang, Q. F., & Han, B. J. (2007). *Jieji,Jieji Yishi Yu Jieji Douzheng- Lun Mao Zedong Shixian Marxism Zhongguohua De Jiben Luoji Huanjie* [Class, Class Consciousness and Class Struggle: The Basic Logical Links in Mao Zedong's Understanding of Marxism]. *Nanjing Social Science,* (6), 18–24.

Shen, Y. (2006). *Shehui Zhuanxing Yu Gongren Jieji De Zaixingcheng* [Social Transformation and the Re-formation of the Working Class]. *Sociological Research, 2,* 13–36.

Shirk, S. L. (1993). *The Political Logic of Economic Reform in China.* University of California Press.

Solinger, D. J. (1999). *Contesting Citizenship in Urban China: Peasant Migrants, the State, and the Logic of the Market.* University of California Press.

———. (2009). *Contesting Citizenship in Urban China* (C. G. Wang & L. Q. Shan, Trans.). Zhejiang People's Publishing Houses.

Song, S. C., & Li, R. H. (2001). Globalization and the Construction of Socialism with Chinese Characteristics. *Social Science in China,* (06), 4–13, 204.

Stacey, J. (1983). *Patriarchy and Socialist Revolution in China.* University of California Press.

State Council. (1986a). *Guoying Qiye Shixing Laodong Hetongzhi Zanxing Guiding* [Provisional Regulations on the Institution of the Labour Contract System in SOEs]. Available on 12th September, 2022, *vide*: http://www.gov.cn/zhengce/content/2016-06/22/content_5084288.htm

———. (1986b). *Guoying Qiye Zhaoyong Gongren Zanxing Guiding* [Provisional Regulations on SOEs Recruiting Workers]. Available on 12th September, 2022, *vide*: ibidem.

———. (2015). *Zhonggong Zhongyang、Guowuyuan Guanyu Shenhua Guoyou Qiye Gaige De Zhidao Yijian* [Guiding Opinions of the Central Committee of the CCP and the State Council on Deepening the Reform of State-Owned Enterprises]. Available on 12th September, 2022, *vide*: ibidem.

———. (2016a). *Guowuyuan Guanyu Yinfa Jiakuai Boli Guoyou Qiye Ban Shehui Zhineng He Jiejue Lishi Yiliu Wenti Gongzuo Fangan De Tongzhi* [Notice on Speeding Up the Divestment of State-Owned Enterprises' Social Functions and Resolving Problems Left Over from History]. Available on 12th September, 2022, *vide*: ibidem.

———. (2016b). *Guanyu Guoyou Qiye Tuixiu Renyuan Shehuihua Guanli De Zhidao Yijian (Zhengqiu Yijian Gao)* [Guidelines on the Socialised Management of Retirees in State-Owned Enterprises, Draft for Comments]. Available on 12th September, 2022, *vide*: ibidem.

State-Owned Assets Supervision and Administration Commission (SASAC). and the Ministry of Finance. (2017a). *Guanyu Guoyou Qiye Zhigong Jiashuqu "Sangongyiye' Fenli Yijiao Gongzuo De Zhidao Yijian* [Guiding Opinions on the Separation and Transfer of the Workers' Family Dependency Areas in State-Owned Enterprise]. Available on 12th September, 2022, *vide*: ibidem.

———. (2017b). *Guanyu Guoyou Qiye Ban Shizheng、Shequ Guanli Deng Zhineng Fenli Yijiao De Zhidao Yijian* [Guidelines on the Separation and Transfer of Functions Such as Municipal Community Management by State-Owned Enterprises]. Available on 12th September, 2022, *vide*: ibidem.

———. (2017c). *Guanyu Guoyou Qiye Ban Jiaoyu Yiliao Jigou Shehui Gaige De Zhidao Yijian* [Guidance on the Deepening Reform of Educational and Medical Institutions Run by State-owned Enterprises]. Available on 12th September, 2022, *vide*: ibidem.

Stockman, N. (2013). *Understanding Chinese Society* (pp. 52–196). John Wiley & Sons.

Sun, J. H. (1998). The Causes of Mao Zedong's Misjudgement on the Class Attribute of Intellectuals. *Journal of the Northwest Normal University, Social Sciences Edition,* (2), 35–40.

Sun, L. P., Wang, H. S., Wang, S. B., Lin, B., & Yang, S. H. (1994). *Gaige Yilai Zhongguo Shehui Jiegou De Bianqian* [Changes in The Social Structure of China Since the Reform]. *Chinese Social Sciences,* (2), 47–62.

Szelenyi, I. (1978). Social Inequalities in State Socialist Redistributive Economies. *International Journal of Comparative Sociology, 19*(1–2), 63–87.

Tong, X. (2002). *Shehui Bianqian Yu Gongren Shehui Shenfen De Chonggou* [Social Changes and the Reconstruction of Workers' Social Identity]. *Sociological Research,* 6, 1–12.

Tong, H., & Ding, X. L. (2009). *"Sanfan' 'Wufan' Yundong De Lishi Jingyan* [The Historical Experience of the "Three Anti" and "Five Anti" Campaigns]. *Journal of Ideological and Theoretical Education,* (11), 25–30.

Tong, X., & Zhang, H. B. (2005). *Shehui Fenceng Yu Shehui Hexie* [Social Stratification and Social Harmony]. *Society, 25*(6), 68–80.

Unger, J., & Chan, A. (1999). Inheritors of the Boom: Private Enterprise and the Role of Local Government in a Rural South China Township. *The China Journal,* (42), 45–74.

Walder, A. G. (1983). Organized Dependency and Cultures of Authority in Chinese Industry. *The Journal of Asian Studies, 43*(1), 51–76.

———. (1988). *Communist Neo-Traditionalism: Work and Authority in Chinese Industry*. University of California Press.

———. (1992). Property Rights and Stratification in Socialist Redistributive Economies. *American Sociological Review, 57*(4), 524–539.

———. (2015). *China Under Mao.* Harvard University Press.

Wang, H. S. (1989). *Jianguo Chuqi Gongye Jianshe Daolu De Huigu Yu Sikao* [A Review on the Industrial Construction Development in the Early Stage of PRC]. *Journal of Henan University: Social Science Edition,* (6), 45–50.

Wang, H. N. (1990). *Shehui Ziyuan Zongliang Yu Shehui Tiaokong: Zhongguo Yiyi* [Social Resources and Social Control: Implications for China]. *Fudan Journal: Social Science Edition,* (4), 2–11.

Wang, S. Z. (1993). *Jianguo Chuqi Sanfan Wufan Yundong Shuping* [A Review of the Three Anti's and Five Anti's Movement in the Early Period of PRC]. *Studies in the History of the Chinese Communist Party,* (1), 70–76.

Wang, Y. Q. (2006). A Political Sociology Research on the Arousing Pattern of the "Four Clean-Ups" Movement. *Journal of Historical Science,* (6), 46–52.

Wang, Y. H. (2007). *Jin Shinian Siqin Yundong Yanjiu Zongshu* [An Overview of Studies on Four Clean-Ups Movement in the Last Decade]. *Chongqing Social Science,* (7), 72–76.

Wang, F. L. (2010). Reviewed Work: The End of the Revolution: China and The Limits of Modernity by Wang Hui. *The Journal of Asian Studies, 69*(4), 1215–1217.

Wang, D. J. (2018, December 26). *Jianli Shehui Zhuyi Shichang Jingji Tizhi Shi Weida Chuangzao* [The Establishment of a Socialist Market Economy Is a Great Creation]. *People's Daily*. Available on 12th September, 2022, *vide*: http://PA-PER.PEOPLE.COM.CN/RMRB/HTML/201812/26/NW.D110000RENMRB_20181226_107.HTM

Wang, L. (2021, September 30). *Gongzi Zhidu Yu Fenpei Zhengyi* [Wage System and Distributive Justice]. *China Social Science Journal,* (A04). Available on 12th Sep, 2022, *vide*: https://epaper.csstoday.net/epaper/read.do?m=i&iid=6142&eid=42378&sid=195337&idate=12_2021-09-30

Weber, M. (1997). *Jingji Yu Shehui* [Economy and Society] (R. Y. Lin, Trans.). Commercial Press.

White, G. (1976). *The Politics of Class and Class Origin: The Case of the Cultural Revolution*. Australian National University: Distributed by Contemporary China Centre.

Whyte, M. K., & Parish, W. L. (1985). *Urban Life in Contemporary China*. University of Chicago Press.

Wright, E. O. (1985). *Classes*. Verso.

Wright, T. (2010). *Accepting Authoritarianism: State-Society Relations in China's Reform Era*. Stanford University Press.

———. (2018). *Popular Protest in China*. John Wiley & Sons.

Wu, Z. M. (2004). *Cong Jieji Fenxi Dao Dangdai Shehui Fenceng Yanjiu* [From Class Analysis to Contemporary Social Stratification Research]. *Academy*, (1), 64–88.

Wu, Q. J. (2008). *Shichang Zhuanxing Shiqi Guoqi Gongren De Qunti Renting Yu Jieji Yishi* [Group Identity and Class Consciousness of SOE Workers in the Market Transition Period]. *Sociological Research, 6*, 58–79.

Wu, J. L. (2018). *Shehui Zhuyi Shichang Jingji: Renshi Jinzhan Yu Tizhi Jiangou* [Socialist Market Economy: Progress in Understanding and Institutional Construction]. *China Finance*, (24), 18–22.

Wu, J. P., Zhang, S. Y., & Zhang, S. G. (1978). *Changzhou Shi 'Da Jiti' Suoyouzhi Gongye De Diaocha* [A Survey of 'Collective Ownership' Industries in *Changzhou* City]. *Economic Research*, (11), 55–60.

Xi, J. P. (2021, October 15). *Zhashi Tuidong Gongtong Fuyu* [Solid Promotion of Shared Prosperity]. Available on 12th September, 2022, *vide:* http://www.qstheory.cn/dukan/qs/2021-10/15/c_1127959365.htm

Xiao, L., Tang, Z. K., & Zhang, T. X. (1980). *Weihai Shi De 'Da Jiti' Gongye* [The 'Collective' Industries in *Weihai* City]. *Chinese Social Sciences*, (1), 213–224.

Xing, F. S. (1996, June 6). *Jianchi Marxism Bu Dongyao - Huaqing Marxism He Anti-Marxism De Jiexian* [Adhere to Marxism Unswervingly, Draws a Clear Line Between Marxism and Anti-Marxism]. *People's Daily*.

Xinhua News. (2021, July 15). *Xi Jinping: Zai Qingzhu Zhongguo Gongchandang Chengli 100 Zhounian Dahui Shang De Jianghua* [Xi Jinping: Speech at the Congress to Celebrate the 100th Anniversary of the Founding of the Communist Party of China]. Available on 12th September, 2022, *vide*: http://www.xinhuanet.com/politics/leaders/2021-07/15/c_1127658385.htm

Xu, J. Z. (2008). *Waiguo Xuezhe Lun Zhongguo Tese Shehui Zhuyi* [Foreign Scholars' Studies on Socialism with Chinese Characteristics]. *Studies on Socialism with Chinese Characteristics*, (03), 39–51.

Xu, C. W. (2010). *Mao Zedong Dui Shihe Zhongguo Guoqing De Shehui Zhuyi Jianshe Daolu De Tansuo* [Mao Zedong's Exploration of Sinicization of the Constructions of Socialism]. *Marxism and Reality,* (3), 133–141.

Xu, Y. L. (2011). *Shehui Zhuyi Shichang Jingji Shi Shenme Moshi- Yu Wu Jinglian Xiansheng Taolun* [The Socialist Market Economy—A Discussion with Mr. Wu Jinglian]. *Contemporary Economic Studies,* (12), 41–46.

Xu, Y.P. and Shi, X.Y. (2006). *Gongren Jieji Xingcheng: Tizhi Nei Yu Tizhi Wai De Zhuanhuan* [The Formation of the Working Class: Transitions within and Outside the System]. *Xuehai* [Studies], *4*, 27–39.

Yan, Y. Q. (2002). *Zhong Su Lunzhan Yu Mao Zedong Guanyu Shehui Zhuyi Shehui Jieji Douzheng Lilun Xing* [An Analysis of The Sino-Soviet War and the Formation of Mao Zedong's Theory on Class Struggle in Socialist Society]. *Party History Research and Teaching*, (3), 30–34.

Yan, Y. X. (2012). *The Individualization of Chinese Society* (Shanghai, Trans.). Shanghai Translation Publishing House.

Yang, J. (2017). *Mental Health in China: Change, Tradition, and Therapeutic Governance.* John Wiley & Sons.

Ye, Q. Z. (1992). *Jiegou, Yishi Yu Quanli: Dui 'Shehui Jiegou' Gainian De Jiantao* [Structure, Consciousness and Power: A Review of the Concept of 'Social Structure']. In *Sociological Theory and Method.* Zhongyang Yanjiuyuan Minzuxue Yanjiusuo [Institute of Ethnology, Academia Sinica].

Ye, S. Z. (2010). *Kaige Kaifang: Po Stalin Moshi Fanli Chuang Zhongguo Tese Shehui Zhuyi* [Reform and Opening Up: Breaking the Barriers of the Stalinist Model to Create Socialism with Chinese Characteristics]. *Exploration and Controversy, 1*(5), 29.

Yip, W. (2010). Disparities in Health Care and Health Status: The Rural–Urban Gap and Beyond. In *One Country, Two Societies: Rural-Urban Inequality in Contemporary China* (pp. 147–165). Harvard University Press.

You, Z. L. (2006). *Guanli Kongzhi Yu Gongren Kangzheng - Ziben Zhuyi Laodong Guocheng Yanjiu Zhong De Youguan Wenxian Shupin* [Management Control and Workers' Resistance—A Review of the Literature on Capitalist Labour Process]. *Sociological Research,* (4), 169–185.

Zhang, Y. (2004). The Acquisition of Chinese Social Status. *Sociological Studies, 4*, 79.

Zhang, J. G. (2008). *'Sanfan' 'Wufan' Yundong Yanjiu Shupin* [Review of Research on the 'Three Anti' and 'Five Anti' Campaigns]. *Journal of Hubei Socialist Academy,* (2), 75–80.

Zhang, W. (2009). *Zhongguo Gongren Jiji 60 Nian* [The 60 Years History of the Chinese Working Class). *Shidai Fengcai* [Time Style], (15), 16.

Zhang, Y. Q. (2011). *Shichang Zhuanxing Yu Danwei Zuzhi Bianqian Fenxi* [Analysis of Market Transformation and Units' Organizational Changes].

Journal of Changchun University of Technology: Social Science Edition, 23(4), 92–94.
Zhang, Y. (2016). *Shehui Zhuyi Zhengzhi Jingjixue De Lishi Yanbian- Jianlun Zhongguo Tese Shehui Zhuyi Zhengzhi Jingjixue De Lishi Gongxian* [The Historical Evolution of Socialist Political Economy—The Historical Contribution of Socialist Political Economy with Chinese Characteristics]. *Studies on Socialism with Chinese Characteristics, 1*(1), 35–41.
Zhao, Z. K. (Ed.). (2008). *Gaige Kaifang 30 Nian Sixiangshi* [The History of Ideology in 30 Years of Reform and Opening Up]. People's Publishing House.
Zheng, H. S. (2002). *Woguo Shehui Jieceng Jiegou Xin Bianhua De Jige Wenti* [Several Issues on the New Changes in the Social Class Structure in China]. *Journal of Central China Normal University: Humanities and Social Sciences Edition, 41*(4), 5–9.
Zheng, J. H. (2016). Review and Reflection: A Review of Research on Salary and Welfare System in New China. *Journal of Baoding College, 29*(03), 45–53.
Zhou, H. H., Jiang, F. Y., & Li, T. W. (Ed.). (1993). *Zhonghua Renmin Gongheguo Dashiji Shiben Mo (1949 Nian 10 Yue – 1991 Nian 12 Yue)* [Significant Events in PRC 1949.10–1991.12] (pp. 335–339). Sichuan Cishu Press.
Zhou, X. G., Tuma, N., & Moen, P. (2002). Guojia Shehuizhuyi Zhidu Xia De Shehui Jieceng Dongtai Fenxi: 1949–1993 Nian De Zhongguo Chengshi Zhuangkuang in Shichang Zhuanxing Yu Shehui Fenceng: Meiguo Shehuixuezhe Fenxi Zhongguo [Dynamic Analysis of Social Classes under the National Socialist System: China's Urban Conditions from 1949 to 1993]. In *Market Transition and Social Stratification: An American Sociologist's Analysis of China*. Joint Publishing.
Zweig, D. (2001). China's Stalled 'Fifth Wave': *Zhu Rongji*'s Reform Package of 1998–2000. *Asian Survey, 41*(2), 231–247.

CHAPTER 2

Theories and Methodology Applied

2.1 Theories

Classical Marx's debate of class and class struggle is the first topic to examine this research's hypothesis that after economic reforms, SOE workers have restructured the class under Marx's class theory, and the class society in China has been reformed rather than fading away because of economic development.

My research uses Marxism to analyse the current Chinese working class and their social status. Therefore, when reviewing Marx's main concepts, it uses Marx's original work as the main material instead of expanding on the analysis of others.[1] Marx's theoretical system is extraordinarily rich and covers a wide range of topics; according to my research question and hypothesis, his thoughts on the proletariat, the exploited working class and the working class's consciousness and resistance will be discussed from Marx's ideology. His other concepts, such as relations of production, surplus value and the alienation of labour that related to the formation of classes and the status of workers, will be mentioned but not as the focus of this theoretical review. From Marx's theoretical logic,

[1] Marx and Friedrich Engels co-authored works on the working-class revolution and their viewpoints of capitalism and communism are highly consistent. Therefore, in this study, Engels' interpretation of Marx theory (mainly cited from his introduction and preface works for Marx) will also serve as the original material of Marx.

S. S. Huang, *The Political Economy of Reforms and the Remaking of the Proletarian Class in China, 1980s–2010s*, Palgrave Studies in Economic History, https://doi.org/10.1007/978-3-031-20455-5_2

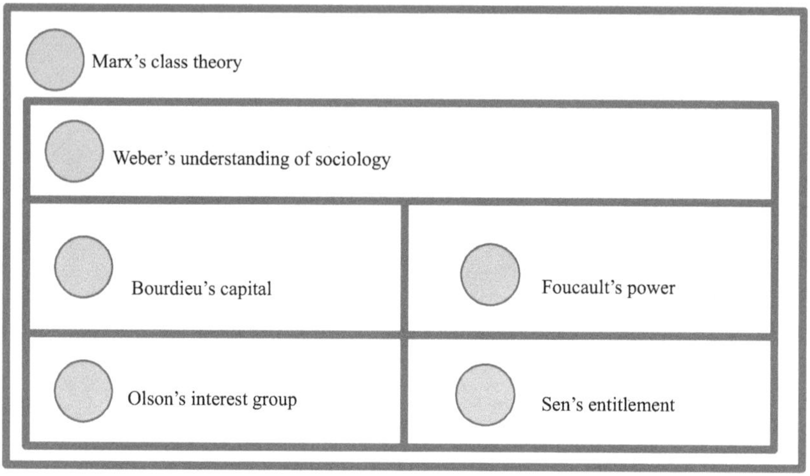

Fig. 2.1 The theoretical framework (*Data Source* The author's original work)

workers (proletariat) need to be consciously awakened and fight because of class antagonism created by exploitation. He then raised up with an ideal concept: a communist society, where class no longer exists.

To deliver my research, it is important to consider a range of approaches. Guided by Marx's class theory, this research takes different approaches to explore SOE workers in China, for example, understanding them from an individual level from Weber's understanding of sociology, relating their rights with Bourdieu and Foucault's sociological concepts: capital and power, regarding them as an interest group from Olson's opinion, and explaining their essence of behaviour from Sen's entitlement. The theoretical framework is shown in Fig. 2.1.

In addition to the theoretical framework of this research, this chapter will also discuss how the methodology and research methods such as the case study and interviews are supported by theory and applied.

Macro Guidance: Marx's Debate on Class and Class Struggle

Marx's analysis of the proletariat: the modern wage labourer emphasises the situation of the exploitation of the workers and the exploitation will exist as long as capitalist production relations exist.[2] The situation of exploitation could be summarised as follows. First, the social power of the working class is only numerically superior. There is inevitably competition among workers (Marx, [1866] 2009).[3] There are differences in labour prices (wages) for workers in different industries. A worker competes with the fellow workers, making the fellow workers competitors, who also sell themselves under poor conditions, creating competition within the working class (Marx, [1932] 2009).[4] Workers' superiority in numbers is destroyed by their decentralised form. Secondly, in terms of struggle over wages, the capitalists often win because workers are in a subordinate relationship to the capitalists. When capitalists make profits, workers do not necessarily benefit from this; while when capitalists make a loss, workers will also suffer from the losses. The labour price (wage) is more stable than the price of the means of subsistence. The two are often inversely proportional. When subsistence prices are expensive, wages fall as the demand for labour falls and rise as the price of the means of subsistence rises. When prices are cheap, wages rise because of the higher demand for labour and fall because of the lower price of the means of subsistence. Therefore, wages and subsistence prices cancel each other out (Marx, [1932] 2009). No matter whether the prices are high or low, there would always be a certain number of workers who suffer. Engels ([1891] 2009) further explained that even though the means of subsistence decrease at a higher rate than wages, i.e., workers can buy more goods for less money, more goods require more labour to produce. Capitalists pay workers less in

[2] See Marx and Engels' (1848) statements in *The Communist Manifesto*, that the bourgeoisie possesses the means of production and uses wage labour, while the proletariat has no means of production of its own and needs to sell its labour to make ends meet. Also see Marx's discussion (1867) on the general laws of capitalist accumulation in *Capital, vol. 1*, such a labour-capital relation, labour is incorporated into capital as a means of value appreciation, sold to the capitalist and is subordinate to capital. The worker does not own the products he produces but receives the means of subsistence through wages (Marx, [1844] 1932). Cited from *Marx and Engels Collection, Vol. 2 1848–1859* (2009).

[3] See Marx's arguments on work union's past, present and future in *Instructions from the Provisional Central Committee to Delegates on A Number of Issues in 1866*. Cited from *Marx and Engels Collection, Vol. 1 1843–1848* (2009).

[4] See Marx's arguments on wage in *Economic and Philosophic Manuscripts 1844*, firstly published in 1932. Cited from *Marx and Engels Collection, Vol. 1 1843–1848* (2009).

exchange for their labour.[5] The inequality of labour-capital relation allows capitalists to dominate a larger amount of labour with the same amount of capital, i.e., capitalists' right to dominate the working class increases, and workers' social status become lower and the gap with capitalists is greater than before. Lastly as Engels (1891) mentioned, workers can leave capitalists who employ them if they want, and capitalists can dismiss workers at will. When capitalists can no longer benefit from workers or obtain expected profits, workers may be dismissed. However, workers who sell labour as the only source of income cannot leave the whole buying class, the capitalist class, if they do not want to starve to death.

Marx ([1844] 1932) used alienated labour to explain why the more wealth the worker produces, the greater the impact and scale of production, the poorer he becomes.[6] The more the worker creates, the more he becomes a cheap commodity. The product of labour does not depend on the producer and is in opposition to labour. Workers lose ownership of the product and are enslaved to it. Even labour itself becomes an object that workers can only possess through maximum effort and extremely irregular intervals. The alienation of labour means workers' relation to the product of their own labour is a relation to an alien object. The more power workers expend in labour, the stronger the power of the alienated object (which is created by workers' hand and against workers themselves), and the poorer themselves, the less they can occupy.

This is because the worker is also alienated into commodities in the process of commodity production. In Marx's analysis, workers can only benefit in societies where wealth is in a period of growth.[7] Marx ([1844] 1932) discussed three main forms of social status of workers. In addition to the favourable position in the period of growth (discussed in the main text), the other two forms are: (1) workers suffer the most when social wealth is in decline; (2) when social wealth reaches its possible peak, both wages and capital interests would be low. Competition among workers for employment would lead to wages shrinking to just enough to sustain the existing number of workers, beyond which the segment is doomed to die.

[5] See Preface of Marx's (1849) *Wage Labourer and Capital* wrote by Engels for the 1891 publication version. Cited from *Marx and Engels Collection, Vol. 1 1843–1848* (2009).

[6] See *Alienation of Labour and Private Property* in *Economic and Philosophic Manuscripts 1844*.

[7] See Marx's arguments on Wage in *Economic and Philosophic Manuscripts 1844*.

In summary, in a declining society, the poverty of workers grows, and they become oppressed. In a growing society, the wealth produced by workers leads to the physical destruction of the workers. And when social wealth reaches a peak, the poverty of workers continues unchanged. The only and most favourable social condition to workers is from the consequences of the increasing in social wealth.

In this period, capitalists compete due to the fact that the demand for workers exceeds the supply of workers. However, driven by the desire to earn money, workers need to sacrifice their time to engage in excessive labour, which shortening the life of workers. Hence, in Marx's view, the working class has always had to sacrifice to gain benefits.

Moreover, Marx argued that even though workers struggle with capitalist for wages, the wages only cover part of the products produced by workers. The other part that remained in the hands of the capitalists is the profit sought by capitalists. Marx ([1865] 1898) uses surplus value to explain this.[8] The worker is required to perform additional work in addition to the hours that compensate for wages or the value of labour. The extra work time is the surplus time, which creates value as well but does not receive any corresponding equivalent. Under the capitalist system of production (wage labour), the labour-capital relation can never be concluded on fair terms. The surplus value embodies the surplus and unpaid labour of the worker, which can be used by the capitalist for the monopoly of land to obtain rent or obtained the surplus value in the name of interest through lending. In either form, the worker is exploited. To Engels (1880), the discovery of surplus value by Marx uncovered the secret of capitalist production. He stated that the appropriation of unpaid labour is the basic form of the capitalist mode of production and the exploitation of workers through this mode of production. Even if capitalists buy the labour of workers at the full value that it has as a commodity on the commodity market, they squeeze more out of the labour than they pay for it. This surplus value ultimately constitutes the value accumulated by the increasing amount of capital in the hands of bourgeois. This is the process of capitalist and capital production.

The accumulation of capital involves the constant increase of labour (i.e., the increase of the proletariat), and the pursuit of profit by the

[8] See Marx's arguments on *Production of Surplus Value* and *The Different Parts into which Surplus Value is Decomposed in Value, Price and Profit* ([1865] 1898). Cited from *Marx and Engels Collection, Vol. 3 1864–1883* (2009).

capitalists involves the constant extraction of surplus value. In such a labour-capital relation, Marx believed that workers were at a great disadvantage in fighting with the capitalists. Thus, in Marx's view, there is an inevitable confrontation between the bourgeoisie and the proletariat (modern wage workers) in the society in capitalist relations of production. Marx used a dualistic structure to describe the society. In his class theory, the working class is the only class that produces all value (Engels, 1891) and the only revolutionary class in opposition to the bourgeoisie. The rest of the classes are declining and dying with the development of big industry, but the proletariat is a product of big industry itself (Marx, [1844] 1932). The rest of the classes are classes between the bourgeoisie and the proletariat, including industrialists, small merchants, craftsmen and peasants. They struggle against the bourgeoisie to preserve their survival from extinction. They are not revolutionary but conservative, and more than that, they are even reactionary, for they seek to turn back the wheel of history. If they are revolutionary, it is because they are going to join the proletariat. In this way, they are going to defend, not their present interests but their future interests. They are going to leave their original position and occupy the position of the proletariat (Marx, [1844] 1932).

Therefore, Marx emphasised the need for an ideological awakening of the working class ([1844] 1932). According to Marx, capitalism not only dominates the workers through the coercive system of production, but also through the superstructure, the ideology of the class. However, workers were not aware of their advantages but struggle where they are least good at, and where they are sure to lose, such as destroying the machines or occupying factories. This kind of protest can only express feelings of anger, but it cannot help them gain the sympathy of the public. Destroying machines, occupying factories or going on strike cannot improve the status of the working class or gain sympathy from the public; instead, it causes inconvenience for other citizens. This might place workers in a dilemma. These are what Marx defined as "*class-in-itself*" level, while workers should know how to use the ideological tool to struggle from "*class-for-itself*" level.[9] "For" means they have class consciousness and identification.[10]

[9] See Marx ([1847] 1920), *The Poverty of Philosophy*, p. 194.

[10] There are two important concepts in Marxist class theory, one is class consciousness and the other is class struggle. Lenin attached great importance to the key role of the

Regarding the class struggle from "*class-for-itself*" level and eliminating exploitation, Marx also provided ideas. Marx and Engels (1848) proposed that the first step of the working class's revolution is to raise the proletariat to the ruling class and fight for democracy. The proletariat would use its political rule to seize the entire capital of the bourgeoisie step by step, to concentrate all the means of production in the hands of the state, the proletariat organised as the ruling class, and to increase the total amount of productivity as quickly as possible. When class differences disappear in the process of development and all production is concentrated in the hands of united individuals, public power loses its political nature. Political power, in its original sense, is organised violence used by one class to oppress another class. If the proletariat, in its struggle against the bourgeoisie, must unite as a class, make itself the ruling class through revolution and destroy the old relations of production by violence in its capacity as the ruling class, then in destroying such relations of production it also destroys the conditions of existence of class antagonism, of the class itself, and thus of its own rule as a class.[11] Eventually, a classless society is formed.

This classless society is the communist society conceived by Marx: eliminate the exploitation of some people by others, eliminate private ownership[12] and realise people's true control over themselves. Marx

formation of working-class consciousness in the contemporary political struggle and the cultivation of advanced intellectuals (Shang & Han, 2007). Raymond Aron (2003, p. 17) discussed that social classes exist only when they are self-conscious and there can be no class consciousness without acknowledging the class struggle. A class is self-conscious only when it finds itself fighting against other classes.

[11] Marx (1871) and Engels (1871) separately stated that the emancipation of the working class is to destroy all class domination. The emancipation of the working class should be fought for by the working class itself. The struggle for the emancipation of the working class is not for class privileges and monopolies, but for equal rights and duties, and the destruction of all class domination. The economic domination of the workers by the monopolists of the means of labour, i.e., the sources of life, is the basis of all forms of slavery, of all social poverty, spiritual sinking and political dependence, and therefore the economic emancipation of the working class is the great goal to which all political movements should be subordinated as a means. See Marx (1871) *Resolutions of the International Congress of Workers' Associations* and Engels (1871) *On Working Class Political Action*, available on 12th September, 2022, *vide*: https://www.marxists.org/chinese/marx-engels/17/048.htm.

[12] See Marx's arguments on *Private Property and Communism* in *Economic and Philosophic Manuscripts of 1844*, and Marx and Engels (1848) *The Communist Manifesto*. Cited from *Marx and Engels Collection, Vol. 1 1843–1848* (2009).

(1848) mentioned that the communists can summarise their theory in one sentence: the elimination of private property. The characteristic of communism is not the abolition of the general ownership, but the abolition of bourgeois ownership. It is not about the deprivation of the right of possessing the social products, but the deprivation of the right to use that possession to enslave the labour of others. Communist ownership is a positive renunciation of private property (the self-alienation of man) (Marx, [1844] 1932).

A classless society (communist society) that replaces the capitalist society is a Marxist idea of how the society develops linearly.[13] Because the productive forces determine the relations of production, and the relations of production correspond to the ideology, a social revolution will come when the material productive forces of society reach a certain stage of development that contradicts the existing relations of production (Marx, 1859). Communist relations of production can well resolve the incompatibility of socialised production and capitalist appropriation in capitalist relations of production. The products and production produced according to socialisation under the capitalist relations of production are socialised, but the relations of appropriation are such that those who use the social means of production and produce these products do not possess them, but rather they go to the capitalists. In communist relations of production, once the means of production are in social possession, commodity production will be eliminated, and with it the domination of the product over the producer. The anarchy in social production would be replaced by a planned and conscious organisation. The struggle of the individual for survival would cease. Thus, the individual would no longer be controlled to some extent by alien forces but would dominate themselves and become the true master of society (Engels, 1880).

After Marx put forward the conception of communism, the orthodox Marxist: Lenin implemented Marx's ideas and wanted to build socialism in one country, Lenin was not concerned with the problem of class exploitation, or rather he fully accepted and agreed with Marx's analysis of class and the workers' struggle. Socialism is viewed as the primary stage of communist development, and the ultimate goal of national development of a socialist state is a communist state. Marx ([1875] 1891)

[13] The laws of social development are primitive society, slave society, feudal society, capitalist society and communist society. See Marx (1859) *Critique of Political Economy* and Lenin ([1919] 1929) *On the State*.

in *Critique of the Gotha Programme* discussed that communism is the end state of socialism in terms of equity, classlessness and allocation on demand. Socialism is the lower stage of communist development. This difference was accepted by Lenin (1917) and stated in *The State and Revolution*. China also accepted the "two stages of communism".[14]

Lenin's focus is on how to achieve communism in a country in a brief period of time. Through the wartime economy (the construction of heavy industry and military industry), one country can break through the siege of capitalism and build a communist state and then lead all other countries on the path to communism.[15] However, problems were discovered with applying Lenin's theoretical practice in the Soviet Union, Eastern Europe and China. These socialist states established national ownership of the means of production that were held by the party-state, guaranteed full employment, granted welfare benefits (under the concept of communism) to workers and eliminated classes (or the so-called exploiting antagonistic classes) artificially. The common problem is that this path is economically unsustainable. The rapid accumulation of productive forces cannot reach the conceived, and the classless society cannot be achieved in a short time.

Marx's analysis of class and the exploitation of the proletariat is based on "positivist research" and the conclusions are accurate.[16] However, Marx did not expect whether it is possible to achieve the ultimately idealised society at once. His logic chain: from exploitation to class antagonism, to resistance and to the establishment of communism, might need further discussion. In other words, it may be possible that the production in economy can always progress, but whether the class could be eliminated in social relations required further thought. Learnt from history, countries that practised communism, the problem of inefficiency arose when they tried to concentrate their efforts to build communism within one to two generations under public ownership, for example, Hungary and Yugoslavia.[17] These countries needed to choose whether continuing the

[14] See Mao Zedong (1940), *On New Democracy* (*Xin Minzhu Zhuyi Lun*).

[15] Lenin's practical theories on how to build the socialist state can be derived from Lenin's works- *Military Program of Proletarian Revolution* (1916) and *On the European Federal Slogan* (1915).

[16] Positivism is the opposite of normativism, which involves a lasting philosophical debate. This study will not involve in this debate.

[17] See *Explore and Selection: A History Evaluation of Hungary and Yugoslavia* at China Reform Data (tansuo yu xuanze: dui nansilafu xiongyali de lishixing kaocha, zhongguo

socialist path of equity, which eliminated the private ownership and class but cannot improve the efficiency of production or introducing competition in the market by taking economic reforms. The result is they chose efficiency at the expense of socialist fairness. So, after sacrificing fairness, will the working class be exploited by the management class? Does such exploitation pull the workers back to the proletariat under Marx? With such a theoretical connection, this study can apply Marx's theory of the proletariat and class to analyse current Chinese workers.

To look further at the practical theory of Lenin guided by Marx, it did not consider the inefficiency problem of communist fairness either. Before Deng Xiaoping's economic reform, China followed the path of construction proposed by Lenin (the Soviet path to socialism). China's society which was built according to Marx's class theory and Lenin's practice of building socialism was faced with the problem that the ideal pathway may not work. From Deng's discourses at the Eveleth Plenary Session of the Third Central Committee, when it came to solving the problem of fairness and efficiency, Deng chose efficiency.[18] This means, the labour-capital relation carefully needs reconsideration in China.

gaige xinxiku), 1 October 2010, available on 12th September, 2022, *vide:* http://www.reformdata.org/2010/1001/1812.shtml.

[18] See Deng's speech—*Emancipating the Mind, Seeking Truth from Facts and Uniting as One in Looking to the Future* (jiefang sixiang, shishi jiushi, tuijie yizhi xiangqian kan), 13 December 1978, available on 12th September, *vide:* http://www.people.com.cn/item/sj/sdldr/dxp/B101.html.

"Not to talk about more work and more profit, not to attach importance to material benefits is fine for a few advanced elements but not for the masses, is fine for a period of time but not for a long period of time" (*bujiang duolao duode, bu zhongshi wuzhi liyi, dui shaoshu xianjin fenzi keyi, dui guangda qunzong buxing, yiduan shijian keyi, changqi buxing*);

"The revolution arises on the basis of material benefits, and it would be idealism to talk only about the spirit of sacrifice and not about material benefits" (*geming shi zai wuzhi liyi de jichu shang chansheng de, ruguo zhijiang xisheng jingsheng, bujiang wuzhi liyi, na jiushi weixinlun*);

"Not only should every workshop director and production team leader be made responsible for and think about production, but every worker and peasant must be made responsible for and think about production" (*budan yinggai shi meige chejian zhuren, shengchan duizhang dui shengchan fu zeren, xiang banfa, erqie yiding yao shi meige gongren nongmin dou dui shengchan fu zeren, xiang banfa*);

"We should allow some regions, some enterprises and some workers and peasants to have more income and a better life first because of their hard work and great achievements. If a part of the population gets better off first, it is bound to produce a great demonstration force" (*yao yunxu yi bufen diqu, yi bufen qiye, yi bufen gongren nongmin,*

The privileges granted to workers in the constructed socialist enterprises: SOEs, especially workers in heavy and military industries and workers in central government-managed SOEs, were given the best advantages and became the aristocratic workers among workers. When policies no longer favoured these industries, SOEs' inefficiency problem dragged down the rapid development of the economy. The proposed economic reforms would allow a new labour-capital relation (the conflict between professional managers and workers) to be defined. The privileges of workers were taken away. If it can be found in my empirical research that even workers in central managed SOEs in heavy and military industries have regressed back to the proletariat in Marx's theory, then the situation of workers in other industries and sectors can be inferred. This links to my research hypothesis: workers are exploited after economic reforms, and they reconstitute themselves as the proletariat. Then, would this reconstitution make the reformed workers conscious of the shift from "*class-in-itself*" to "*class-for-itself*"? Has Chinese society regressed back to a class society after significant economic growth? This can be answered by exploring the working class and their social status in this research.

Marx's theory is in line with my research question and hypothesis and is consistent with the current situation in China. In Xi Jinping's article "*Solidly Promoting Common Prosperity*" (*zhashi tuidong gongtong fuyu*),[19] China's current social problems are sharply manifested in the polarisation and gap between the rich and the poor, capital expansion without limits and the consolidation of classes. The article addresses that "Make efforts to expand the size of the middle-income group" (*zhuoli kuada zhongdeng shouru qunti de guimo*), and "Raise the wages of skilled workers to attract more highly qualified people to join the skilled workforce" (*tigao jishu gongren gongzi daiyu, xiying gengduo gao sushi rencai jiaru jishu gongren duiwu*), which are actually talking about the wage claim of the working class.[20] Therefore, it is applicable to explain the current Chinese working

youyu xingqin nuli chengji da er shouru xian duo yixie, shenghuo xian hao qilai. yi bufen ren shenghuo xian hao qilai, jiu biran chansheng jida de shifan liliang); etc.

[19] See *Qiushi*, 15 October 2021, available on 12th September, 2022, *vide*: http://www.qstheory.cn/dukan/qs/2021-10/15/c_1127959365.htm.

[20] Chinese leader Xi Jinping has promoted "common prosperity" in China which clearly shows that Chinese communist leadership is fully aware of the increasing income gap in society, which is not compatible with the ideology that the CCP follows. Although very positive, Xi's "common prosperity" will be a long-term goal beyond the current class

class and class issues by Marx's arguments and analyse the relationship between the labour and capital from Marx.

It is important to note this because the subject of my study is on the workers, there are some points of views that are not in the scope of my discussion. First, some Marx's concepts have been revised or downplayed in China. For example, Marx's class theory emphasises class struggle. Many scholars no longer use class as a leading factor to analyse Chinese social structure to avoid political sensitivity (Lin Chun, 2015, pp. 24–53; Yan, 2012, pp. 278–279) or replace class with other concepts, such as *suzhi*, which was discussed in the last chapter. The other example is the core socialist values education (*shehui zhuyi hexin jiazhiguan jiaoyu*) of Chinese students. As a compulsory module for all Chinese students, though it is about moral education, it links ideology and politics closely and Marxism serves as the core value and the guiding ideology rather than a theory that could be debated and questioned (Gao Yan, 2017, pp. 11–14; Lin Chongde, 2017, pp. 66–73; Liu Zheng, 2012; Min Yongxin, 2010, pp. 80–87; Zhang Yaochan, 2005, pp. 4–10 and 2010, pp. 3–6).

Secondly, I also learned the critique of Marx's class theory from some scholars. For instance, Bourdieu argued that Marx ignored the middle class and critiqued Marx's social structure dichotomy. While class analysis formerly portrayed society as a one-dimensional hierarchy, Marxism imagined the social world as simply organised around the opposition between two blocs—exploiting class and exploited class. Bourdieu regarded the class analysis as more complex than that and thus he pictured society as a "social space". He proposed questions about the one-dimensionality, the boundary between these two blocs, about the "labour aristocracy" and the "embourgeoisement" of the working class (Bourdieu, 1991; Hjekllbrekke & Prieur, 2018, p. 76). Nevertheless, Burawoy (2018, p. 390) discussed both Marx and Bourdieu recognised the conflict between these two fractions and cast conflict in terms of struggles over categories of representation as classification struggles.

Berlin (1978, pp. 84–85, 101 and 104) analysed and summarised Marx's class theory and compared Pierre-Joseph Proudhon with Marx. He stated that in Proudhon's opinion, workers and bourgeoisie must seek through purely economic pressure to impose their own pattern on the rest of society and the process should be gradual and peaceful. Proudhon

division highly visible in China. In other words, Xi's ideal will be a long-term development not a short-term fix.

suggested that workers must on no account have recourse to coercion; not even strikes were to be permitted, since this would infringe upon the individual worker's right to the free disposal of the person's labour. However, Marx's opinion is opposed to this. According to Marx, workers should resist. If a ruling class exists, despotism will remain. The purpose is the total abolition of classes themselves. Marx's opinion on capitalism, which emphasised the crushing and distortion of the lives of millions of workers, is more related to the topic of my research.

Edward Palmer Thompson also challenged Marxists in the material tradition: that they overemphasise material determinism at the expense of social or cultural agency, and thus ignore the complexity of the class subject as well as class consciousness (McLennan, 1982). For Thompson, the "positivist historiography" ignores culture, industrialisation, polity and the qualitative change process of the subjectivity of the working class (McLennan, 1982; Pan & Ren, 2006, pp. 106–123). From Thompson's idea, people's common interests and experiences can therefore help to build class. His point is that class is a historical phenomenon, not a "structure" or "category". It is a real element within people's relationships, and it can be calculated precisely based on an understanding of the historic context within which they are living, which the historian must capture and describe. This "thing" is people's common interests or experiences (Pan & Ren, 2006, pp. 106–123; Thompson, [1963] 2016). Nevertheless, Thompson referred to Marx's account of class consciousness (*class-for-itself*) in which a group of people drew conclusions from common experience, either from their predecessors or personal experience, feel and explicitly state their common interests among themselves and begin to realise that their interests are opposed to those of the rulers and employers, thus forming a class. In brief, class generates itself from practice. Thompson also referred to the Marxist view of the working class, i.e., the subjectivity and various experiences of the working class will provide us with the evidence to understand class itself and no one can become the working-class historical actor except itself (Pan & Ren, 2006, pp. 106–123).

I am concerned with the way in which the workers, under Marx's set of logic, confront the exploitation of power to build a classless society. Criticisms of Marx's dichotomy of social structure, or whether the class should be defined as a historical phenomenon or as a structure, are irrelevant to my research; some of the mentioned scholars shared Marx's analysis on the working class. Marx's vision of a classless society when the proletariat comes to power is clearly not yet realised in China. Then, if a worker's situation after the economic reforms can be described as a kind of exploitation, can this exploitation redefine these "masters" of socialism? And do Chinese workers return to their proletarian status in the old labour-capital relation?

Micro Approaches to Explore

Marx's analysis of class and workers provide me with macroscopic theoretical guidance for this research; beyond that, from a microscopic level, I use different approaches to explore the research question on SOE workers' statuses and capital relation after the economic reforms and examine the research hypothesis: whether SOE workers in China return back to the proletarians in the old labour-capital relation, or at least they are not in the constructed labour-capital relationship in socialism or communism, and a class society has returned to China.

Weber's Understanding of Sociology

Weber's understanding of sociology explains why a large proposition about the class reconstruction in China and the SOE workers' status after economic reforms can be understood in a microcosmic way. Weber emphasised the importance of human individuality in sociology, so that the task of sociological research is to "understand" the intentions or tasks contained in phenomena. In the sense, unlike the strict, uniform, and exclusive way of knowing the natural sciences, "understanding" is at the heart of Weber's methodology and is a unique way of researching a unique object. Distinguished from the causality, precisely formulaic logic of the natural sciences, causality in sociology is a specific and unique grasp of relevance for a specific time. The task of sociology is therefore not to discover laws that explain a series of similar phenomena once and for all, but to try to grasp a relatively plausible cause in each specific case. In real life, there are existences that are purely accidental acts or actions. Therefore, it is the task of sociologists to seek the situational causality behind phenomena, distinguish accidental actions from social actions, and grasp social actions and their intentions and values behind them (Wang Bin, 2016, pp. 12–21).

Weber's understanding of sociology justifies that this study can go back to individual cases, examining macro issues from a micro perspective and exploring the underlying connections. If a case could be found to refute the existing conclusions, it would show what Weber refers to as the special circumstance that exists in society, and it would be valuable to grasp the logic behind these special circumstances. Therefore, this study can start with a case study to answer the research question and test the research hypothesis.

Weber ([1922] 1978, p. 4) argued that sociology is a science: its intent is to gain an interpretative understanding of social action and causal explanation of the process, the results and the consequences of social action. Therefore, in understanding sociology, the personal "meaning" of action is a key point for understanding and interpretation and a key point of understanding sociology as well. Weber suggested that personal action and interpretation unconsciously construct a society (Bendix, 1977). His methodological individualism assumes that individuals are aware of the motives and subjective states of their actions. In terms of the sociological interpretation of the subjectivity of action, collective constructions must be seen as nothing more than modes and results of the organisation of action, since these individuals are the only bearers of subjectively comprehensible actions (Weber, [1922] 1978, p. 16). Therefore, by taking to each individual as an independent case in this study, learning their stories and experiences is a way to create a picture of the society.

Bourdieu's Material and Symbolic Capital

Bourdieu's "capital" is different from Marx's "surplus value", although his economic capital is related to Marx's definition of capital, for Bourdieu, capital itself is a symbolic concept. It is associated with financial capital but has many other meanings. Bourdieu defines capital as either material or symbolic. Material capital may refer to money or property (Feng, 2009, pp. 287–288), while symbolic capital could be cultural, social, political or religious, all aspects that are less tangible. These forms of capital are power resources, meaning they make a difference to people's identities and positions and, more specifically, material capital can enable distinction, domination, and consecration. Neveu (2018, p. 347) suggested that Bourdieu's capital is a collection of goods and skills, of knowledge and acknowledgements belonging to an individual or a group that can be mobilised to develop influence, gain power or bargain for other elements.

Bourdieu's symbolic capital can only be valued and related to differences between people when their practical power is activated by recognition (Grenfell, 2004, p. 28). As Bourdieu argued, "Agents possess power in proportion to their symbolic capital, i.e., in proportion to the recognition they receive from the group" (Bourdieu, 1991, p. 106). Thus, such capital is symbolic in that there is an "audience" of people who are able to interpret its meaning and share the understanding of that meaning among themselves in ways which are communicable and comprehensive. This also relates to people's own self-identity, where they are the audiences of their own capital. Capital of any sort needs to be understood and to avail itself of interpretive frameworks. In other words, capital can only really function with labour, and those different forms of capital can be obtained by accumulating labour (Bourdieu & Wacquant, 1998; Feng, 2009, pp. 287–288; Lin & Li, 2007, pp. 63–68). This is similar to Marx's view that the labour of workers creates values.

Bourdieu's explanation of capital, especially symbolic capital, can flexibly be applied to this research to distinguish SOE workers' different forms of capital which related to their status. The ownership of various forms of capital, be it economic, cultural and social, constructs the class (Bourdieu, 1977; [1979] 1984). This has been recognised and applied by various sociologists, e.g., David S. G. Goodman (2014, p. 29).[21] Bourdieu suggested that capital brings power to the one who holds it. It enables a person to achieve things and do things in society. The ruling class occupies the largest amount of all kinds of capital, while the working class has only an exceedingly small amount of capital. The differences between different classes are clear because people compete with different combinations of capital in the society. Even within the same class, subgroups exist (Lin & Li, 2007, pp. 63–68). Bourdieu's description of capital can help to analyse the rights that SOE workers want to gain and the interest behind the rights. It can also classify workers' demands and the resources used by workers in their actions.

Foucault's Power Concept

When Foucault spoke about power, he did not regard it as guaranteed, as is the case with a political institution or a ruler, but instead spoke about "relationships". For Foucault, power is a relationship that is in a cyclical process. This means that power never fixes its location in the hands of some people, and it cannot be regarded as one person's property. Foucault compared power to a crisscrossing network; everyone is in

[21] His classification of class in contemporary China is based on economic configuration, political behaviour, social mobility and symbolic construction.

the network nodes. This network does not have a subject or a centre, but it is relative, and everyone can apply the power or be controlled by the power. The network is uncertain (Chen Binghui, 2002, pp. 84–90). He further critiqued the traditional concept of power, which presents a binary opposition, with people simply divided into the ruling class and the controlled class. Foucault suggested that power should be a network that is always engaged in strained activities. In addition, Foucault emphasised the symbiotic nature of power and knowledge. He suggested that knowledge is an important method by which power gains legitimacy and an important means of disciplining power as well (Yan Feng, 1997, p. 55). Foucault focused on how power operates. In his book *Discipline and Punish*, he discussed disciplining power and the use of technical power to control people's bodies, actions and so on, making individuals submit to a disciplined action mode (Foucault, 1999).

SOE workers were privileged in the constructed socialist enterprises, but their privileges were withdrawn after economic reforms. Foucault's concept of power can be used to help understand how workers' power is acquired and controls their understanding of themselves, their class and their behaviours in production within networks in factories. According to Foucault's understanding, the realisation of man's true freedom does not lie in the breaking of external chains and the elimination of all relations of power that control and oppress, but in the awakening of man to himself (Li Jing, 2013, pp. 60–68; Wang Xizong, 2013, pp. 5–6). To some extent, Foucault shares the idea of class consciousness that Marx wanted to evoke in workers.

Olson's Interest Group

Mancur Olson used an individual analysis approach like Weber. His theories are based on microscopic individuals pursuing their own interests (Li Zenggang, 2002, pp. 77–81). In applying Olson's interest groups in the Chinese context, Zhang Yuyan (1994, pp. 97–106) analysed that interest groups use government to profit, use government regulation to prevent the entry of new competitors and use national legislation to seek group interests. This description applies to the analysis of SOEs and SOE workers in a particular historical period, who existed as privileged enterprises and privileged groups that constructed their interest groups.

Olson's interest groups can influence policies to a certain extent (Olson, [1982] 2008). A small and highly organised group can often control the expression of the public interest when sufficiently funded because they seek their own interests from specific laws and rules. An interest group is Olson's practice of analysing collective action, and collective action is the premise of an interest group. Olson ([1965] 2012) argued that collective action is easier to generate when the number of collectives is small; however, as the number of collectives grows, it becomes increasingly difficult to generate collective action because it is exceedingly difficult to negotiate how to share the costs of collective action within large collectives of large numbers. Moreover, the larger the group, the lower the per capita benefit, the stronger the incentive to free rider, and the more difficult it is to detect free-riding behaviour (Wang Jingxian, 2010, p. 15; Zheng Zifeng, 2011, pp. 42–66). Olson's concept of interest groups can be used to explain whether workers act collectively to defend their interests after economic reforms, and whether their class consciousness fight for the class rather than just their individual interests.

Sen's Entitlement Approach

Amartya Sen shared a consistent concern with Marx on whether people are free or exploited. They both regarded it as an important motivating factor in judging socio-economic development. Existing research argued that SOE workers have become the new urban poor. Their poverty can be seen in the economic loss of income of the laid-off workers, and also in their social status transformation from the "master" and "leading class" to the ordinary "population" in terms of political rights (Chen Feng, 2009; Cho, 2013; Li Peilin, 2004; Li Qiang, 2002; Lee, 2007; Solinger, 2006, pp. 177–193; Thornton, 2017, p. 257; Wright, 2010; Wu Qingjun, 2008, p. 64; Yan, 2012, p. 50). From a sociological perspective, the new poor are a part of the population whose ability to live, enthusiasm for work, willingness to learn and willingness to consume are gradually decreasing under the influence of the overall social consumption environment, resulting in a delayed improvement in personal income and quality of life, and thus eventually entering the "underclass" (Bauman, 1998, p. 93). Sen focused on the causes of poverty and his "entitlements approach" can also be applied to explain the SOE workers, aristocratic workers, who had been disenfranchised after economic reforms. The poverty of SOE workers and what they want to fight for is not only economic.

Sen believes that the essence of poverty is the deprivation of capabilities, more precisely the deprivation of "viable capabilities", i.e., the deprivation of the freedom to perform activities that lead to worthwhile life, ranging from basic material things such as food, clothing, housing and transport, to deeper levels of access to education, social participation and decent life (Jiang Jinshen, 2017, pp. 41–45; Sen, 2002, pp. 62, 85). Income is a manifestation of poverty. It is a cause and a means and a tool to identify poverty. However, it is important to recognise that the deprivation of entitlements is the essence of poverty (Wu Ling & Zhang Fulei, 2018, pp. 28–35; Chen Shiyong & Qin Meng, 2017, pp. 33–43). Sen mentioned that not only those who are extremely poor need attentions, but also those who are just below the poverty line (Sen, [1983] 2016, pp. 191–192). The entitlement approach proposed by Sen is a system of rights in which political, economic and social systems all influence the distribution of rights and determine the fate of different groups (Ma Xinwen, 2008, pp. 69–74). It is not only those who are in extreme poverty that are likely to remain in poverty, but different classes of people can be in poverty for varied reasons. Sen's social stratification is based on the possession of similar resources (Qu Hui & Yu Guoming, 2019, pp. 150–157).

SOE workers are suffering from poverty because "they lack the capability and entitlements to access goods" (Sen, [1983] 2009, p. 58; Zou Libing, 2011, pp. 24, 27). SOE workers are in a very passive position in terms of both access to wages and political status. As my research hypothesis mentioned—the current Chinese society is in fact still a class society and the capability of SOE workers to change their status and fight for their entitlements after they have been reintegrated into the proletariat is extremely limited. The consequence of this lack of capability is that they have to accept the loss of the welfare benefits they had before economic reforms and accept they were deprived of their privileges as "masters of the country" as well. SOE workers' material changes caused by the changes in political status made it impossible for SOE workers to obtain the satisfaction and security of their previous standard of living and failed to reach the "'minimum' of their recognition" (Sen, [1983] 2016, p. 202) of the status of SOE workers, making them the new urban poor.

In conclusion, I carefully selected Marx's theory as the research guidance but use multiple approaches to undertake this research, studying a classical question of class with modern approaches. The use of micro approaches is based on Weber's understanding of sociology, which explains and explores social problems and processes in terms of individuals' actions.

2.2 Methodology

The theoretical framework states why case and individual can be used as the unit of research in the theory. The methodological framework will further discuss the details of research methods: case study, data collective methods, data analysis methods and the use of NVivo to assist the analysis, and how to overcome challenges in fieldwork research. How this research applies these methods, and statistical analysis together with my findings will also be discussed in this chapter.[22]

Sociologists proved that besides statistics, there are other methods that can be used to understand social reality. Qualitative research has a desire to understand the participants' viewpoints on their own terms as well as understand their viewpoints in terms dictated by pre-existing categories. It can represent a data-driven approach and a theory-driven approach (Watts, 2014, pp. 1–14). This research will take qualitative research methods to answer the research question of how the economic reforms in China influence workers' status and examine the research hypothesis, that through the SOE workers returned to the proletariat, the reconstruction of a class society in China after economic reforms can be proved.

Qualitative Research Methods—Case Study, Oral History and More

The value of any case study is that it can help to generate new theories, disprove overly deterministic theories and shed light on previously unknown processes (Thaxton, 2008, p. 9). Based on Weber's theoretical understanding of sociological research methods from the perspective of individuals, it is suitable to use the case study method to explore this research's question: the status of SOE workers after economic reforms. As stated in Chapter 1, SOE workers were in a privileged position compared to others in the working class. If workers in a particular policy and financial supported SOE can be examined and it shows that their status has returned to the proletariat, inferences can be drawn from the situation of other workers.

A case study is a strategy for doing research which involves an empirical investigation of a particular phenomenon within its real-life context using multiple sources of evidence (Yin, 2013). From the philosophical

[22] More detailed information on the fieldwork site will be dealt with later in Chapter 3—Introduction to EGC.

perspective, the whole is constructed by independent parts and a part reflects the whole, and each part shows the whole's fundamental rules (Burawoy, 2008). A case study method allows me to "retain the holistic and meaningful characteristics of real-life events - such as individual life cycles, small group behaviour, organisational and managerial processes, neighbourhood change, school performance, international relations, and the maturation of industries" (Yin, 2013, p. 4).

I note that there are a number of anthropological explorations in the study of reformed Chinese society using case study, oral history and ethnography research methods. For instance, Du Shi (2018, p. 6) did a case study of a state-owned car factory in an old industrial base in Northeast China based on fieldwork in the anthropological sense. In Du's opinion, such an industrial ethnography can help to understand the transformation stories of SOEs as well as urban societies. An industrial ethnography encompasses multiple dimensions of workers' working and living experiences and is oriented towards the identification of practical problems in the field. Du thinks that the sociological paradigm and framework focus on the impact of factories on social structure and control at the macro level, or the study of unit societies and workers' communities at the meso level, while the nature of his case study is that of micro-level survey texts.

"Anthropological economics" or "cultural economics" is also a common perspective in studies of SOEs. For example, Zhang Xiaojun (2011, pp. 1–12) explores the dilemma between monopoly and privatisation and marketisation of SOEs in the context of economic reforms. His choice of such a research perspective aims to go beyond the horizon of economics and situate the discussion in a broader socio-cultural economic perspective. Wang Shaojie and Tu Yulong (2021, pp. 13–18) also applies an economic anthropology approach to the investigation of three SOEs in South China. By making long-term observation records of the fieldwork site and interviewing the employees to obtain research data, Wang and Tu's research demonstrates that the path of choice of the property rights model directly influences the choice of different paths of human economic behaviour, and also explains the different fates of the three SOEs.

Another example is a case study of *Wanli* Factory (*wanli chang*), a large SOE in Lanzhou, Gansu Province (Liu Fan, 2016, pp. 39–54). Liu interviewed ten retirees and selected different interviewees on different research questions to understand the medical choices of retired SOE workers and the institutional weaknesses of the health insurance system from a medical anthropological perspective.

In fact, these methods: case study, oral history (obtained through interviews), observation and even ethnography, are not unique to anthropology. These methods have been widely used in the study of SOEs and SOE workers from a sociological point of view, to make a historical overview of an enterprise or study a group of people. The sociological approach can also be used to examine and analyse issues from a microscopic perceptive.

Sun Dongbo's research (2015, pp. 91–95) is based on several interviews with one person by using the oral history method and archival materials to describe the process of a factory's construction process and detailing the person's feelings and perceptions about the enterprise's closure and lay-off policy. It presents a case study of an SOE established during the Cultural Revolution in a border town in Yunnan Province. Liu Xiao and Liu Wankun (2020, pp. 5–13) use oral histories to explore changes in enterprise management and the formation of industrial workers' skills. The oral histories of 20 workers, technicians and cadres are recorded in audio form, and the oral data are collated and summarised to present the characteristics of the micro-management elements of enterprises at different historical stages from a historical perspective. Xu Xuanguo et al. (2020, pp. 217–241, 246) studied a special group of community cadres who have been transformed from cadres in SOEs to cadres in communities.[23] An oral history research method was used. By taking in-depth interviews and documentation as data collection methods, they collected data from eight community cadres in Shanghai. From the perspective of institutional change, a moderate change in the relationship between the state and the individual is constructed, focusing on the government-led transition of cadres from units to communities to alleviate the plight of workers laid off, unemployed and re-employed as a result of SOE reforms. There is another study of an SOE established during the Third Line construction period (Xu Youwei & Yang Huaguo, 2015, pp. 17–25). Xu and Yang explored the profit and loss of small Three Line enterprises in Shanghai in the 1980s and the transformation of the enterprises from military to civilian production. It is based on the corporate archives of the case enterprises in Shanghai: *Qianjin* Machinery

[23] The original text of community cadres is *she sao*, literally means the older sister in the community.

Factor (*qianjin jixie chang*), *Xietong* Machinery Factory (*xietong jixie chang*) and *Xinguang* Metal Factory (*xinguang jinshu chang*), as well as Shanghai's urban archives and oral histories.

In general, oral history reflects the history of change and development of the organisation and society through the historical review of the individual. It can reveal detailed information that reflects the changes in the wider context. If SOE workers are considered as an ethnic group, an ethnography of SOE workers can be constructed (or an SOE itself can be regarded as the subject of ethnography). An ethnography refines the understanding of a group to a deeper level. The use of the case study method and autobiographical ethnography in the studies mentioned above provides methodological support for this sociological research.

This study uses these research methods flexibly, exploring the changes in SOEs from the individuals' histories, more importantly, reflecting on the changing status of workers in SOEs from personal perceptions and facts gathered from archival research. This research does not intend to define how these research methods should be applied differently in different disciplines, but to use these methods of collecting research data and materials to make a multifaceted analysis of the proposition of the status of SOE workers from multiple levels and dimensions.

It is important to note that the above-mentioned anthropological and sociological studies on Chinese SOEs or certain types of SOE workers during the reform period do not address my research question. Therefore, applying similar research methods flexibly to explore SOEs and SOE workers from a class perspective expands the field of research that can be covered by case study and interview research methods. The empirical research that uses these methods is not limited to studying enterprise management and personal development but can be applied to explore social change and the composition of class.

Data Collection Methods

Secondary Data Collection

The fieldwork research took place between February and September 2018. The first three months were used to collect related documents, such as documentation, including administrative documents: progress reports and other internal records; news clippings and articles from the mass media or community newspapers; archival records, including public use files, census and other statistical data made available by industry sector, local and central government; service records that show the number of clients served over a given period of time; organisational records, such as budget or personnel records; and maps and charts of the geographic characteristics of the fieldwork site and the located city and demographic data of employment. For instance, news reported that on 17 September 2016, the advertising board of E Group Company (EGC) at the top of the marketing building was moved due to the sale of the property to pay for SOE reform costs. This building is located at the main road crossing in D city. In the past, every car that entered the city centre, either from the outside or driving past to other cities, could clearly see the sign "The Marketing Department of EGC" on this building, which used to be a remarkable symbol. The silent disappearance of this led to a significant informal discussion among the employees within the enterprise. A while later, an official announcement was made that EGC's marketing department had sold its building's fourth to the sixth floor to a company and had to move the advertising board away. Web news like this was used in the interviews to explore the respondents' memories of a particular time period or reform policy.

The multiple data sources strengthen the reliability of this research's findings and analysis. In particular, there was a discussion about the conflicts between different groups of workers and workers' entitlements on an online platform during the workers' strike and resistance movement. This discussion has been selected to support this research's analysis.[24] The full list of documents related to the fieldwork site is in Appendix B. For anonymisation, the links will not be presented.

Although this research takes qualitative methods, the contextual data that provides evidence of the case study includes both qualitative and quantitative data.

Primary Data Collection

The primary data can be divided into two parts: from my previous research and this research in 2018. The first time I undertook a quantitative research project on SOE workers was in 2012, when I used questionnaires to investigate how SOE restructuring influenced on employees' choices; this was then followed by a qualitative research project in

[24] The discussion took place in September 2014 (in Chinese) through *Baidu Tieba* (an internet discussion platform). In later chapters, I will directly quote some of the discussion to further discourse EGC and EGC workers.

2015 to understand the workers' situation after collective activities by using internet-based interviews. The previous research contributed to my knowledge of the shifting situation of SOE workers in various times and the information about SOE reform policies between 1990 and 2010s.

The research in 2018 is empirical research based on open observation and semi-structured interviews to collect first-hand data. My participatory observation began when I lived in the living area of this case study site. The open observation provides a good opportunity for me to learn about the workers' daily routine, observe the working and living areas as well as broadly determine the breakdown of the composition of the people to be interviewed.

For instance, in the morning, workers are asked to arrive at work at 8 am, after that the main enterprise gate closes and only a gate with strict entrance review is open. After 8 am in the morning, registration is needed to get into the workplace, and lateness may be punished with a fine. I lived about 15 minutes walking distance from the case SOE, so the broadcast could be heard from the SOE. In the morning, this plays music for around 20–30 minutes before 8 am, and in the evening, the broadcast announces the enterprise news, at finishing work time: 6 pm until around 6.30 pm. The working life in the case SOE is quite regular. Although there is overtime work in this enterprise, the broadcast and the living area provided the researcher with a better understanding of how and when to find available interviewees.

Two other helpful pieces of information gained from the observation are:

1. Free bicycle sharing provided by the enterprise. The family area can be very crowded at rush hour, as thousands of people head in the same direction. To avoid the traffic, the enterprise provides free bicycle sharing—*mobai danche* (Mobike) to its employees. The annual fee for the Mobike is 240 Yuan and the deposit is 299 Yuan; the case enterprise covers these fees. Mobike is very easy and convenient to use; all you need is a smart phone and a downloaded app, then you can open any Mobike you want to use and park it at any place that is convenient. Hence, many Mobikes were parked in the living community and people used their phones to unlock them at rush hour. I also took photos of this phenomenon and attached them in Appendix F. Photos Collected from Fieldwork Research. Later in the interview phase, I also used a Mobike

to meet the respondents and the shared bicycle became a useful point of reference to build a comfortable and relaxing conversation atmosphere.

2. Popular activity—*guangchang wu* (square dance)—mostly organised by early retirees and retirees from the case SOE. It was found from the participant observation that the workers organised a lot of activities after work in the living area. The most popular was the *guangchang wu*; along the roads of the enterprise's main gate, there is a lot of open space; and the space was divided into several squares for different dance groups. The dancers, most of them SOE workers and retirees, were there every night to dance and engage in aerobic exercise. One commented, "We only have three days off per year, two days for the College Entrance Examination, one day for the Chinese New Year's Eve" (Interviewee 009). I participated in some of their activities, taking photos and videos for them. This provided another approach to getting to know the workers and learning about their lives through informal conversations, as well as finding potential interviewees. From these casual conversations, I developed an impression of how EGC workers currently evaluate their (life) situation.

As soon as I entered the fieldwork site and began the research, I clarified my identity as a PhD researcher and the interviews will only be used for academic purposes. Based on previous research experiences in SOEs, I have contacts with some manager-level employees in the case enterprise. After explaining the purpose and the content of the research, they helped me to gain access to the fieldwork site and conduct the first few interviews by putting me in touch with their colleagues and friends. With their help, I won the trust of the respondents in the region. This research was thus able to develop frank conversations with the interviewees.

The semi-structured interview can support this research to obtain as much information as possible and individualise each case by asking open questions and controlling the pace and core theme of the interview with the use of some structured questions. The structured questions are used to collect the interviewees' information, the general information on the enterprise's reforms and the workers' status. While the open questions are followed according to the interviewees' narratives to explore their working experiences and the workers' collective activities, etc., this method is also helpful in briefly reviewing the respondents' information.

The basic information of the interviewees is summarised in Appendix A, Table A.1. The semi-structured interview questions are attached to Appendix C.[25]

The respondents were reached by utilising the snow-balling method. Two of the interviewees helped a lot with introducing respondents for interviews. Due to "friend introductions", most of the respondents were willing to talk and answered the questions with as many details as they were asked for.

I conducted in-depth interviews with 23 people total and the average length of each interview is over 75 minutes. They are from various sectors and their ages ranged from 23 to 89. They all had clear memories of their lives and histories, as well as some of the landmark events the case SOE had experienced in its history of over 60 years. People from different job positions and different workplaces help diversify the respondents. I undertook two to four interviews with three respondents to explore more information. Besides the interviewees' working and life stories, the 23 respondents provided reliable stories of their co-workers as well. This kind of information contributed to enriching the research data, ensuring that the analysis was not limited by the number of interviews, but instead developing a broader picture of this case SOE and its workers. The participants can be distinguished as follows:

1. Still-employed state sector workers, including, rank-and-file workers (front-line workers and second-line workers), technicians and managers (17 people).
2. Early retired state sector workers.[26] Based on the data, the case SOE doesn't "lay-off" people, but these are people who left the enterprise earlier than their official retirement age and so, according to the

[25] Note here: the interviews always started with small conversations that were not related to the research topic. The opening conversation helps to build a relationship with the respondents and creates a more spontaneous start to the interview. For instance, I have a phone number that was issued in Beijing City. When using this number to call the interviewees to arrange interviews, I got many enquires when met in-person as to why it was being used in the case site. This type of simple conversation helps to start talking but is not recorded in the transcripts or used for analysis.

[26] This group of people will be discussed in detail in the next chapter in the fieldwork findings as well as later in the analytical chapters to address the particularity of this case study.

reform policy, they fit into this group (4 people. I took 2 interviews with one interviewee as she is in the first group of early retirees).
3. Pensioners, people who retired at their official retirement age (2 people. I took 4 interviews with one interviewee, and 2 interviews with the other to learn about the history of the enterprise establishment and work and life in SOE before the Reform and Opening up).

All the participants in the interviews were still associated with the case SOE during the fieldwork research period.

Data Analysis Methods and Application of NVivo

The criteria for interpreting the findings and the unit(s) of analysis are the other two important components of a case study research (Yin, 2013). NVivo software is used in this research to assist me in the analysis of qualitative research data.[27] All the interviews' transcripts are imported to NVivo. Individuals will be considered as analysis units in this research, that is every single interview is regarded as a case in NVivo.

To interpret this research data, I first transcribed (in Chinese) all the interviews.[28] By doing so, I became refamiliarised with the data and discovered valuable analysis points. Each case represents a unit of interviews, the respondents. The case classifications record information about cases, such as individuals' job positions and demographic data, which differentiate the interviewees in a concise and clear way by using attributes like gender and age.

I used various nodes to code my interview data. In NVivo, nodes are containers for coding by themes and topics, which gather related material in one place and interpret both data and theory-driven codes. The interviews' transcripts are narrative data provided by the participants and are coded according to themes. The first level of coding is descriptive coding, which gathers data and the second level of coding is interpretative coding, which reflects my preliminary thoughts on the interviews. Table 2.1 presents nodes I created in NVivo and also shows the number

[27] NVivo does not automatically make the qualitative data analysis better, more reliable or "objective". It will not do the analysis but assist in my analysis of qualitative research.

[28] The transcripts are in Chinese. In the analytical chapters, the extracts of interviewees are translated to English.

of related interviews and how many times the themes and topics are discussed by the interviewees.

NVivo can also be used to take notes during the qualitative data analysis. I created memos to record my primary analysis while using NVivo to do the analysis. Memos build the relationships among the nodes and the interviews. The table of memos is attached as Appendix D, Table D.1. It shows my reflections on the fieldwork data and the analysis inspirations I got from the interviews.

Annotations were added to the transcripts. Annotations help to link the interviews with the fieldwork collected documents, for instance, internal documents, newspaper and internet articles, the enterprise's public annual

Table 2.1 Nodes in NVivo

Coding categories	*Name of nodes*	*Related number of interviews*	*Number of reference*
Descriptive coding	Classification	9	10
	EGC's technique school	5	8
	Family background	18	34
	Female's promotion	2	4
	Job and unit allocation	21	64
	Movement	9	12
	New blood	13	18
	Opportunities to promote or change	19	50
	Original SOE tradition (welfare)	17	34
	Peer workers' stories	10	14
	Poor years (statement)	11	19
	Rich years (statement)	9	15
	Self-identity	4	4
Interpretative coding	Attitude towards SOE	20	119
	CCP	11	22
	Changes of state workers' identity	20	32
	Decided factors	19	31
	Relationship	14	39
	SOE reform	20	111
	Workers attitude towards leaders	14	55
	Working experience	20	93

Data source Fieldwork research

reports, the local government statistics, and tables and charts about the enterprise's construction situation, employees' situation, annual profitability, etc. The annotations support the further analysis and arguments. Annotations table is attached as Appendix E, Table E.1.

Overcoming Challenges

Dialect and Terms

I speak Mandarin as my mother language, but in a few cases the interviewees could only speak Sichuanese, which is difficult to understand if they are talking fast and due to the local dialect makes it even more difficult to understand. To avoid misunderstanding and confusion, I repeated their words and sentences back to them when they were difficult to understand, and then the interviewees corrected and provided further explanations on certain statements. By doing so, the dialect/accent problem was overcome.

Besides overcoming the accents, it was necessary for me to learn the common terminology that workers use before starting the interviews, as this constructs the "small society", differentiating "us" and "other" identities, and this could also be applied to prevent sensitive questions. After conducting several interviews, I was able to copy and apply some words and concepts learnt from the interviewees, to reduce the gap with the respondents as well as to protect their privacy in case they did not want to address some issues. For instance, concepts like "strike" and "demonstration", "cadres" and the "early retirement policy" were sensitive to EGC workers; it was better to describe them using other terms, such as "*yundong*" (movement), "*dangguande*" (leaders) and "*huijia*" (back home). When using their language to ask the interview questions, the respondents were more open and spoke more.

Research Ethics and Safety

I provided background information and gained consent from participants verbally instead of written information and consent forms. I always gave an introduction about myself and this research at the start of the interviews. A summary of questions and the request for permission to record the interviews were stated at the beginning as well. I explained the anonymisation carefully by stating how I would use the information that the respondents provided in this research. All the interviewees were adults, and they were informed and understood the research aims and topic from the substantive explanations; they all voluntarily participated in this research and provided information from their personal perspectives. In the interviews, I went back to questions that had not been completely answered and repeated questions when the answers lacked evidence. However, the interviewees were not forced to answer any questions that they did not want to.

To manage the researcher-respondent relationship and keep their contacts in case they needed to be contacted again, I created a new WeChat account for exchanging messages. This meant that the interviewee and I both had each other's contacts for any follow-up interviews and for reviewing the research report; this exchange of contacts also helped to introduce new interviewees. One of the interviewees used WeChat to communicate with his friends and colleagues to see whether he could find more people to participate and once he got a response, he contacted me via WeChat and shared the contact information details: for instance, the person's job position, industry, age and education background. This enabled me to prepare and adjust the interview questions before arranging the interview.

Most of the interviews were conducted in public venues, ensuring the safety of the female researcher at the fieldwork site. I offered to buy the drinks or paid for the food if the interview took place in an area serving food. These were not undue incentives but were considered necessary due to the interview length. Most still-employed state sector workers only have time to talk after work. For them, this time is about being at home and having dinner. The enterprise is also located in quite a central area within the city, so for the sake of convenience, most of the interviews were held in shopping mall cafés or restaurants nearby. To Chinese people, both official business and private relationships can be built at the dining table. I attempted to construct a casual and relaxing atmosphere for the interviewees. After a long workday, rather than an official talk in a meeting room, interviews during meals are more comfortable. Even though buying meals increased the fieldwork expenses, this was a worthwhile expense. The participants felt less pressured in the interviews, and this was an efficient way to build a good relationship with the respondents. In some cases, based on what was convenient for the interviewees, I visited their houses or offices. In this situation, the introducer confirmed the safety of this approach.

Anonymisation
This research ensures that the personal data about the interviewees are held securely and in a separate place from the interview transcripts. When using the documents and interview data, the interviewees and the case site are not identified. When using the "introducer" and "snow-balling" methods to gather the interviewees, this research continued the anonymisation rule among the interviewees. After the interviews, neither the introducer nor I would discuss the details of any other interviewees. Due to the introducers often introducing several participants at one time, anonymisation was guaranteed by preventing access to uniquely identifying information. In the following analytical chapters, interviewees will be given pronouns or referred to as their codes in the interviews.

Despite my explanations about the anonymisation, some of the interviewees also engaged in this strategy when they talked about workers' strikes and protests. Even though they know the organisers very well, they refused to name them. In the words of one interviewee, "He did this for all the workers, how can I reveal his personal information?" (Interviewee 021). The same situation occurred when talking about their managers, especially if they voiced negative evaluations of the managers. Many workers complained that a lot of workers left after the reform but based on their experience, they did not notice the number of managers change, which, to the workers, suggests that the managers can still enjoy the benefits of EGC since the SOE reform. Although the respondents were willing to provide information about a specific manager's inappropriate behaviour, they preferred to refer to a group of managers' characteristics by using the plural, leaders (in their narratives, ***dangguan de men***), rather than referring to one person. Hence, on both the researcher's and the participants' side, anonymisation was applied in this research.

References

Aron, R. (2003). *Jieji Douzheng: Gongye Shehui Xinjiang* [La lutte de classes. Nouvelles leçons sur les sociétés industrielles] (Y. G. Zhou, Trans., 2003 ed., p. 17). Yilin Press.

Bauman, Z. (1998). *Work, Consumerism and The New Poor*. Open University Press.

Bendix, R. (1977). *Max Weber: An Intellectual Portrait*. University of Berkeley.

Berlin, I. (1978). *Karl Marx His Life and Environment* (4th ed.). Oxford University Press.

Bourdieu, P. (1977). *Outline of a Theory of Practice*. Cambridge University Press.
———. ([1979] 1984). *Distinction: A Social Critique of the Judgment of Taste* [La distinction: Critique sociale du jugement (1979)] (R. Nice, Trans.). Harvard University Press.
———. (1991). *Language and Symbolic Power* (J. B. Thompson, Ed., G. Raymond & M. Adamson, Trans.). Harvard University Press.
Bourdieu, P., & Wacquant, L. (1998). *Dui Fansi Xing Shehuixue De Yaoqing* [An Invitation to Reflexive Sociology] (M. Li & K. Li, Trans.). Central Compilation and Translation Press.
Burawoy, M. (2008). *Manufacturing Consent: Changes in the Labor Process Under Monopoly Capitalism* (R. R. Li, Trans.). Commercial Press.
———. (2018). The Poverty of Philosophy: Marx Meets Bourdieu. In T. Medvetz & J. J. Sallaz (Eds.), *The Oxford Handbook of Pierre Bourdieu* (pp. 375–397). Oxford University Press.
Chen, B. H. (2002). Foucault De Quanliguan [Foucault's View of Power]. *Journal of Xiamen University: Philosophy and Social Sciences Edition* (4), 84–90.
Chen, F. (2009). Guojia, Zhidu Yu Gongren Jiji De Xingcheng – Xifang Wenxian Jiqi Dui Zhongguo Laogong Wenti Yanjiu De Yiiyi [The State, Institutions and the Formation of the Working Class—Western Literature and Its Implications for the Study of Labour Issues in China]. *Sociological Studies, 5*(1).
Cheng, S. Y., & Qin, M. (2017). On Multidimensional Poverty Measurement of Urban Migrant Workers in China and The Choice of Precise Poverty Alleviation Strategies. *Teaching and Research, 4*, 33–43.
Cho, M. Y. (2013). *The Specter of "the People": Urban Poverty in Northeast China*. Cornell University Press.
Deng, X. P. (1978, December 13). *Jiefang Sixiang, Shishi Jiushi, Tuanjie Yizhi Xiangqian Kan* [Emancipating the Mind, Seeking Truth from Facts and Uniting as One in Looking to the Future]. Available on 12th September, 2022, *vide*: http://www.people.com.cn/item/sj/sdldr/dxp/B101.html
Du, S. (2018). An Investigation of the Ethnography of the Old Industrial Enterprises in Northeast China and its Reflections—Based on Fieldwork of Car Factory in C City. *Journal of Changchun University of Technology* (Social Science Edition), 6.
Engels, F. (1871). *On Working Class Political Action*. Available on 23rd June, 2022, *vide*: https://www.marxists.org/chinese/marx-engels/17/048.htm
———. (1880). *Shehui Zhuyi Cong Kongxiang Dao Kexue De Fazhan* [Socialism from THE Imaginary to the Scientific]. Available on 12th September, 2022, *vide*: https://www.marxists.org/chinese/engels/marxist.org-chinese-engels-1880a.htm

———. (1891). *Daoyan* [Introduction to Wage Labourer and Capital] (1891 ed.). Available on 12th September, 2022, *vide*: https://www.marxists.org/chinese/marx/mia-chinese-marx-184904.htm

Feng, J. K. (2009). Dui Bourdieu Shehuixue Lilun Zhong "Ziben" Gainian De Jiedu [Interpretation of The Concept of "Capital" in Bourdieu's Sociological Theory]. *Journal of Inner Mongolia Agricultural University: Social Science Edition, 11*(6), 287–288.

Foucault, M. (1999). *Guixun Yu Chengfa* [Discipline and Punish: The Birth of the Prison] (B. C. Liu & Y. Y. Yang, Trans.). Joint Publishing.

Gao, Y. (2017). Kecheng Sizheng- Kecheng Sizheng Jianshe De Guanjian Wenti Yu Jiejue Lujin [The Key Problem and Solution in Ideology Education]. *Chinese Higher Education* (15), 11–14.

Goodman, D. S. (2014). *Class in Contemporary China*. Wiley.

Grenfell, M. (2004). *Pierre Bourdieu: Agent Provocateur*. A&C Black.

Hjekllbrekke, J., & Prieur, A. (2018). On the Reception of Bourdieu's Sociology in the World's Most Equal Societies. In T. Medvetz & J. J. Sallaz (Eds.), *The Oxford Handbook of Pierre Bourdieu* (pp. 68–87). Oxford University Press.

Jiang, J. S. (2017). Lun Amadiya Sen dui pinkun lilun de biange [Amartya Sen's Transformation of Poverty Theory]. *Social Scientist* (5), 41–45.

Lee, C. K. (2007). *Against the Law: Labour Protests in China's Rustbelt and Sunbelt*. University of California Press.

Lenin, V. (1915). *Lun Ouzhou Lianbang Kouhao* [On the European Federal Slogan]. Available on 12th September, 2022, *vide*: https://www.marxists.org/chinese/lenin-cworks/26/044.htm

———. (1916). *Wuchan Jieji Geming De Junshi Gangling* [Military Program of Proletarian Revolution]. Available on 12th September, 2022, *vide*: https://www.marxists.org/chinese/lenin-cworks/28/006.htm

———. (1917). *Guojia Yu Geming* [The State and Revolution]. Available on 12th September, 2022, *vide*: https://www.marxists.org/chinese/lenin/191708-09/index.htm

———. ([1919] 1929). *Lun Guojia* [On the State, Speech at Sverdlovsk University]. Available on 12th September, 2022, *vide*: https://www.marxists.org/chinese/lenin-cworks/37/004.htm

Li, J. (2013). Chuanboxue Shiyu Zhong De Foucault: Quanli, Zhishi Yu Jiaowang Guanxi [Foucault in Communication: Power, Knowledge and Relations of Communication]. *International Journalism* (2), 60–68.

Li, P. L. (2004). *Huashuo Shehui Fenceng* [Talking About Social Stratification]. China Social Science Literature Press.

Li, Q. (2002, October 23). *Zhongguo Shehui De Fenceng* [Chinese Social Stratification]. Ai Sixiang [Thinking]. Available on 12th September, 2022, *vide*: http://www.aisixiang.com/data/1894-2.html

Li, Z. G. (2002). Olson Jingji Sixiang Shuping [A Review of Olson's Economic Thoughts]. *Economic Review* (5), 77–81.

Lin, C. (2015). The Language of Class in China. *Socialist Register, 51*, 24–53.

Lin, C. D. (2017). Goujian Zhongguohua De Xuesheng Fazhan Hexin Suyang [To Construct Sinicized Core Competencies and Values for Students' Development]. *Journal of Beijing Normal University (Social Sciences), 1*, 66–73.

Lin, K. L., & Li, Q. S. (2007). Guangyi Ziben He Shehui Fenceng—Bourdieu De Ziben Lilun Jiedu [Capital and Social StratifiCation—Bourdieu's Capital Theory]. *Journal of Yantai University, Social Science Edition, 20*(4), 63–68.

Liu, F. (2016). The Deficiency of the Current Medical Security System for the Retired Workers and Its Support of Local Community: A Field Report from a State-Owned Enterprise in Lanzhou. *Journal of Northwest Normal University: Social Science Edition* (4), 39–45.

Liu, X., & Liu, W. K. (2020). Qiye guanli zhidu bianqian yu chanye gongren jineng xingcheng- jiyu H sheng Z qiye 20 ming chanye gongren de koushushi yanjiu [Changes of Enterprise Management System and Skill Formation of Industrial Workers: An Oral History Study of 20 Industrial Workers in Enterprise Z, Province H]. *Journal of Wuhan Vocational Technology College, 19*(4), 5–13.

Liu, Z. (2012). *Daxuesheng Rentong Yu Shijian Shehui Zhuyi Hexin Jiazhiguan Yanjiu* [Research on University Students' Identity and Practice of Socialist Core Values]. Available on 12th September, 2022, *vide*: https://cdmd.cnki.com.cn/article/cdmd-10533-1012474438.htm

Ma, X. W. (2008). Amartya Sen De Quanli Pinkun Lilun Yu Fangfa Shupin [A Review of Right-Based Poverty Theory and Methodology of Amartya Sen]. *Foreign Social Sciences* (2), 69–74.

Marx, K. ([1844] 1932). *1844 Economic and Philosophic Manuscripts.* Available on 12th September, 2022, *vide*: https://www.marxists.org/chinese/marx/marxist.org-chinese-marx-1844.htm. Also Available on 12th September, 2022, *vide* in *Collections of Marx*. Translated by Bureau for the Compilation and Translation of the Works of Marx and Engels, Lenin and Stalin, Central Committee of the CCP. Beijing: People's Press. 2000 Edition.

———. ([1847] 1920). *The Poverty of Philosophy* (pp. 194–195). Foreign Language Publishing House.

———. ([1849] 1891). *Guyong Laodong Yu Ziben* [Wage Labourer and Capital]. Available on 12th September, 2022, *vide*: https://www.marxists.org/chinese/marx/mia-chinese-marx-184904.htm

———. ([1859] 2009). Zhengzhi Jingjixue Pipan [Critique of Political Economy]. In *Marx and Engels Collection Vol. 2 1848–1859* (pp. 588–594, 595–606). Translated by Bureau for the Compilation and Translation of the Works of Marx and Engels, Lenin and Stalin, Central Committee of the CCP. People's Publishing House.

———. ([1865] 1898). Gongzi, Lirun He Jiage [Value, Price and Profit]. In *Marx and Engels Collection, Vol. 3 1864–1883* (pp. 25–78). Translated by Bureau for the Compilation and Translation of the Works of Marx and Engels, Lenin and Stalin, Central Committee of the CCP. People's Publishing House.

———. (1867). *Ziben Lun* [Capital] (Vol. 1). Available on 12th September, 2022, *vide*: https://www.marxists.org/chinese/marx/capital/index.htm

———. (1871). *Resolutions of the International Congress of Workers' Associations*. Available on 23rd June, 2022, *vide*: https://www.marxists.org/chinese/marx-engels/17/048.htm

———. ([1875] 1891). *Geda Gangling Pipan* [Critique of the Gotha Programme]. Available on 12th September, 2022, *vide*: https://www.marxists.org/chinese/marx/marxist.org-chinese-marx-1875-4.htm

———. (2009). *Marx Engels Wenji* [Marx and Engels Collection] (Vol. 1: 1843–1848, Vol. 2: 1848–1859, Vol. 3: 1864–1883). Translated by Bureau for the Compilation and Translation of the Works of Marx and Engels, Lenin and Stalin, Central Committee of the CCP. People's Publishing House.

Marx, K., & Engels. F. ([1848] 2009). Gongchandang Xuanyan [The Communist Manifesto]. In *Marx and Engels Collection Vol. 2 1848–1859* (pp. 3–67). Translated by Bureau for the Compilation and Translation of the Works of Marx and Engels, Lenin and Stalin, Central Committee of the CCP. People's Publishing House.

Mao, Z. D. (1940). *Xin Minzhu Zhuyi Lun* [On New Democracy]. Available on 12th September, 2022, *vide*: https://www.marxists.org/chinese/maozedong/marxist.org-chinese-mao-194001.htm

McLennan, G. (1982). EP Thompson and The Discipline of Historical Context. In *Making Histories* (Vol. 117). Hutchinson.

Min, Y. X. (2010). Da Xuesheng Sixiang Zhengzhi Jiaoyu Youxiaoxing Yanjiu De Xianzhuang He Zhanwang [The Research on the Effectiveness of Ideological and Political Education for College Students]. *Journal of Ideological and Theoretical Education* (1), 80–87.

Neveu, E. (2018). Bourdieu's Capital(s): Sociologizing an Economic Concept. In T. Medvetz & J. J. Sallaz (Eds.), *The Oxford Handbook of Pierre Bourdieu* (pp. 347–374). Oxford University Press.

Olson, M. ([1965] 2012). The Logic of Collective Action. *Contemporary Sociological Theory*, 124.

———. ([1982] 2008). *The Rise and Decline of Nations*. Yale University Press.

Pan, Y., & Ren, Y. (2006). *Gongren Zhutixing De Shijian: Chongshu Zhongguo Jindai Gongren Jieji De Xingcheng* [The Practice of Workers' Subjectivity: Restatement on the Construction of Chinese Working Class in Modern Times]. *Open Times* (03), 106–123.

Qu, H., & Yu, G. M. (2019). Xinxi "Xin Qiongren" Yu Meijie Chanye Jiegou De Gonggong Weiji- Jiyu Amartya Sen "Quanli Lilun" Shijiao De Fenxi

[The "New Poor" of Information and The Public Crisis of Media Industry Structure: An Analysis Based on Amartya Sen's "Rights Theory" Perspective]. *Dongyue Series, 8*, 150–157.

Reformdata Org. (2010, October 1). *Tansuo Yu Xuanze: Dui Nansilafu Xiongyali De Lishixing Kaocha, Zhongguo Gaige Xinxiku* [Explore and Selection: A History Evaluation of Hungary and Yugoslavia. China Reform Data]. Available on 12th September, 2022, *vide*: http://www.reformdata.org/2010/1001/1812.shtml

Sen, A. K. (1983). *Poverty and Famines: An Essay on Entitlement and Deprivation* (2009 ed., p. 38 and/or 2016 ed., pp. 191–192, 202). Commercial Press.

———. (2002). *Yi Ziyou Kandai Fazhan* [Development as Freedom] (J. Ren & Z. Y. Yu, Trans., 2002 ed., pp. 62, 85). Renmin University Press.

Shang, Q. F., & Han, B. J. (2007). Jieji,Jieji Yishi Yu Jieji Douzheng- Lun Mao Zedong Shixian Marxism Zhongguohua De Jiben Luoji Huanjie [Class, Class Consciousness and Class Struggle: The Basic Logical Links in Mao Zedong's Understanding of Marxism]. *Nanjing Social Science* (6), 18–24.

Solinger, D. J. (2006). The Creation of a New Underclass in China and Its Implications. *Environment and Urbanization, 18*(1), 177–193.

Sun, D. B. (2015). Reformation Process of Mid-Small State-Owned Enterprise in Southwest China: A Case Study of D Factory Based on Oral-History and Archives. *Journal of Honghe College, 13*(3), 91–95.

Thompson, E. P. ([1963] 2016). *The Making of the English Working Class.* Open Road Media.

Thornton, P. M. (2017). A New Urban Underclass? Making and Managing "Vulnerable Groups" in Contemporary China. In *To Govern China: Evolving Practices of Power* (pp. 257–281). Cambridge University Press.

Thaxton, R. A., Jr. (2008). *Catastrophe and Contention in Rural China: Mao's Great Leap Forward Famine and the Origins of Righteous Resistance in Da Fo Village.* Cambridge University Press.

Wang, B. (2016). Bei Wudu De Weber Shehuixue Renshi Lun: Lijie Fanshi Zhu Yinsu Jiqi Neibu Lianxi [Misinterpreted Weberian Sociological Epistemology: Understanding Paradigmatic Factors and The Internal Connections]. *Sociological Review* (1), 12–21.

Wang, J. X. (2010). Qiantan Olson De Jiti Xingdong Lilun- Jiti Xingdong De Luoji Dushu Biji [An Introduction to Olson's Theory of Collective Action—The Logic of Collective Action]. *Law and Society*, 15.

Wang, S. J., & Tu, Y. L. (2021). Ziben Kongzhi Yu Chanquan Gaige- Jiyu Huanan Sanjia Guoqi Yanhua De Jingji Renleixue Kaocha [Reform on Capital and Property Rights: An Economic Anthropological Study of the Evolution of Three SOEs in South China]. *Finance and Accounting Newsletter* (06), 13–18.

Wang, X. Z. (2013). Lun Gongchang Changyu Zhong De Guixun Quanli [The Discipline of Power in The Factory Field]. *Modern Communication: The Second Half of the Month* (8), 5–6.

Watts, S. (2014). User Skills for Qualitative Analysis: Perspective, Interpretation and The Delivery of Impact. *Qualitative Research in Psychology, 11*(1), 1–14.

Weber, M. ([1922] 1978). *Economy and Society: An Outline of Interpretive Sociology* (Vol. 1, p. 4). University of California Press.

Wright, T. (2010). *Accepting Authoritarianism: State-Society Relations in China's Reform Era*. Stanford University Press.

Wu, L., & Zhang, F. L. (2018). Jingzhun Fupin Beijing Xia Nongcun Shuzihua Pinkun Jiqi Zhili [Rural Digital Poverty and Its Governance in The Context of Precise Poverty Alleviation]. *Contemporary Issues in World Socialism, 2*, 28–35.

Wu, Q. J. (2008). Shichang Zhuanxing Shiqi Guoqi Gongren De Qunti Renting Yu Jieji Yishi [Group Identity and Class Consciousness of SOE Workers in The Market Transition Period]. *Sociological Research, 6*, 58–79.

Xi, J. P. (2021, October 15). *Zhashi Tuidong Gongtong Fuyu* [Solid Promotion of Shared Prosperity]. Available on 12th September, 2022, vide: http://www.qstheory.cn/dukan/qs/2021-10/15/c_1127959365.htm

Xu, X. G., Tang, X. Q., & Yang, W. W. (2020). Institutional Change, Role Construction and Evolution Logic of State-Individual Relation—Based on The Oral History Study of "Community cadres" in Shanghai. *Journal of Social Development* (02), 217–241, 246.

Xu, Y. W., & Yang, H. G. (2015). Zhengfu Rangli Yu Qiye Zizhu: 20 Shiji 80 Niandai Shanghai Xiao San Xian Jianshe De Ying Yu Kui [Government Concessions and Enterprise Autonomy: Profit and Loss in the Construction of the Small Third Line in Shanghai in the 1980s). *Jiangxi Social Science* (10), 17–25.

Yan, F. (1997). *Quanli De Yanjing—Foucault Fangtanlu* [Eyes of Power: An Interview with Foucault] (Vol. 1, p. 55). Shanghai People's Publishing Houses.

Yan, Y. X. (2012). *The Individualization of Chinese Society*. Shanghai Translation Publishing House.

Yin, R. K. (2013). *Case Study Research: Design and Methods*. Sage.

Zhang, Y. C. (2005). Sixiang Zhengzhi Jiaoyu De Tedian He Guilv Tanxi [Exploring the Characteristics and Laws of Ideological and Political Education]. *New Moral Education. Theory of Thought Education: Comprehensive Edition* (2), 4–10.

———. (2010). Tuijin Sixiang Zhengzhi Jiaoyu Yanjiu Fanshi De Renxue Zhuanhuan [Promoting an Anthropological Shift in the Paradigm of Ideological and Political Education Research]. *Research in Ideological Education* (7), 3–6.

Zhang, Y. Y. (1994). Liyi Jituan Yu Zhidu Fei Zhongxing [Interest Groups and Institutional Non-neutrality]. *Reform, 2*, 97–106.

Zhang, X. J. (2011). The Vision of Cultural Economics: "Privatization" and "Marketization"-Also on Coase Theorem in a Broad Sense and Equality in Property Right. *Jiangsu Social Sciences* (06), 1–12.

Zheng, Z. F. (2011). Jiti Xingdong Lilun De Kunjing Yu Chulu- Du Olson Jiti Xingdong De Luoji [The Dilemma and Solution Collective Action Theory: Reading Olson's The Logic of Collective Action]. *Southern Journal* (6), 42–44.

Zou, L. B. (2011). Pinkun De Ling Yizhong Quanshi: Quanli De Huode Yu Boduo- Jianpin Amartya Sen Pinkun Lilun [Another Interpretation of Poverty: The Acquisition and Deprivation of Rights: A Review of Amartya Sen's Theory of Poverty]. *Neijiang Science and Technology, 32*(2), 24, 27.

CHAPTER 3

The Case of E Group Corporation—an SOE in Sichuan, Post-1949

3.1 Sichuan: Artificial Establishment of SOEs in a Farming Province

"The Third Line" was put forwarded by Mao Zedong in 1964. From the mid-1960s to the early 1980s, a large-scale economic construction movement was conducted out in the southwest interior areas (the Third Line) of China. Nationally, the First Line refers to the northeast and coastal provinces, and provinces bordering a neighbouring country (such as Xinjiang, Tibet and inner Mongolia). Besides Sichuan Province, the Third Line includes provinces such as Qinghai, Gansu, Ningxia, Shanxi, Shaanxi, Henan, Hubei, Hunan, Chongqing, Yunnan, Guizhou and Guangxi. These provinces' geographical positions are in the interior of China as well as in the west. Between the First Line and the Third Line is the Second Line. Besides, each province also has its own first, second and third lines. The national scale is called "*da sanxian*" (large Third Line), and the provincial scale is called "*xiao sanxian*" (small Third Line). Large Third Line and small Third Line are collectively referred to as the Third Line construction and this construction is historically named as "three-line construction" (*sanxian jianshe*).

The reasons for constructing the three lines can be concluded from the existing research into the following points: (1) Tensions around China in

S. S. Huang, *The Political Economy of Reforms and the Remaking of the Proletarian Class in China, 1980s–2010s*, Palgrave Studies in Economic History, https://doi.org/10.1007/978-3-031-20455-5_3

the 1960s and the potential threat to national security increased[1]; (2) China's industrial layout was unreasonable. Around 70% of the industries were concentrated on the southeast coast and the 1950s' construction focused on northeast China. The construction of the interior was not enough[2]; (3) to prevent the restoration of capitalism "*fan xiu fang xiu*".[3] The first two points considered the external international situation, and the third point was tending to the internal situation. According to Mao's idea, besides the nationally Third Line, each province must establish its three lines. If revisionism appears in the central government, each province can rebel (Sun Dongsheng, 1995; Dong Baoxun, 2001; Duan Juan, 2012; Li Caihua & Jiang Dayun, 2005). Besides the reasons, the existing research elaborated the characteristics of location selection, the statistics on investment and industrial growth, especially identifying and analysing the international relations in which these decision-making processes took place.

Li Caihua (2002, pp. 43–51, 126) found that between 1964 and 1978, China's total industrial output value increased from 52% to 59.4% in the total output value of the national economy, and the percentage of workers in the industrial sector in the total number of workers in the society increased from 6.4% to 12.6%. A total of 205.268 billion Yuan was invested in the Third Line areas between 1965 and 1980, accounting for 39.01% of the national investment within the same period. During the Third Five-Year Plan period (1965–1970), the peak of the Third Line construction, the percentage reached 49.43% (Xu Youwei & Chen Xi, 2015, pp. 81–92, 127).

Research (Li Caihua, 2002, pp. 43–51, 126; Xu Youwei & Chen Xi, 2015, pp. 81–92, 127) pointed out that the Third Line construction had enabled Sichuan Province, as a core province of the Third Line construction, to develop into a pioneer in the industrialisation and

[1] The tensions can be divided as follows: tensions between the Soviet Union and China began in the late 1950s, and the Sino-Soviet border strategic confrontation; the U.S.-Vietnam war approached China's southern gate in 1964; issues in the Taiwan Strait in the southeast coastal area and China-India issues; in the northeast, US troops stationed in South Korea and Japan pose a threat to China.

[2] Third line construction also allowed the completed construction factories to move to the interior areas.

[3] "Xiu" refers to "xiuzheng zhuyi" (the revisionism). It means distort, falsify and deny Marxism.

urban modernisation development of inland China, and its status in the national industrialisation and urbanisation system had also been greatly improved. Between 1965 and 1967, the state's investment in Sichuan Province accounted for 14.5% of the country's total. In 1968, Sichuan's capital construction investment increased by 169% over the previous year (Xu Youwei & Chen Xi, 2015, pp. 81–92, 127). Sichuan was also a pilot province to conduct leader Zhao Ziyang's SOE reform project in 1978 in the first stage of SOE reform between 1978 and 1984 (China Labour Bulletin, 2007).[4] By the end of 1979, heavy industry (machinery, metallurgy and chemicals) accounted for 49% of Sichuan's manufacturing industry and in 2018, industry contributed 37.6% of Sichuan's economic growth (Sichuan Provincial Bureau of Statistics, 2019a).

In Fig. 3.1 and Fig. 3.2, I comparatively looked at the national and provincial statistics about the industrial structure. Years 1952 (earliest national statistics to be found), 1978 (launched the Reform and Opening Up) and 2018 (Fieldwork research time) are selected to compare the data clearly and concisely.

Figure 3.1 and Fig. 3.2 show that though the primary industry was the dominant industry in Sichuan Province until 1978, the secondary industry had explosive growth during the construction of the Third Line in Sichuan. Learnt from statistics, in 1988, the secondary industry surpassed the primary industry for the first time and became the dominant industry in Sichuan Province from 1991 to 1999 (Sichuan Statistical Yearbook, 2018, 2019a and 2020). Between 1979 and 1991, the secondary industry's contribution to Sichuan's GDP was 45.8%–47.8% (Sichuan Zhengbao, 1993).

From an interior province whose industry relied mainly on sugar, paper and salt (*baitang, baizhi, baiyan*—"*san bai*", three whites), the

[4] Zhao Ziyang, Premier of State Council between 1980 and 1987; General Secretary of the Central Committee of the CCP between 1987 and 1989, quoted from China Labour Bulletin (2007), during the first stage of SOE reform (1978–1984, management reform), "in October 1978, the Sichuan provincial government, spearheaded by future Party Secretary Zhao Ziyang, launched a pilot project to expand enterprise autonomy in six selected enterprises. Instead of submitting all profits to Beijing, these enterprises were allowed to keep a proportion of their profits, and when they produced more than the state-set quota, they were free to use that profit to re-invest in production and technical innovation, provide workers and staff with individual bonuses and collective welfare, or to use the profit to maintain a reserve fund".

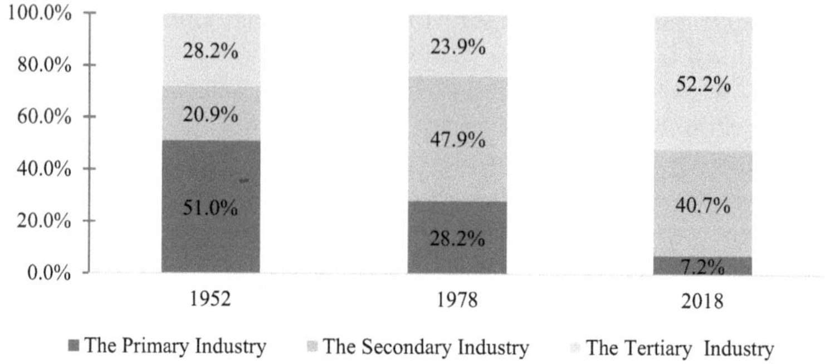

Fig. 3.1 Proportion of the three industries in Gross Domestic Production (GDP) in China, 1952 versus 1978 versus 2018 (*Data Source* National Bureau of Statistics, 2016 and 2020; China Statistical Yearbook, 2019[5])

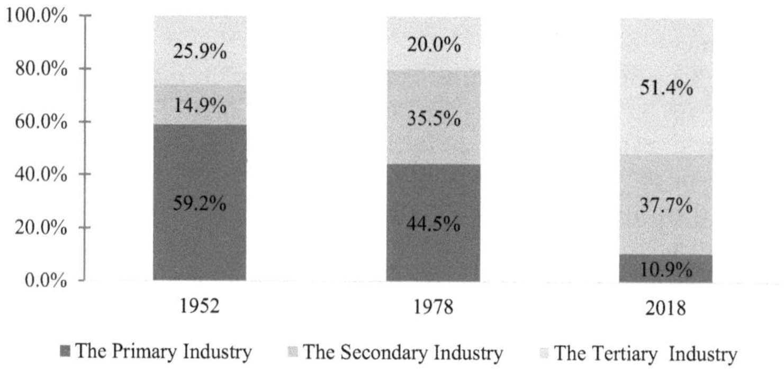

Fig. 3.2 Proportion of the three industries in Sichuan's GDP, 1952 versus 1987 versus 2018 (*Data Source* The State Council Information Office of the P. R. China 2009; Sichuan Provincial Bureau of Statistics, 2018[6])

[5] The chart does not show a historic and positive change in the structure of China's three industries happened in 2013, when the share of the tertiary sector in GDP raised to 46.1%, surpassing the secondary industry for the first time for 2.2% (National Bureau of Statistics, 2016). This change marks that China's economic development entered a new stage of transformation from an industrial-led economy to a service-oriented economy.

[6] The increase of the tertiary industry started from 1999. In 2018, it firstly reached over 50% in the provincial GDP (Sichuan Statistical Yearbook, 2018, 2019a and 2020).

establishment of manufacturing industry in Sichuan was the result of artificial policy guidance and embodied the characteristics of state control of economy plan in this period. In the study of national industrial layout, around 70% of the industries were concentrated on the southeast coast in 1950s, and the 156 key projects in the 1950s were distributed in northeast China and transportation hubs in north China, such as Taiyuan and Xi'an (Sun Dongsheng, 1995; Dong Baoxun, 2001; Duan Juan, 2012; Li Caihua & Jiang Dayun, 2005).[7] The state kept focusing on the development of heavy industry and the characteristics of the locations of the Third Line construction: "backer, scatter and hide" (*kaoshan, fensan, yinbi*), giving Sichuan a good opportunity to develop heavy and military industry. So, Sichuan has become a typical province with a high concentration of SOEs and where traditional heavy industries were based, just like Liaoning, Heilongjiang and Hebei (China Labour Bulletin, 2007).

Changes in the structure of industries are accompanied by changes in the number of people employed. In Fig. 3.3 and Fig. 3.4, I compared percentages of people employed in the three industries nationally and in Sichuan. Same as the last two figures, years 1952, 1978 and 2018 are used.

Statistics show that those working in industry in Sichuan have always been the minority. Hurst (2009, p. 25) said that a sizeable portion of the early Upper Changjiang working class consisted of workers "imported", along with their factories, from other regions—usually the Northeast or Central Coast during the Third Line construction period. This made the workers in this region very different. They were more closely tied to

Press conference on Sichuan's Economic and social Development achievements in 60 Years of P.R. China, Sep 30th, 2009. ("xin zhongguo 60nian Sichuan jingji shehui fazhan chengjiu" xinwen fabuhui). Available on 12th Sep, 2022, *vide*: http://www.scio.gov.cn/m/xwfbh/gssxwfbh/xwfbh/sichuan/Document/427606/427606.htm.

A Journey of Progress A Great Leap Forward—2nd in a series of reports on the achievements of Sichuan's economic and social development in the 40 years of Reform and Opening up, August 31st, 2018. (fengjin de lichen weida de kuayue—gaige kaifang 40nian Sichuan jingji shehui fazhan chengjiu xilie baogao zhi er). Available on 12th Sep, 2022, *vide*: http://www.sc.gov.cn/10462/10464/10465/10574/2018/8/31/10458035.shtml.

[7] The 156 Key Projects (*156 xiang zhongdian gongcheng*) established with Soviet aid in 1950s. The 156 Key Projects were aimed to initially establish China's industrial economic system during China's first Five-Year Plan (1953–1957). The 156 projects cover the major fields: industrial, mining infrastructure, energy, pharmaceutical, chemical, national defense, etc., that were introduced from the Soviet Union and Eastern European countries.

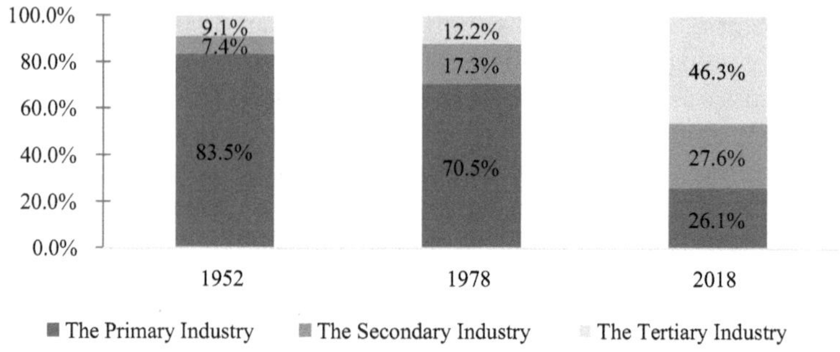

Fig. 3.3 Employment ratio of the three industries in China, 1952 versus 1978 versus 2018 (*Data Source* National Bureau of Statistics, 2016; China Statistical Yearbook, 2019)

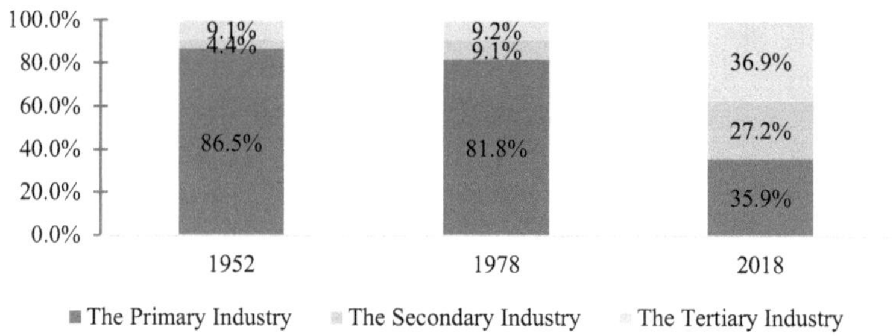

Fig. 3.4 Employment ratio of the three industries in Sichuan, 1952 versus 1978 versus 2018 (*Data Source* Sichuan Provincial Bureau of Statistics, 2019b[8])

their enterprises. For example, the overall urbanisation rate of Sichuan at this stage was not high, and even the level of urbanisation lagged behind industrialisation and was gradually decoupled from industrialisation. The rate of urbanisation in Sichuan is -1.15% from 1965 to 1975 (Li Caihua, 2002). However, the "work unit society" (*danwei shehui*)

[8] *Experience a better life and witness the great changes in Tianfu—8th out of A series of Sichuan's economic and social development achievements in the 70th anniversary of the founding of P.R. China* (ganshou meihao shenghuo jianzheng Tianfu jubian—xin zhongguo chengli 70 zhounian Sichuan jingji shehui fazhan chengjiu xilie zhi ba), August 22nd, 2019. Available on 12th Sep, 2022, *vide*: http://tjj.sc.gov.cn/scstjj/c105849/2019/8/22/4eab6dc77ecd4ee7b5bcd8d917c390f6.shtml.

with advantages made SOE workers' living much better than the local community. The infrastructures, welfare, housing, education and health care were provided by the enterprise. The small number of SOE workers became the regional aristocracy with access to resources that were not available to other residents in that backward region.

Sichuan is a good example of the changing industrial structure of China. Building industry in what was then an agricultural country, and for objective reasons such as war preparations, choosing an agricultural province like Sichuan to build industry from scratch, Sichuan represents a good laboratory perspective on analysing how to concentrate state's power to develop industry in places that had no industrial base. The development of these enterprises drove the local infrastructure and developed the bases of these SOEs from villages and towns into cities. Especially those SOEs directly under the central government (*yangqi*) were in fact privileged in that they had weak links with the municipal governments of their jurisdictions, but strong links with the central government, even to the extent of implementing central government policies over and above the municipal governments. At the same time, due to its remote location and inaccessibility, Sichuan naturally forms an isolated laboratory where it is possible to observe these SOEs, mainly heavy industry and military industry, that have developed thanks to the financial, human resources and technical support provided by completely artificial policy guidance. These SOEs have over-provided either "imported" or local workers with the benefits of a socialist society. This minority, in turn, became an aristocracy, enjoying preferential treatment not available to the local population. These SOE workers were able to live in completely disconnected from the local economy in an artificially created socialist society (i.e., the SOE work unit society) that transcended the economic conditions of China at the time, so that the socialist economy (SOEs) and the working class (SOE workers) could hardly be integrated into the local society and the local economy. Enterprises' raw materials and products were directed to the outside and workers' needs can be met in the unit society.

3.2 E Group Company: Privileged SOE–cum–Financial Burden

D City[9]

The case SOE- EGC is located in D city, Sichuan. D city transformed from an ordinary county town to a nationally renowned city of heavy industry because of EGC's construction (Xu Youwei & Chen Xi, 2015, pp. 81–92, 127). The construction of EGC backed to 1950s while D City only started to build on its urban scale in 1983. The city is within 30 min by high-speed rail from Chengdu, Sichuan's provincial capital. Besides EGC, it has two other large-scale SOEs and many manufacturing industries. The employees contribute to the population of the city and each SOE or work unit also has their owned internal hospitals, schools, public places of entertainment, residence areas and a series of services that support living. SOEs in this city divide residents into different small societies. The work unit characteristic in this city is significant. Below is a map of the SOEs in D City's urban area: The star indicates where EGC is located. The other large-scale SOEs in this city are D and R companies. The other three, T, J and G, have comparatively fewer employees and smaller scale. The sketch map illustrates EGC's location in the downtown (Fig. 3.5).

E Group Company's History[10]

EGC is an essential manufacturing base and major technical equipment base for complete metallurgical equipment, complete castings for nuclear power, hydropower, thermal power, heavy pressure vessels, large transmission parts and large aviation die forgings in China (Jingwei Wang, 2013). It is China's largest and one of the most important new energy equipment manufacturing bases (EGC Website, 2013). EGC is a large central government managed SOE and has always been under the direct jurisdiction of the central government department till 2013.

[9] For the sake of anonymous, the fieldwork city will be referred to as D City.

[10] Data sources in this section are mainly obtained from the fieldwork research and will be quoted directly in this section. As EGC does not publish its annual report every year, there is no way to use the data from the research year 2018 when doing some data comparisons.

The completed list about the internal documents found in fieldwork research will be attached as Appendix B.

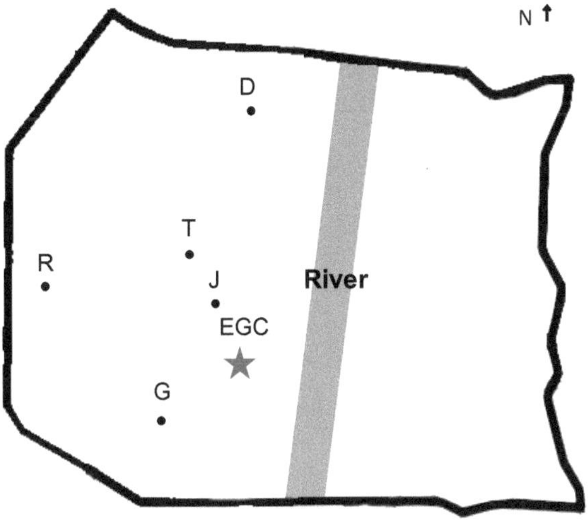

Fig. 3.5 Sketch map of SOEs in D City (*Data Source* The author's fieldwork)

Then, China National Machinery Industry Corporation (SINOMACH) gradually took over this central-managed enterprise since 2009, EGC and SINOMACH have restructured and SINOMACH has become the biggest stockholder of EGC in 2013, which means they are directly managed by the State-owned Assets Supervision and Administration Commission (SASAC) which was replaced by indirectly institutionally management.[11] In other words, EGC became a wholly owned subsidiary of SINOMACH. EGC also undertook internal reorganisation in 2014, reducing the sub-companies and industries from 37 to 24 and reorganising five independent business units (EGC Annual Report, 2014). A further reform on ECG happened in early 2018; SINOMACH reorganised EGC's main business of equipment manufacturing with its heavy equipment sector and formed a national flagship platform of high-end heavy equipment integrating science, industry and trade. EGC became a participating shareholder of the new formed platform (Fig. 3.6).

[11] In Chinese text: *Zhongguo jixie gongye jituan youxian gongsi*. SASAC is directly managed by the State Council. It represents the state to supervise and manage the central government controlled SOEs (exclude the financial institutes).

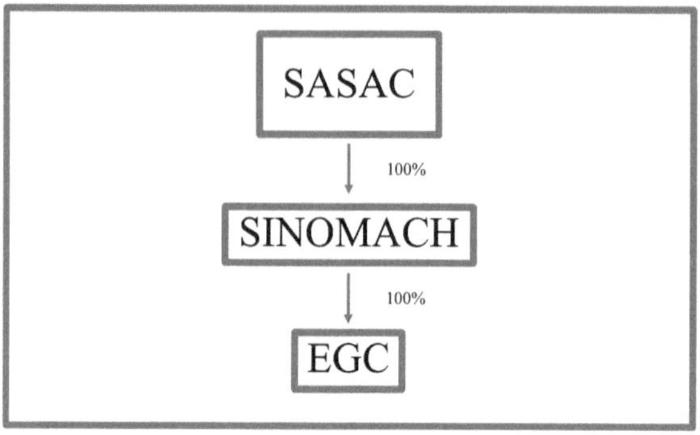

Fig. 3.6 Graph of Property Rights and Control Relations between EGC and The Actual Controller (*Data Source* The author's fieldwork)

The location of the large manufacturing industry in D City could be described as a pilot project for the Third Line construction. It was planned and established before the start of the Third Line construction programme. In the middle of the 1950s, based on research into the old industrial bases in China's northeast and cadre training courses in Beijing, the central government finally decided to construct the second biggest manufactory industry in D city. The construction of EGC started from 1958. According to EGC's Yearbook, the construction of EGC slowed down in 1960 because the Central Committee of the Communist Party of China decided to implement the eight-word policy of "adjusting, consolidating, enriching and improving (*tiaozheng, gonggu, chongshi, tigao*)" the national economy, reducing the infrastructure front and compressing projects, and restarted in 1962.[12] The construction was completed and EGC put into production in 1971. The Third Line construction increased the policy bias as well as resources investment in EGC. Evidence can be found in historical records showing that during the Third Line construction period, EGC imported 200 skilled workers from Shanghai Heavy Machinery Factory in 1966 and additional 200 people in the following year (Xu Youwei & Chen Xi, 2015, pp. 81–92, 127).

In addition to the construction of the factory infrastructure, the construction of the work unit society is also taking place at the same

[12] 1959–1961 was the "three years of hardship period (*sannian kunnan shiqi*)". There were not enough resources for EGC's construction.

time. EGC provided life services for the enterprise employees and their families. It had a hospital, a theatre, several meal halls, accommodation areas and markets, which were referred to by number, for instance, "No.3 living community". Utilities, living support services and education institutes were also established to make EGC more like a society. EGC had *zidi xiaoxue* (*zidi* primary school), *hongwei zhongxue* (*hongwei* secondary school), EGC's high school, a technical school and *zhigong daxue* (employees university).[13] The education system was complete for employees' children, allowing them to entirely copy their parents' footsteps. By doing this, the SOE society did not need new people from the outside world in order to develop. This also meant that almost all the personal activities, organisational activities and the construction of social networks took place within the unit environment. All these were constructed close to different enterprise gates. In Fig. 3.7, a map shows the layout of the EGC community.

EGC separated its social responsibilities and handed these over to the local government during the SOE reform period. For instance, since 2000s, the city's education sector took over EGC's employee schools and colleges; the employees' hospital has also been managed by the city and living-supporting services that originally belonged to this enterprise, were gradually moved out of its jurisdiction and then taken over by the city government.

EGC started as a military and heavy industry SOE. After launching the reconstruction in 1962, with a guiding philosophy focused on preparation for war, on 20 January 1964, the central leading group meeting decided that the investment in military construction projects would be increased to prepare for the construction of an aviation forging production line and an artillery production line in EGC. In general, EGC's main business units can be divided into casting, welding, testing, metalworking, military and other production departments, and it had its own sub-enterprises in charge of the market, propaganda and after-sale services in order to cooperate with the production units. EGC's main products are large die forgings and so the metallurgical industry directly influences EGC's profits. It has steel scrap, pig iron and nonferrous metals as its upstream

[13] As suggested by the name, the primary school is for EGC employees' children. *Hongwei* means Chairman Mao's Red Guards. It has a very typical political and historical characteristic. The central government-managed enterprise shows these political characteristics in many ways—in this case, showing in their education system.

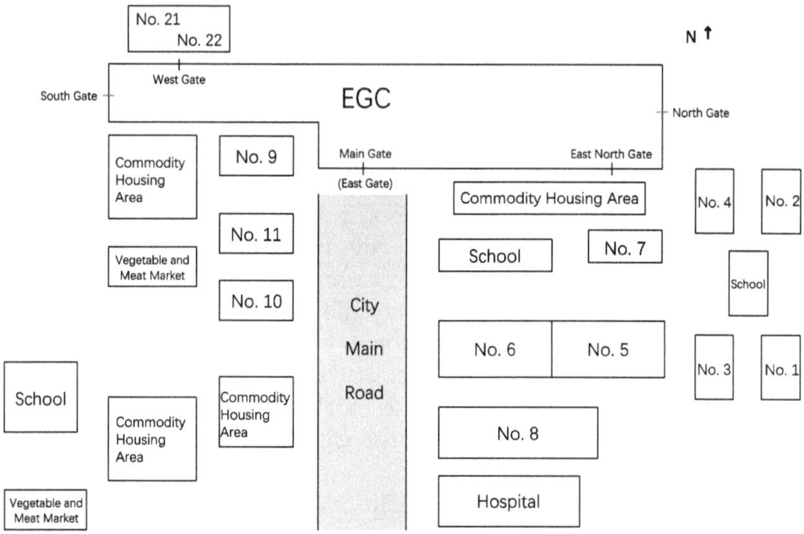

Fig. 3.7 Sketch map of EGC living communities (*Data Source* The author's fieldwork)

industry and reaches industries that are vital to the economy, such as iron and steel, petrifaction and electricity as its downstream industry (Li Chao, 2014). Its main services involve metallurgy, mining, energy, petrochemicals and other basic raw materials and energy fields. In the SOE reform period, which started from the 1990s, some of EGC's productions have transformed into light industry, but the enterprise is still mainly in heavy machinery manufactory. In 2009, EGC won the bid to undertake an aeroplane project, which aims to master the key technologies in the air industry rather than depending on exports.[14] In 2018, this research found EGC has new sectors on nuclear energy and space technology.

As of 2018, EGC divides its business into three main locations. D City is where the main manufacturing industries based and where this research fieldwork took place. It is the original construction base. The construction of the design centre in Chengdu began in 2008 to meet the requirements of development. It is a modern 34-floors building covering over 120,000

[14] The period for completing this project was 10 years. Interviewee 015 who works at the aircraft industry said that this project was successfully completed on time in 2018.

square metres. Although an accurate cost of the construction is not available, the decoration company went to EGC at the end of 2014 requesting 28 million Yuan as the balance due for decorating the design centre. The people who work at the design centre take shuttle buses to get there every day, and these run for free. A new manufacturing base in Jiangsu Province was established in 2009. The new manufacturing base is close to the East China Sea, aiming to save on the transportation costs that industries in D city accumulate. The management level thinks the new base is located in the core area of China's industry business and has the congregate customers there. The investment budget for the new industrial base is 5.73 billion Renmin Bi (Chinese currency RMB/Yuan), but the base is not at full production capacity due to the whole manufacturing industry experiencing a problem with a lack of orders (He Weiguang, 2015; Guo, 2015). This industrial base aims to produce nuclear power-related machines. However, influenced by Japan's Fukushima nuclear leakage accident in March 2011, the State Council has stopped approving nuclear power projects. This was a big shock to EGC, and it has been reflected in the reduced number of orders. According to the records, the order value decreased from 14.97 billion RMB in 2009 to 5.8 billion RMB in 2013. The new industrial base lost over 143 million RMB in five years. Moreover, due to the request for environmental protection, part of EGC's business has had to stop (Guo, 2015).

E Group Company: Economic Booster-Cum-Financial Burden

EGC was the main power to boost the city's GDP. From the late 1980s till 2008, EGC performed well in the local business revenue ranking. In the afternoon of 6 January 1987, the enterprise and the government of D City signed the contract of economic efficiency and the agreement of increasing profits for the first time. According to EGC's historical recording, from 1987 onwards, on the basis of the profits which handed over in 1986, EGC's profits would hand in at a rate of 9% per year to D City, and contracts would be made every four years. From 2000 to 2008, EGC's total value of output experienced a rapid growth, from 620 million to 12.8 billion RMB. In 2008 and 2009, EGC's profits separately were 500 million RMB and 788 million RMB. It ranked 2nd in 2008 in D City with business revenue over two billion RMB, which is EGC's highest rank in recorded statistics. EGC's profits and taxes ranked 4th in

D City in 2008 and 3rd in 2009, which were in the range of five hundred million to one billion RMB.

The whole heavy manufacturing industry had a fast development in 2008, with the increase rate reaching 32% but the industry order quantity decreased by 20% (China Heavy Machinery Industry Association, 2009).[15] EGC did not correctly estimate the trend and more investments coming in made the situation more serious. Also, the initial investment in the aeroplanes project in 2009 added a significant burden to EGC's finances.

After reaching the peak, EGC's profits has continued decreasing since 2010 (see Table 3.1, p. 93). EGC has been looking to transform the metallurgical industry into clean energy. However, this has not been a successful trial. Although EGC had kept having business revenue over two billion and sometimes five billion RMB, EGC's gross profit for a complete set of metallurgical equipment and equipment accessories was deducted from 500 million RMB in 2009 to minus 458 million RMB in 2013. It faced 272 million RMB loss in 2013 (Guo, 2015). EGC had its initial public offerings (IPO) in 2010. Since 2011, EGC faced a problem of a lack of orders, from both the domestic market and the foreign market. In 2011, EGC lost 140 million RMB. It was entitled to special treatment (*ST) in 2013, which means it lost profits over the subsequent two years as the stock was under special treatment within the stock market (stock with the title "*ST" is at the risk of delisting). In 2014, EGC lost 7.8 billion RMB in profits and the loans reached 653.6 million RMB. From 2012 to 2014, EGC was not in the List of Enterprises with Total Profits and Taxes beyond Tens of millions in D city's statistical yearbook. The new supervisor of SINOMACH tried to help EGC solve its financial problems with extra funding and subsequently provided 1.3 billion RMB (Guo, 2015), but this did not change the delisting in 2015. By April 2015, EGC owed over 8,000 million RMB in bank loans and had to voluntarily delist according to the general meeting of stockholders. Table 3.1 shows EGC's profits changes between 2010 and 2013.

[15] Source: Report from China Heavy Machinery Industry Association (CHMI) (*zhongguo zhongxing jiexie xiehui*). Available on 12th Sep, 2022, *vide*: http://navi.cnki.net/KNavi/YearbookDetail?pcode=CYFD&pykm=YZXJX&bh=N2010060053.

Table 3.1 EGC's operating income and Net profits 2010–2013 (Unit: Billion RMB)

Year	*Operating income*	*Net profits*
2010	6.7	0.27
2011	7.2	– 0.14
2012	3.9	– 2.6
2013	4.8	– 3.2

Data Source Xinjing Bao 2015

Even with a heavy financial burden, EGC differs from other SOEs that in its 60 years history from 1958 to 2018, it has not in fact laid-off workers.[16] Even when the first "laid-off wave" (*xiagang chao*) took place in 1997 in response to Zhu Rongji's policy—"bring SOEs back to profit in three years"—EGC took different measures to solve the labour cost problem.

Firstly, when the enterprise does not have enough workload to operate at full capacity, EGC will take "*xigong*" (stop working and taking a vacation), "*lungang*" (job rotation), "*daigang*" (await job assignment) and "*peixun zhuangang*" (job-transfer training) to save the labour and operation cost. Some of these measures had been studied in Hurst's research (2009, pp. 77–79) on Chinese laid-off workers. The differences between Hurst's findings and this case SOE are obvious. From Hurst's research, he found that workers in northeast China were giving long vacation (*fang chang jia*) from the 1980s till 2001 or 2002. Some workers from the central coast area were cheated to leave their job positions and have never been called back to SOEs. Workers from the north-central area and upper Changjiang area were given the promise to wait for a post if new positions are available. From Hurst's view, these strategies are forms of lay-off. However, EGC workers who were requested to "*xigong*", "*lungang*", "*daigang*" or "*peixun zhuangang*" have the opportunities to return to their job positions or be assigned to new jobs and continue work for EGC. Moreover, transparent information about workers' temporarily leave was released to the workers. There has been no case in EGC that workers were

[16] Laid-off workers are still SOE workers nominally and they need to negotiate with the work unit on whether keeping their labour relations. They have no salary and are unemployment in a passive way.

asked to leave their jobs cheating through deception. EGC established its own labour service company (*laowu gongsi*) for re-employments and job training for its employees. Measures that are mentioned in this paragraph once implemented, workers' basic salaries were provided to cover the basic living expenses according to the local standards of consumption. Workers still enjoy the same welfare and insurance as the others who are in a working position.

Dingti (replacement) was applied after Cultural Revolution to provide jobs for the knowledgeable youths who returned from the villages. EGC kept this measure till the early 1980s. It is a gentle way to let the first generation of EGC's workers and also cadres leave their jobs early by keeping and providing these job opportunities to their children. The replacement strategy allows employment and recruitment to be dealt with within the work unit society.

Other than controlling the number of employees, one solution that EGC has engaged to solve the redundant personnel problem is referred to as "*dingyuan dinggang*" (the related employees are decided by the personal qualities, and the job positions are clarified by the job responsibilities). As every job position and every employee is allocated work contents and responsibilities, EGC wants to ensure their effectiveness and avoid the waste of human resources as much as possible.

The measures mentioned above mainly moderate policies. After EGC was reconstructed with SINOMACH in 2013, more measures were applied, and those measures do not expect to bring any workers back to the enterprise once a decision has been made. Early retirement (*tiqian tuixiu*) and internal retirement (*neibu tuixiu* or describe as "*tuiyang*" in EGC) can be discussed together. These two allow people to retire earlier than the official retirement age. The difference between early retirement and internal retirement in EGC is that early retirement is for people who are within 5 years of their official retirement age, and it is according to legitimate document, while the internal retirement can be extended to within 7–10 years and it is the enterprise's internal policy. People who choose early retirement can receive their full pensions while internal retirement can only guarantee people a fixed monthly salary till their official retirement age or in a certain period 80% (from the empirical research) of their monthly salary when they were at their job positions. Not only workers but also cadres can voluntarily choose whether they want to end their services early. However, learnt from fieldwork research, cadres normally do not choose to do so. This can be explained by the interviews that workers think if EGC can still pay for their insurances and welfare, they want to stop working as early as they could have a rest or even find a higher salary job outside of EGC, while from their perspective, cadres' work is not as hard as workers and cadres will not leave SOEs till their official age to obtain the higher annual income. There is also another common measure applied in SOEs called "*tingxin liuzhi*" (stop the wages, keep the position) (Hurst, 2009, p. 77); many workers use this as a strategy to keep enjoying SOEs' welfare and insurance support but find a new job outside of SOEs. EGC does not approve of this. Workers have to choose whether to be in the SOE system or end their contracts with the SOE before they leave. However, interviews revealed some under-the-table operations where the worker and their teams agreed to conceal the fact that the worker was working outside by paying other colleagues in the team to help with the person's work, but still retaining the employment contracts with EGC.

All the measures mentioned above actually still keep the labour relations between the employees and the enterprise. However, "*maiduan*" (buyout) does not serve that purpose. The buyout policy does not have an age limitation; people who would like to end their labour contracts with EGC are offered a one-time off subsidy for their years of service. The amount of severance payments is depended on the workers' years of employment (*gongling*). By doing so, EGC no longer affords these workers' insurance and welfare; in other words, these workers no longer belong to the enterprise and end their labour contracts with the enterprise.

As I mentioned in the last chapter about the interviewees' categories (p. 48), laid-off workers are not the focus of my research nor workers who buy out their years of employment. These two groups of people no longer belong to SOE workers, nor do they have labour contracts with SOE. This research interests in workers that still have labour relations with SOE (including early retirees and internal retirees). These people depend on SOE to pay for their insurance and get welfare, and the profits of EGC to some extent will impact their situation. Although these people are still being taken care of by SOE, they do not have too many choices on employment. Once they leave EGC, re-employment can only be found in the service sector, such as waiters and gatekeepers according to the interviews. Moreover, their understanding of their class has also changed. Therefore, this group of people deserves to be studied.

3.3 E Group Company Workers

Going back to what was mentioned in the research background section about work unit (gongzuo *danwei*), unit presents a kind of "dependence"; the individual depends on the unit and the unit depends on the state. In the context of interdependence, those organisations or groups in a superior position can influence, dominate and control the organisations or groups in a disadvantaged position. In the relationship between the state and the unit, the state fully controls social resources and is in an absolute superior position. In terms of the relationship between units and individuals, units fully occupy and control the development opportunities of unit's members and almost all the resources members need, forming a dominating relationship over unit members (Li lulu, 2002; Li Hanlin, 1993; Huang Jie, 2014, pp. 15–19). The emphasis on industry and the Third Line construction made the benefits of EGC workers very pronounced before economic reforms and SOE reforms.

Before D city was constructed, thousands of people across the country moved to this small town to engage in EGC's construction. In particular, experts and technicians who had previous work experience in the industrial area in the northeast of China were allocated to support the construction work of EGC. They helped with various aspects of the construction work, from the basic construction of industry and factory workplaces, to managing and guiding the process of production. The first generation of EGC employees contributed a lot to the city and the enterprise. At that time, D City was about the size of a town. Most of its residents worked in the primary industry, agriculture. Due to the different backgrounds and industries, EGC's employees distinguished themselves from the local residents. Within EGC, the first generation supported each other, not only in work, but also in life, due to their shared identity as the new immigrants to D City and the fact that they did not have the support of family and friends here.

Figure 3.8 shows EGC's employees accounting for a significant proportion of workers in D city within a certain period.[17] In 2018 research, the number of EGC workers has shrunk to less than half. Regardless of the period, EGC workers were a minority group in the city. This allows SOE's

[17] "The number of workers in D city in 1987" reflects workers in the industry while "the number of workers in D city in 2018" especially refers to the manufactory industry.

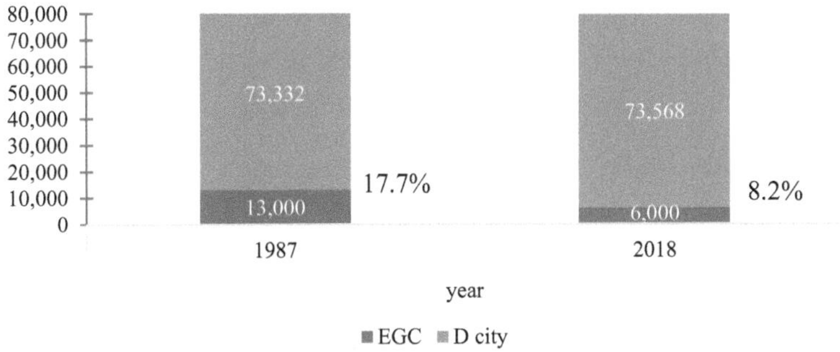

Fig. 3.8 Comparison of numbers of EGC employees and people in (manufactory) industry in D City, 1987 versus 2018 (*Data Source* 1987 D City Statistical Yearbook; 2019 D City Statistical Yearbook; 1984–1988 EGC History Book; 2018 Fieldwork interviews)

special care of their workers that can be granted in EGC and EGC workers can access the privileges.

The impact of SOE reforms on EGC workers is evident in two broad aspects: the proportion of workers in the factory and workers' wages. Firstly, in terms of the proportion of workers, I have taken the year 1997 as a reference because it was an important year for the nationwide SOE reform and saw a massive lay-off of SOE workers. Figure 3.9 and Fig. 3.10 show the composition of the non-managerial workforce at EGC in 1997, when there was a wave of lay-offs nationwide. There were 2.5 times more workers than technicians.

For the post-reform data, I have taken the year 2014, the first year after restructuration with SINOMACH. In Fig. 3.11, by the end of 2014, EGC only had around half of the workers who were in the production sector. The type of job coded as "other" is not clear in EGC's statistics. The labour contractors who work to support the production work might be allocated into this group.

From EGC's annual year report (2014, pp. 13, 18 and 51–52) of 2014, 2,500 employees had left EGC through early retirement, "*daigang*" (wait for job assignment) and buyout. Of the remaining employees, professionals accounted for 30.22%, engineering and technical personnel accounted for 10.63% and there were 2,023 leading cadres, which means though 1407 people belong to the management group, the actual cadres in workplaces and industry are over 2000. It again proved the declining number of workers.

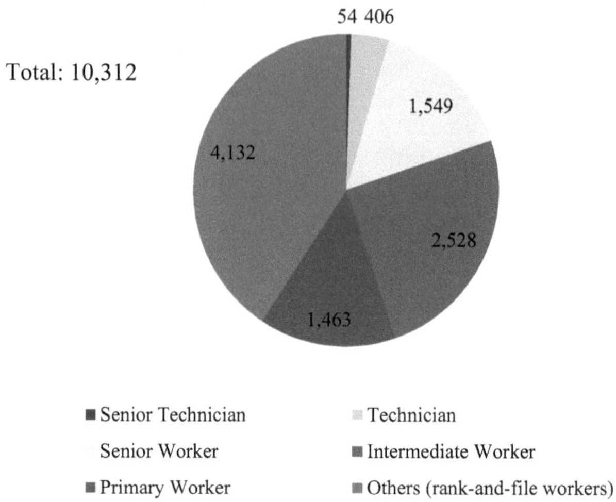

Fig. 3.9 EGC number of workers in 1997 (*Data Source* EGC history book for 1989–1997, pp. 77)

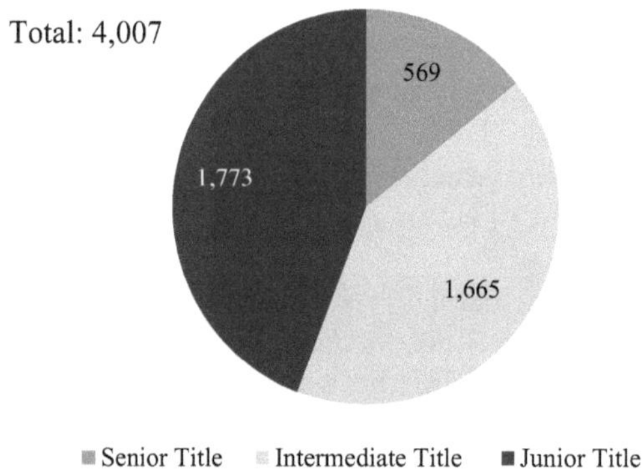

Fig. 3.10 EGC number of professionally technical cadres in 1997 (*Data Source* EGC history book for 1989–1997, pp. 76)

Also in 2014, Table 3.2 shows a breakdown of EGC's workforce by employment relationship with the enterprise. It clearly reflects the significant burden of retirees for EGC.

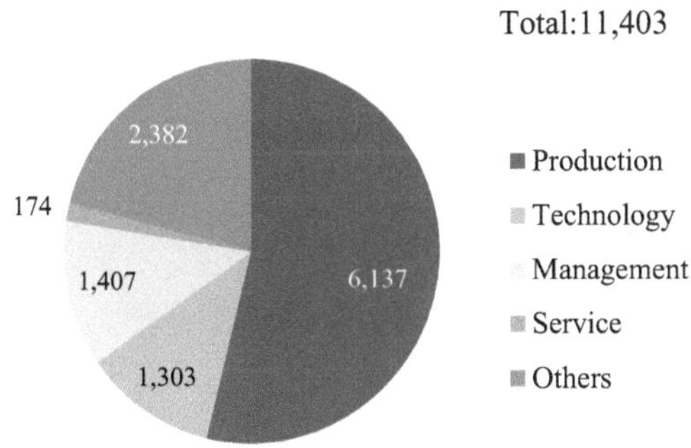

Fig. 3.11 EGC statistics on employees job type in 2014 (number of people) (*Data Source* EGC annual report, 2014, p. 52)

Table 3.2 EGC and Main Sub-companies' Statistics on Employees in 2014 (number of people)

Employees at EGC	8,664
Employees at Main Sub-companies	2,739
The Total Number of On-position Employees	11,403
The Total Number of Retirees	8,779

Data Source EGC Annual Report 2014, p. 52

From the above charts, the staff changes at EGC were not significant till 2014. The number of employees at EGC remained above 10,000.

Secondly, in terms of workers' wages, in the late 1990s, EGC employee incomes comprised a standard wage, overtime wage, allowance and bonus. Figure 3.12 reflects the change in wages, with wages for EGC workers having an advantage over the city or other SOEs in 1997, which has turned into a significant disadvantage in the 2016 statistics.

The gap in both the number of workers and wages can be seen in the 2015 reform of EGC as a dividing line. In that year, in addition to the delisting, the number of workers at EGC fell from 13,000 to 6,000, and workers staged a mass strike over wages. Although restructured with SINOMACH in 2013 brought EGC investments to solve the problem, the external investment has not made a significant change.

On 21 April 2015, EGC published a document entitled Termination of Labour Contracts Implementation Measures (Draft for Comments)

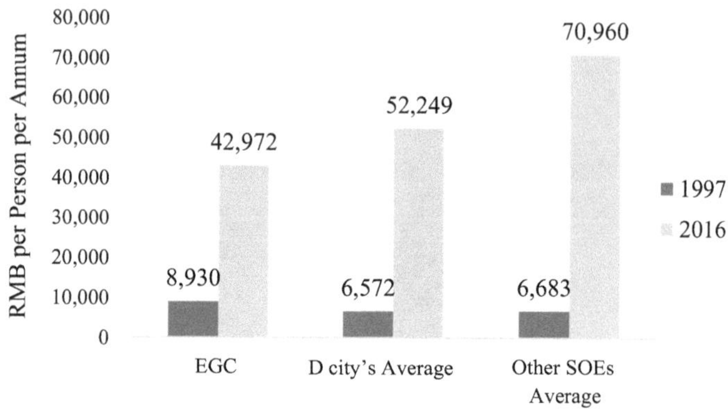

Fig. 3.12 Average income comparison among EGC, D City and other SOEs in 1997 and 2016 (*Data Source* 1997 D City statistical yearbook[18]; 1998 D City statistical yearbook; 2017 D City statistical yearbook; EGC's history book for 1989–1997, p. 27; EGC's Recruitment Information in 2016)

(*jiechu laodong hetong shishi banfa (shengyigao)*).[19] This document became the direct cause of the resisting of reform on the workers' side. Even before SOE reform started, workers acted passive and slow down in work when they found they were unable to receive proper incomes and benefits. When this Draft was revealed to be about ending labour contracts with some workers who failed to compete in the internal job recruitment, the workers' resistance became more aggressive, with a strike, procession and demonstrations in public.

On 11 May 2015, workers organised a large protest, which had never happened before in EGC's history, and it became a landmark differentiating between the phases of SOE reform within EGC. This labour activism ultimately had thousands of people participate in it, including retirees and workers' family members. Workers put up signs with the slogan "corruption among the leaders and the incapable management that had ruined EGC". The trigger for this event was the bad profits that caused workers' average pay to decrease to 1,000 RMB per month;

18 "Other SOEs average" in Fig. 3.12 refers to the employees' average income of SOE workers in other SOEs in D city.

19 This document will be referred to as "Draft" in the following.

some workers were only able to get 360 RMB after the insurance and housing fund was deducted.

According to news reports,[20] EGC workers sought help from society, experts and scholars who had previously organised and had helped workers protect their interests in the southeast of China. EGC workers learnt about cases of successful negotiation with enterprises and strategies on how to negotiate as a group according to the law and the facts.[21] The experts' help was eventually reflected in the workers' requirement of salaries that were according to the rules and the law. Workers made demands of EGC clearly and accurately, rather than just making an announcement. They did not destroy the machines and public property, but instead engaged in a reasonable strike and protests within the EGC area only and not in the city. They addressed the legality and legitimacy of striking. On the fifth day of this strike, EGC agreed to apply an "internal retirement" policy to people who had failed to compete for the post or abandoned the competition. EGC also agreed to continue

[20] These reports have 14 series, which were published along with the process of the strike movement on the Blog for the Workers' Support Group. They will be listed in Appendix B, internal documents about EGC.

[21] The Labour Law and the Trade Union Law. According to the provisions of article 8 and article 33 of the Labour Law, workers have the right to elect workers' representatives, convene workers' group meetings, meetings for workers' representatives and workers' congresses, and they have the right to consult and negotiate on an equal footing with the management on the settlement plan. When conditions permit, the general congress of workers of the factory may be convened. The general congress of workers is the highest organ of power for protecting workers' collective rights. When the general congress of workers is not in session, the meeting for workers' representatives may exercise the functions and powers of the workers' general congress. In accordance with the provisions of article 27 and article 53 (4) of the Trade Union Law, if the company refuses to negotiate with the workers on an equal footing, the workers shall have the right to prompt the management to negotiate through collective actions such as stopping work or slowing down work, and they shall have the right to send representatives to the people's government above the county level to ask the government to order correction and deal with the matter according to the law. (*genju laodongfa dibatiao, disanshisantiao zhi guiding, gongren youquan xuanju gongren daibiao, zhaokai gongren xiaozu huiyi, gongren daibiaohui he gongren dahui, youquan yu zifang jiu anzhi fangan pingdeng xieshang tanpan. You tiaojian shi, keyi zhaokai quanchang gongren dahui, gongren dahui shi gongren jiti weiquan de zuigao quanli jiguan, gongren dahui bihui qijian, gongren daibiao dahui keyi xingshi gongren dahui de zhiquan. Genju gonghuifa diershiqitiao, diwushishantiao disixiang zhi guiding, ruguo gongsi jujue yu gongren pingdeng xieshang tanpan, gongren youquan tongguo tinggong, daigong deng jiti xingdong cushi zifang tanpan, youquan xuanpai daibiao dao xian yishang renmin zhengfu, yaoqiu zhengfu zeling gaizheng, yifachuli.*).

supporting these workers' social insurance according to the average level of the EGC employees and pay them two months' pay annually as their settlement allowance.

In the course of the 30-day protest, workers introduced further requirements, especially after their meetings with scholars, experts and representatives of EGC. For instance, the minimum guaranteed wage should be 1,200 RMB per month after deducting the insurance and housing funding and the standard of the insurance and housing funding could not be decreased; people who left the enterprise earlier than their retirement age should receive compensation of around 10,000–15,000 RMB per year; cadres should have the right to choose whether they wanted to leave or stay, EGC could not force them; the enterprise should publicise the annual income of all employees in EGC (including workers and middle- and high-level managers) to ensure they calculate the average pay openly; workers should get payment for overtime work retroactively; EGC should reduce the number of managers to a rate of 1: 30 (managers verse the rank-and-file workers); and the employees' representatives should contain at least 80% workers and should be selected by anonymous voting among all employees.

After one and a half months of the workers' movement, EGC published two documents through the Congress of Employees: 2015 EGC Measures for the Termination of Labour Contracts (*2015 EGC jiechu laodong hetong shishi banfa*) and 2015 EGC Worker Off-Position and Rest Measures for its Implementation (*2015 EGC zhigong ligang xiuyang shishi banfa*). (This is actually the internal retirement policy.) According to these two measures, workers could sign the contract to end their labour relationship with EGC within 30 days and the enterprise would pay the related settlement allowance. Meanwhile, in these documents, the "buyout" employees could get compensation of 6,413 RMB per year (the total amount varied according to their seniority), plus one-off compensation of 25,000 RMB.[22] For people who received salaries below EGC's average, they would receive an extra one month's pay per year as their allowance. It should be mentioned that the calculation started from 2008 and the measures were published in 2015. For example, people who joined EGC before 2008 and got a pay that was lower than the average level could receive the maximum eight months' pay as a subsidy.

[22] Some interviewees mentioned that the subsidy is 10,000 RMB per year.

People who joined EGC in 2014 and received the lower pay could apply for two months' pay as a subsidy. The amount of the month's pay was according to the person's wage standard of that year. Furthermore, people who reach their retirement age before the end of 2025 can apply for "off-position and rest" (internal retirement) in 2015. Their insurance and housing funding will be sponsored by EGC, but they can only receive 1,000 RMB per month as living expenses; the amount increases 8% per year until they reach the official retirement age and receive a pension.

Among those people who ended contracts or buyout, workers at the rear service account for a large number, proving that during a recession, the core worker's job position will be protected, but the fringe workers are easy to be laid-off (Friedman, 1977; You, 2006, p. 9). The total number of employees was down to 7,500 in 2017 based on the official report (Sina Finance, 2017). The Chairman of SINOMACH said at the first forum on Reform and Development of Chinese Enterprise (*zhongguo qiye gaige fazhan luntan*) that EGC's reduction in its number of employees has saved it 500 million RMB annually in the cost of labour. He also noted that the management group has decreased by 40% since the reorganisation and the loss of leading staff were within 10% (Sina Finance, 2017).

It is important to note that strikes by workers at EGC regarding pay issues are not exceptional across the country. Reviewing the national strike map from January 2008 to December 2018, strikes by workers for over payment, management or lay-offs and unemployment issues are frequent. Sichuan is the province with the most strikes among the traditional Third Line construction areas.[23]

Despite the tougher policies implemented by EGC in the 2015 reform and the fierce resistance, EGC has not laid-off workers, and the company continues to provide jobs for 6,000 people, as well as welfare and support to retirees of around the same number of on-position employees. In a most recent statistic, EGC ranked 4th in the List of Business Revenue Ranking and 5th in the List of Enterprises with Total Profits and Taxes beyond Tens of millions in D city in 2017. Although SOE reform removed the social responsibility from SOEs, EGC still provides an

[23] *Data Source* China Labour Bulletin. Available on 12th Sep, 2022, *vide*: https://maps.clb.org.hk/?i18n_language=en_US&map=1&startDate=2008-01&endDate=2018-12&eventId=&keyword=&addressId=&parentAddressId=&address=&parentAddress=&industry=&parentIndustry=&industryName=

annual "Chinese New Year Gift" and "Winter Heating Allowance" to all its current and former employees. The work unit society characteristic doesn't disappear in this SOE. In other words, due to the specificity of its industry and field of production, EGC is still to some extent an SOE that enjoys the state policy bias, and its workers still receive some benefits by association within this reformed SOE.

3.4 Summary on E Group Company

In comparison with those in the Northeast SOEs that have closed down, or the coastal and riverine enterprises that have asked for lay-offs, and the emerging factories that attract migrant workers, EGC is in fact is a utopia for the existence of a socialist conception of the state enterprise society. It does not have laid-off workers (means the full employment characteristic in socialism), still has the SOE aura with continued policy bias. As my interviewee Xu (Interviewee 015) mentioned "it is important to recognise the potential of the enterprise, that there are good times and bad times, but subconsciously the SOE will always go back to the way it was back then".

EGC provides a lot of meaningful data; for example, in the context of the SOE reform, EGC tried to transform from military to heavy industry, abolished the military branch, aimed to transform into new energy and light industry, and added monopolistic industries such as nuclear power and aerospace. These changes reflect the political tendencies of the state and the changes in management, from a planned state enterprise to a market-oriented one, and now back to the military heavy industry. The more tangible manifestation for workers is in the restoration of benefits such as staff canteens. The essence of the transformation is that socialist fairness is being challenged by market competition and price mechanisms, the need for efficiency and the inevitable change to meet benefits, and the most intuitive consequence of this change is the loss of workers.

Workers miss the period when they enjoyed privileges as aristocratic workers, though such privileges are in contradiction with the "socialism" or so-called socialism with Chinese characteristics. The essential requirement or characteristic of socialism is the elimination of classes and the creation of a classless society. Before SOE reform, state presidents and prime ministers successively visited EGC, and it obtained a lot of honours. Workers, as the main force of EGC, have been the main motivation for the enterprise's glory for its 60 years' development. Mao Zedong privileged a sense of a particular kind of satisfaction by giving people status: "Only political mobilisation could unleash the creativity of the masses of workers" (Walder, 2015, p. 98). However, the status that workers look for in a "socialist enterprise" is a job to live without worrying, stability, a long-term contract, etc. This status gradually broke down after SOE reform, and to EGC workers, their aristocratic status is replaced by civil servants, which require a degree to enter, need social connections to get a good job, have less tiring work and income and benefits are guaranteed.

After the reform of the SOEs, workers were caught in a whirlpool of meaning: contributing to the state and being part of the nation building versus working for the money-making machine of the market economy, which in practice means contributing to the efficiency of the enterprise and saving the cost of production for the enterprise. Products produced by workers cannot be directly incorporated into consumption but need to enter the market, and then, workers get paid through wages to buy consumer goods in exchange for the labour they put into production. While peasants produce consumer goods that can be directly consumed, workers need to pay in with the commune and the state and can only make ends meet, so peasants realised earlier than the workers that even though they are given higher prestige and status politically, they were not at all the leading class or masters of society. When SOE workers begin to realise that "the working class is the leader" and "the alliance of workers and peasants as the masters of socialism" are in fact contradictory to their status, they became class-conscious. It is the transformation of what the Marxian called from "*class-in-itself*" to "*class-for-itself*" and it will lead to a revolt.

In qualitative research, the empirical evidence is expected to prove the research hypothesis through facts. SOEs, especially heavy and military industry, were once in an advantaged position. However, SOE workers are not the beneficiaries of the economic reforms. They have lost more than they have gained. EGC workers had enjoyed good welfare benefits until EGC underwent radical SOE reforms, and even after the SOE reforms, EGC workers still have a degree of security. If empirical research can prove that these workers (few of the few, privileged of the privileged workers) in this ideal SOE were substantially returned to the proletariat and need to resist, strike and march against to gain their rightful power and benefits, then the situation of other workers can be inferred. Such a crisis, confirming the reconfiguration of the proletariat, and the formation of a class society can be demonstrated. Then, the following analytical chapters are expected to verify my observations of this enterprise and the inferences mentioned here from a societal perspective. Paradigms such as socialist development and the working class in China are challenged empirically.

References

China Labour Bulletin. (2007). Reform of SOEs in China. Available on 12th September, 2022, *Vide*: https://clb.org.hk/content/reform-state-owned-enterprises-china.

———. (2011). Strike Map. Available on 12th September, 2022, *Vide*:: https://maps.clb.org.hk/?i18n_language=en_US&map=1&startDate=2018-01&endDate=2018-12&eventId=&keyword=&addressId=&parentAddressId=&address=&parentAddress=&industry=&parentIndustry=&industryName=.

China Heavy Machinery Industry Association (CHMI). (2009). 2008 China Heavy Machinery Industry Yearbook. Available on 12th September, 2022, *Vide*: http://navi.cnki.net/KNavi/YearbookDetail?pcode=CYFD&pykm=YZXJX&bh=N2010060053.

Dong, B. X. (2001). *Yingxiang Sanxian Jianshe Juece Xiangguan Yinsu De Lishi Touxi* [An Historical Analysis of The Associated Factors of The Policy Marking of The Third Line Construction]. *Shandong University Journal (Shandong Daxue Xuebao), 1*, 89.

Duan, J. (2012). *Jin 20 Nian Lai Sanxian Jianshe Jiqi Xiangguan Wenti Yanjiu Shupin* [A Review of Studies on The Third Line Construction and Related Issues in The Past 20 Years]. *Studies in Contemporary Chinese History, 6*, 100–109.

E Group Company (EGC). (1988). 1984–1988 EGC History Book.

———. (1997). 1989–1997 EGC History Book

———. (2013). EGC Official Website Page.

———. (2014). EGC 2014 Annual Year Report

———. (2015a). EGC *Zhigong Ligang Xiuyang Shishi Banfa Cao'An* [EGC Worker Absences Cultivation Measures for Its Implementation Draft]. June 24th, 2015a.

———. (2015b). EGC *Jiechu Laodong Hetong Shishi Banfa* [EGC Measures for The Termination of Labour Contracts]. June 30th, 2015b

———. (2015c). EGC *Zhigong Ligang Xiuyang Shishi Banfa* [EGC Worker Absences Cultivation Measures for Its Implementation]. June 30th, 2015

———. (2016). 2016 EGC's Recruitment Information.

Friedman, A. L. (1977). *Industry and Labour: Class Struggle at Work and Monopoly Capitalism* (Vol. 82). Macmillan.

Guo, Y. (2015). *Cong EGC Tuishi Kan Zhongji Hangye Zhe Jinian* [Look at The Heavy Industry In Sight Of EGC]. March 25th, 2015. *Zhongguo Gongye Xinwen Wang.*

He, G. W. (2015). EGC *Ni Caiyuan Zao Zhigong Kangyi* [EGC Workers' Protests]. May 16th, 2015. Caijing Wang.

Hurst, W. (2009). *The Chinese Worker after Socialism.* Cambridge University Press.

Huang, J. (2014). *Danwei Tizhi: Yizhong Xiandai Guojia Goujian De Fangan* [The Work Unit System: A Pathway to Construct the Modern State]. *Theory, 5*, 15–19.

Li, C. (2014). *EGC Huocheng Dierge Changyou: EGC Guanligang He Gongren Bizhong Dadao 1:1* [The Ratio of Management and Workers Reached 1:1]. September 5th, 2014, *Jingji Guancha Bao*, quoted from *Sina Finance.*

Li, C. H. (2002). *Sanxian Jianshe Tiaozheng Gaizao De Lishi Kaocha* [A Historical Examination of The Adjustment and Transformation of the Third Line Construction]. *Studies in Contemporary Chinese History, 9*(3), 43–51.

Li, C. H., & Jiang, D. Y. (2005). *Woguo Da Sanxian Jianshe De Lishi Jinyan He Jiaoxun* [The Historical Experience and Lessons of The Construction of the Third Line in China]. *Journal of Northeast Normal University: Philosophy and Social Science Edition, 4*, 85–91.

Li, H. L. (1993). *Zhongguo Danwei Xianxiang Yu Chengshi Shequ De Zhenghe Jizhi* [The Integration Mechanisms of Work Unit and Urban Communities]. *Sociological Research, 5*(9).

Li, L. L. (1992). *Shehui Jiegou De Zhuanxing: Jiegou Zhuti He Jiegou Guize De Biange* [The Transformation of Social Structure: Changes in Structural Subjects and Structural Rules]. *Sociological Research, 5*, 16–30.

National Bureau of Statistics. (2016). *2015 Nian Zhongguo Tongji Nianjian* [China Statistical Yearbook 2015]. Available on 12th September, 2022, *Vide*: http://www.stats.gov.cn/tjsj/ndsj/2015/indexch.htm.

———. (2020). *2019 Nian Zhongguo Tongji Nianjian* [China Statistical Yearbook 2019]. Available on 12th September, 2022, *Vide*: http://www.stats.gov.cn/tjsj/ndsj/2019/indexch.htm.

New Youth- Youth Reviews (*Xin Qingnian- Qingnian Pinglun*). (2013). *Xiri Mingxing *ST EGC Jukui Shi Zenme Zaocheng De* [The Large Losses of EGC]. June 19th, 2013. Quoted from *Jingwei Wang.*

———. (2014). *EGC Gongren De Xinsheng (Ruogan Wangyou Tiezi Jihe)* [Voices Of EGC Workers [A Collection Of Posts By Several Netizens]]. New Youth.

———. (2015). *Guanyu EGC Gongren De Zonghe Baodao Xinxi Yiji Baogao* [Comprehensive Report Information And Report On The Workers Of EGC]. New Youth.

Sichuan Provincial Bureau of Statistics. (2018). *Fengjin De Lichen Weida De Kuayue—Gaige Kaifang 40nian Sichuan Jingji Shehui Fazhan Chengjiu Xilie Baogao Zhi Er* [A Journey of Progress A Great Leap Forward—2nd in A Series of Reports on The Achievements of Sichuan's Economic and Social Development in The 40 Years of Reform and Opening Up]. 31st August, 2018. Available on 12th September, 2022, *Vide*: http://www.sc.gov.cn/10462/10464/10465/10574/2018/8/31/10458035.shtml.

———. (2019a). *2018 Sichuan Statistical Yearbook*. Available on 12th September, 2022, *Vide*: http://tjj.sc.gov.cn/tjnj/cs/2018/indexch.htm.

———. (2019b). Ganshou Meihao Shenghuo Jianzheng *Tianfu Jubian—Xin Zhongguo Chengli 70 Zhounian Sichuan Jingji Shehui Fazhan Chengjiu Xilie Zhi Ba* [Experience A Better Life and Witness The Great Changes in Tianfu—8th Out Of A Series Of Sichuan's Economic and Social Development Achievements in The 70th Anniversary of The Founding of PRC]. 22nd August, 2019. Available on 12th September, 2022, *Vide*: http://tjj.sc.gov.cn/scstjj/c105849/2019/8/22/4eab6dc77ecd4ee7b5bcd8d917c390f6.shtml.

———. (2020). *2019 Sichuan Statistical Yearbook*. Available on 12th September, 2022, *Vide*: http://tjj.sc.gov.cn/tjnj/cs/2019/indexch.htm.

———. (2021). *2020 Sichuan Statistical Yearbook*. Available on 12th September, 2022, *Vide*: http://tjj.sc.gov.cn/tjnj/cs/2020/indexch.htm.

Sichuan Zhengbao. (1993). *Sichuan Sanda Chanye Fazhen Gaikuang (1979–1991)* [The three industries in Sichuan 1979–1991], 01, 42.

Sina Finance. (2017). *EGC Chongzu Wu Yili Zhigong Shangfang Susong Shijian* [Official Report to Summary EGC's Status After The 2015 Labour Activism]. 23rd February, 2017. Sina Finance.

Standing Committee of the National People's Congress. (1992). The Trade Union Law of the People's Republic of China. Available on 23rd June, 2022, *Vide*: http://www.law-lib.com/law/law_view.asp?id=554.

———. (1995). The Labour Law of the People's Republic of China. Available on 23rd June, 2022, *Vide*: http://www.gov.cn/banshi/2005-05/25/content_905.htm.

State Council Information Office. (2009). *"Xin Zhongguo 60nian Sichuan Jingji Shehui Fazhan Chengjiu" Xinwen Fabuhui* [Press Conference on Sichuan's Economic and Social Development Achievements in 60 Years of PRC]. 30th September, 2009. Available on 12th September, 2022, *vide*: http://www.scio.gov.cn/m/xwfbh/gssxwfbh/xwfbh/sichuan/Document/427606/427606.htm.

Statistical Bureau of D City. (1988). *1987 D City Statistical Yearbook*.

———. (1998). *1997 D City Statistical Yearbook*.

———. (1999). *1998 D City Statistical Yearbook.*
———. (2018). *2017 D City Statistical Yearbook.*
———. (2019). *2018 D City Statistical Yearbook.*
———. (2020). *2019 D City Statistical Yearbook.*

Sun, D. S. (1995). *Woguo Jingji Jianshe Zhanlue Buju De Da Zhuanbian-Sanxian Jianshe Juece Xingcheng Shulue* [The Great Change in The Strategic Layout of China's Economic Construction—A Brief Account of The Formation of The Decision on The Construction of The Three Lines]. *Party Literature, 3*, 42–48.

Walder, A. G. (2015). *China Under Mao.* Harvard University Press.

Xin Jingbao. (2015). **ST EGC Tuishi Yading Guming Qihu Nanxia* [EGC Delisting in Stock Market]. 2nd March, 2015. *Xin Jingbao.*

Xu, Y. W., & Chen, X. (2015). *Sanxian Jianshe Dui Zhongguo Gongye Jingji Ji Chengshihua De Yingxiang* [The Impact of The Third Line Construction on China's Industrial Economy and Urbanization]. *Studies in Contemporary Chinese History, 4*, (81–92), 127.

You, Z. L. (2006). *Guanli Kongzhi Yu Gongren Kangzheng—Ziben Zhuyi Laodong Guocheng Yanjiu Zhong De Youguan Wenxian Shupin* [Management Control and Workers' Resistance—A Review of The Literature on Capitalist Labour Process]. *Sociological Research, 4*, 169–185.

CHAPTER 4

Workers' Returning to a Proletariat Position in Post-1978

4.1 Research into SOEs Before Economic Reforms

Research into the industry in the initial period of the founding of PRC demonstrated the necessity and rationality of the development of heavy, military and defence industries. Dong Baoxun (2001, pp. 92–93) summed up the patterns previous research had found about when and how different countries start modernisation. He categorised Germany, Japan, Russia and China as a group due to these countries' initial inducing and stimulating factors of modernisation which are mainly derived from severe challenges of the outside world. Therefore, these countries will put national independence and national security at the top of the list in the process of modernisation and choose to give priority to the development of the defence industry to promote the process of industrialisation. He then assembled Britain, France and the United States to a different group as their motivations of modernisation came from their own countries and are the result of the interaction between the economic base and superstructure, their productive forces and relations of production.

However, Dong's summary work is not well differentiated in taking the opposing camps; capitalism and socialism camps, between 1950s–1990s into consideration, nor did he distinguish the purpose of building the defence industry. Though Japan and China both prioritise heavy

S. S. Huang, *The Political Economy of Reforms and the Remaking of the Proletarian Class in China, 1980s–2010s*, Palgrave Studies in Economic History, https://doi.org/10.1007/978-3-031-20455-5_4

and military industries when starting modernisation, their purposes are different. The former is for the reform of the national system and the latter is for national economy development and defence of war. Other scholars (Song Shichang & Li Ronghai, 2001, pp. 4–13; Wang Huasheng, 1989, pp. 49–50; Wu Li & Wen Rui, 2006; Xu Juezai, 2008, pp. 39–51; Yan Yongqi, 2002, pp. 30–34) agreed with the fact that countries from different camps (socialism and capitalism camps) between 1950s–1990s took different development paths, especially socialism countries followed the Soviet industrial development mode.

Research studied China's reflection on the socialist model when exploring its development path, especially the problems caused by taking the Soviet industrial development mode (Chen Guoqing, 2000, pp. 7–10). Ye Shuzong (2010, pp. 29–37) summarises China's way of historical exploration on socialism by evaluating of Mao Zedong's judgement on international relations and his vision and plans for the development of China's industrialisation. The formulation of the country's main policies during this period reflected Mao Zedong's thoughts. Xu Congwen (2010, pp. 133–141) pointed out that in Mao's report in 1956; On the Ten Major Relationships (*lun shida guanxi*), the shortcomings and mistakes of Soviet socialist construction had been found and Mao put forward the "two-legged" approach (*liangtiao tui zoulu*) in 1958, which means simultaneous development of industry and agriculture, heavy and light industry, central and local industry, coastal and interior industry, etc., to overcome the shortcomings and mistakes. However, all the studies mentioned above tend to summarise historical policies in industries and lack reflection on SOEs.

In this stage, the state owned all the heavy and light industries. Although existing cases (Soviet and east Europe) showed that bias towards heavy industry would cause excessive demand for agriculture and imbalance development of light industry, despite the "two-legged" approach that was put forward by Mao, there were two periods of intensive construction in heavy and military industries. One is in 1950s; the 156 Key Projects (*156 xiang zhongdian gongcheng*) and the other is between 1960s and early 1980s; the Third Line construction (*sanxian jianshe*).

The existing research did not pay attention to individual workers or only regarded them as a subsidiary of studying Chinese socialism and the characteristics of SOEs, nor infer when a large number of factories, enterprises, employees and cadres moved from the eastern first line areas to the interior of China and when the interior areas needed to develop heavy and military industries from infrastructures, a large amount of central financial funds had been invested in the Third Line area, stimulating construction and giving advantages to workers in the Third Line construction projects. These advantages, such as welfares received by workers, were exclusive and depended on the unit's capacity. Thus, as discussion regarding unit, the distinction between superior and inferior organisations led to SOE workers, who belong to the superior organisation, can access and obtain more resources than other groups of people. Further explanations on how SOE workers passively acquired the status and resources can better infer the loss of workers when these privileges were withdrawn due to the economic reforms.

In fact, SOEs' inefficiency problem had been exposed even before the Reform and Opening Up. In the early 1960s, the strategy "*Guan, Ting, Bing, Zhuan*" (Closing, Stopping, Merging, Converting) was released. Xiao Liang (1990) said this strategy was applicable to the planned economy. In the highly concentrated and planned economy, this strategy was the only way to adjust the industrial and organisational structure. Shirk (1993) agreed that this strategy was designed to lighten the centre's financial burden, eliminate inefficient small-scale factories, strengthen centralised coordination of production and guarantee central revenues. However, in the application of this strategy, it inevitably made some resources idle, causing loss and waste due to the existence of "communal pot".[1]

The historical research and summary of this period reflect the following points. First, the state and party's control over enterprises is obvious. Therefore, construction projects like Third Line can be conducted with concentrated human, material and financial resources. The judgement on the international relation and domestic development by the party and state's leaders, especially Chairman Mao, was direct and powerfully reflected in the economy layout and national development plan. Second, SOEs were in an advantageous position with financial support. Especially, the construction projects in southwest region, not only the construction

[1] Even though SOEs experienced the strategy "*Guan, Ting, Bing, Zhuan*", workers' personal wages will not be affected regardless of whether they do more work or less, do it well or not. This means the wages are still paid regardless of whether the company is operating well or not, profit or loss. Therefore, the inefficiency problem was not solved under the condition of guaranteeing full employment during the planned economy period.

industry were supported, the related infrastructure construction, such as road and railway transportation construction had been promoted. Third, as a typical work unit in the city, SOEs reflect the work unit's dependency. It can be reflected on the dependence of the enterprise on the support of the national fiscal policy, and the dependence of the individual on the enterprise. SOEs that were more related to the construction of heavy industry, military industry and national defence during this period, the larger the scale, the more resources were available to these employees. SOE workers' social status was quite high before the economic reforms.

However, in the historical reflections of this period, there is no trace back to Lenin's opinion which points out the emphasis on heavy industry and military industry is due to the opposition between two camps of socialism and capitalism,[2] and the need to successfully establish socialism to break through the encirclement of capitalism. In the economic structure, China implemented a wartime economy, which uses agriculture to support the development of industry. In the political structure, one party dictatorship concentrates power. However, such a concentrated effort to develop industry and support the establishment of socialism should be realised in a limited time because the time to support the wartime economy at the expense of agriculture is extremely limited. In China, serious shortages of resources were found, in particular, agriculture can no longer be sacrificed for development (e.g., the Great Famine in 1960s). At the same time, an important external factor affecting the transformation of economic structure was the weakening of the opposition to the capitalist West. Therefore, the transition from the wartime economy to the national development economy was expected.

In fact, China's early development path had taken in many Eastern European countries. The difference is that Eastern European countries reconciled with capitalism and established capitalism after market reforms, while China still maintains socialist ideology and the state is still a powerful supreme authority that controls the direction of economic development. Research pointed out that the Third Line construction is a product of a highly state-controlled economy in a special historical period and these factories followed the same model nationwide, but different regions did not face the same problem in the reform era. As a result,

[2] See Lenin (1916), *Imperialism: The highest stage of capitalism* and *The state and revolution*.

Table 4.1 NVivo nodes and memos used in Chapter 4

Nodes	Attitude towards SOE
	Poor years
	Rich years
	Working experience
	Original SOE tradition (welfare)
	EGC's technique school
	Decided factors
	Workers attitude towards leaders
Memos	Allocation job position
	Cadres and workers
	Enterprise and State
	Enterprise Strategy
	Reform
	SOE cost

Data Source Fieldwork research

China has been running economic dualism with a hangover of communism and communism-related entitlement. This study will investigate the communist residual reflected by SOE workers.

In this chapter, I use EGC workers as a sample case to illustrate SOE workers' status in pre-SOE reform and after SOE reform eras, reflecting the changes in the composition of the working class and how these aristocratic workers have returned to the traditional working class under Marx's class theory, that is, they have lost their political halo and privileges in economy and have reverted to the bottom of the social structure. Nodes and memos created in NVivo and used in this chapter are summarised in Table 4.1.

4.2 Iron Rice Bowl and Workers' Privilege Under the Work Unit System

Patricia M. Thornton (2017, p. 257) discussed that the state-directed centrally planned economy characterised the state sector's industrial workers with the so called old three iron-calls (*jie san tie*): "the iron rice bowl (*tie fanwan*)", "iron wages (*tie gongzi*)" and "iron-clad posts (*tie jiaoyi*)" which guarantee not only them but their children with stable jobs. EGC workers were interdependently linked with others and with other work units in pre-reform era, the state's policy bias and economic support to the enterprise also gave them a great advantage in a time of scarcity and separated their lives from the local residents. More specifically, EGC workers were distinguished from non-state sector workers and workers from other SOEs in D city.

However, Chinese economic reforms have brought a transformation, where the market has become the main force to construct and drive Chinese economic and social development (Chen Feng, 2009). Under this circumstance, EGC workers' socio-economic status and the composition of the so-called working class in this SOE has also experienced a reform. Since the announcement of SOE reform, EGC used a different mechanism, instead of making workers directly unemployed and losing their income by lay-offs, a division within the working class was raised in EGC. Technicians with better educational backgrounds (engineers' group as part of the intellectuals) were divided out of the working class as a reserve for the later management class. Cadres (the professional managers in the market system), *de facto*, have a clear difference from the workers even though ideologically or politically they are within the progressive class; the working class. The working class in the SOE has experienced instability and impermanence since the economic reform started. Workers returned to Marx's proletarians, no longer as the vanguard of the proletariat or the master of society.

Privileged Work Unit and EGC Workers' Advantages

"Grow up quickly my daughter, then you can marry an EGC boy. Eat royal grain, live in an apartment, EGC also gives out figured cloth, money is given at New Year and festivals, enjoy dancing and playing cards, the money is inexhaustible".[3] This children rhyme was popular in D city before the 1990s. EGC remained synonymous with the ability to provide good treatment for workers in D city till the 1990s. The rank-and-file workers were able to enjoy benefits brought by the work unit that were advanced for other residents of the area. Xuehua and Xu (Interviewees 009 and 015) pointed out that EGC was the first and only work unit to provide gas to its family area in the 1990s.

[3] The original Chinese text: *nv'er nv'er kuai kuai zhang, zhangda jiajin EGC chang. chihi huangliang, zhu loufang, EGC hai fa hua yishang, fengnian guojie dou faqian, tiaowu dapai yong bu wan.*

> In the past, the water we used was drawn by EGC, not like nowadays, the city installs meters. In the past, the gas and water belonged to EGC, EGC charged you. There was a sub-company called W, which was specifically designed for charging utility fees in family areas.[4] If your house had any problem, for instance, the veiling leaks water, W company would send fixers. W company had many kinds of workers, carpentry, tilers and so on. Because we lived in EGC's living areas before, all the utility fees were taken from our monthly pay; the officer came to our houses every month to write down the numbers on meters. It was very convenient. We didn't have to go to a place to make the payment. (Interviewee 009)

EGC workers' livelihoods were fully covered by the enterprise and the benefits were provided to EGC employees exclusively. ECG workers enjoyed a better quality of life without having to deal with any of the city's departments. The advantages and specific relationship with the state made people in EGC a clique, EGC workers clearly distinguished themselves as workers who work for the state, not just an economy, a business, but the state represented behind this enterprise that provides them with these generous benefits.

Between 1950s–1970s, workers who were "imported" for the construction of the factory, mainly moved from an industrially developed area to D city where agriculture was the main industry at that time. One of the interviewees was allocated by the Heavy Machinery Bureau to help with the construction of EGC.[5] Before he joined EGC, he developed rich work experience in Beijing and the Northeast Industrial Base. He participated in the preparatory group for EGC establishment. He told me that at the very beginning the preparatory group had only five people including him, and he was the only one from Sichuan Province (although not D city); all the others were from Northern China (Interviewee 005). Later then, more experienced workers and technicians came. EGC's construction benefited from the investment of the Third Line and the help of the Construction Corps (*jianshe bingtuan*). In addition to the construction of the factory, workers also joined in the construction of the workers' dormitories. Most of whom came from the North China and did not understand the Sichuanese was naturally isolated from the local population, living in

[4] For the sake of confidentiality, the sub-company is coded as W or W company.

[5] The Heavy Machinery Bureau was managed by the First Ministry of Machinery Industry of PRC, which was established in 1952 to manage the manufactory industry, telecoms and shipbuilding.

EGC's unit society. The completion of the establishment of the workplace, residential area and support facilities made the gap between EGC workers and the city residents much greater. Workers used the phrase "work in the city" to refer to all jobs outside of EGC, no matter whether they were in the government departments or the private sector. EGC as a unique society differentiated from the bigger society, the city. "*Changli*" (in industry) and "*shili*" (in city, which means working outside the SOE system) were used to describe this difference.

The creation of the unit society will also encourage people to stay in the familiar culture and environment and mean that they are less interested in change. Interviewees 021 who grew up in EGC's work unit society and Interviewee 006 who relocated to D city after graduating from university both said that when they get used to their workplace and have built friendly social networks with their colleagues, they feel reluctant to change and are afraid of adapting to a new working environment. They share the common idea that a change to a new factory might entail higher pay. Nevertheless, they said they are comfortable and happy in the place they are familiar with. Individuals' choices such as this will enhance EGC's work unit characteristic and also further contribute to the unit culture construction.

Specific treatment for EGC workers was very generous. Li (Interviewee 005) said that when he came to D city in the early 1950, his pay as an accountant was two Yuan higher than that of the mayor of D city. The iron rice bowl characteristic was evident from the early days of construction. Wages were paid as usual even during the construction suspension period (1960–1962) and even during the Cultural Revolution (1966–1976) when the factory stopped production occasionally. Benefits that EGC provided to its workers include houses according to their length of service, the construction of a community and the provision of housing at a price lower than the market price, trips abroad or within the country, technical schools for children of employees, a university for continuing education, as well as a university for the elderly to enrich their lives after retirement; money and rewards, including performance-related pay and a completion mission allowance, half-yearly bonuses, end-of-year bonuses, annual bonuses (*nianjin*), which contributed to a higher pension after retirement, a monthly subsidy for mobile phones, heating fees in winter, very low cost medical care and schooling for their children, etc. In addition, model workers got extra welfare, such as houses, reward trips and bonuses (Interviewee 001, 007, 008, 009, 010 and 016). EGC also supported workers to pay back their monthly mortgage for housing, which most companies do not provide in D city (Interview 006, 009 and 009). Youfang (Interviewee 001) said that in 2002, her factory repaired the workers' rest area. The factory even installed air conditionings for the workers in cranes. In 2008, EGC reached the peak of its profits earning; this year also marked EGC's 50-year anniversary. To celebrate the anniversary, EGC provided additional welfare to employees; they gave employees two sports suits, a business suit and one pair of sports shoes. Checking with interviewees, these clothes allowances cost over 2,000 RMB per person, which was roughly a rank-and-file worker's monthly pay at that time. By buying goods to encourage the employees to celebrate the 50th glory anniversary, EGC sent a signal to its employees that this enterprise was making a profit and conveying a sense of pride in being a member of EGC.

These benefits were gradually abolished during the late 1990s, or those livelihood-related functions were divided from the corporate functions due to SOE reforms. As Walder (1988) described the work unit system that once provided a lifelong institutional basis for material and emotional support has been gradually dismantled.

Benefits for Workers' Families

The benefits offered by EGC provided not only to the workers themselves, but also to their families. For example, Qilian (Interview 007) relocated to D city in the 1960s as EGC worker's family member. The enterprise offered her jobs in EGC's primary school first and then allocated her to the factory's logistics department when the production started. After applying the "*sangong zhuanzheng*" policy (three types of people who asked for regular identities: part-time workers, temporary workers and labour contractors) in the late 1970s, she obtained a regular position in EGC.

The care for workers' children was even more obvious. As the second generation of SOE, they enjoyed priority in employment and schooling. They also carried a deep social imprint of the work unit society. They lived in the EGC living areas, attended EGC education institutes and most of their family members have been EGC workers, consider themselves more innocent and simpler than people who grew up in a city environment. They noted that in the industrial environment, the social network is simpler, better and easier. To them, "the city" is a more open society and an unfamiliar system.

I correlated the policies enacted by the state in relation to SOEs to understand the employment policies provided by EGC for the children of its workers. First, on 2 June 1978 *State Council Circular on Issuing State Council Temporary Measures on Providing for Old, Weak, Sick and Handicapped Cadres* and *State Council Temporary Measures on Workers' Retirement Resignation*.[6] This notice clearly states that if workers' retirement were to place their family in a difficult financial situation, one of their children, either a high school graduate, or a "*shangshan xiaxiang zhishi qingnian*" (knowledgeable youth back from the countryside) who met the requirements of the original enterprise's recruitment could join in the parent's SOE as an official displacement worker. The notice aimed to help cadres and workers who were not in good health to further work and to solve the financial difficulties of families, but some people took advantages of the policy by getting their children into the system while finding a new job for themselves in the private sector. Therefore, further on 7 November 1981 another notice—*State Council Circular on Strict Implementation of the Interim Measures on Workers' Retirement and Resignation*—was published to limit and restrict retirees and from finding new employment (State Council, 1981).[7]

These polices were applied in SOEs as "displacement" (*ding ti*). Displacement aimed to solve the problem of hundreds of thousands of young Chinese left unemployed after the Cultural Revolution. These young people returned to the cities from the countryside without jobs and many could not pass the University Entrance Examination, making them a very unstable factor in Chinese society. It was also an efficient way of bringing the children back to the cities and getting them jobs within the state sector system. Between 1978 and 1983, over 12, 200,000 people retired in China, among them, around 9 million were displaced by their children (He, 1990, p. 152).

EGC conducted the displacement policy between the 1970s and 1980s to help solve the unemployment problem of its employees' children. A

[6] The original Chinese text: *guowuyuan guanyu banfa 'guowuyuan guanyu anzhi lao ruo bing can ganbu de zanxing banfa' he 'guowuyuan guanyu gongren tuixiu、tuizhi de zanxing banfa' de tongzhi.*

[7] The original Chinese text: *guowuyuan guanyu yange zhixing gongren tuixiu tuizhi zanxing banfa de tongzhi.*

high school graduates could get into EGC by taking a parent's job if one of their parents was willing to retire early. Li (Interviewee 005) said he retired 10 years early (as an accountant) for his daughter's displacement.

> She is a knowledgeable youth. I maintained a good relationship with her cadres to get her back to the city. And after just a few months, the country announced the policy. The first knowledgeable youth back from the countryside among your children could enter the enterprise 'ownership by the whole people' [note: *quanmin suoyou zhi*]; the rest of the children can only be contract workers, not officially within the state sector system, so her older brother then got into EGC. For her, if she displaces my job position, she does not have to go through the internship but is an official SOE worker from the very beginning. And the length of service will be counted from the first day she enters. She cannot get into EGC by tests, and as a displacement, for future job transfers, she could get reimbursed travel expenses. (Interviewee 005)

Youfang (Interviewee 001) commented that she displaced her mother at EGC because of her mother's willingness. "She said she was very tired and wanted to take a rest". She got in without any job or technical skills. She did not literally take over her mother's job, instead she was assigned depending on the lack of labour for that year. For example, in 1978, EGC lacked laboratory technicians and, in 1979, EGC lacked crane drivers. Therefore, when she displaced her mother's job in 1979, she was assigned to learn how to drive a crane. After six months training with a qualified worker as an apprentice (*xuetu*) and then a year of work experience, she became a regular crane driver. She commented that at the time, she did not think about finding a job beyond the state sector; the whole society was eating the "*daguo fan*". She did not even think about what kind of job she would get after graduating from high school, but instead depended on EGC's allocation.

The displacement was not a perfect solution for a family whose parents were still young at the time. By applying the displacement policy, the parents had to shorten their working years to make space for their children.

> "The year after I retired, EGC conferred titles for accountants. I should be a senior accountant ... a normal accountant cannot get job subsidies after retiring, but a senior one can get more pensions after retirement. (Interviewee 005)"

Youfang's (Interviewee 001) mother was still young when retired, worked on her own for a while as a street vendor of books and helped out in EGC's family area council. Due to the lack of an open labour market, the job opportunities for young people were very limited and the parents had to make sacrifices to ensure that the children have good jobs. Due to the fact that this was a "displacement" strategy, the requirements in terms of education level were not strict. "Knowledgeable youth" with high school diplomas were qualified for the displacement in EGC.

On 12 July 1986, four documents were announced: *Provisional Regulations on the Institution of the Labour Contract System in State-owned Enterprises; Provisional Regulations on State-owned Enterprises Recruiting Workers; Provisional Regulations on State-owned Enterprises to Dismiss and Discipline Employees;* and *Provisional Regulations on Unemployment Insurance for Employees at State-owned Enterprises* (State Council, 1986a, 1986b, 1986c and 1986d).[8] Based on the four documents, from 1 October 1986 the displacement policy ended. These aimed to break the "*tie fanwan*" and "*daguo fan*", reward ability, distribute materials according to work, encourage the enthusiasm of labourers and improve their quality. Although these documents pointed out the recruitment should be an open, voluntary, comprehensive merit-based assessment, EGC still had a policy to look after the workers' children. Xuehua (Interviewee 009) joined EGC in 1986 through "*ziran jianyuan*" (natural attrition) after graduating from high school. Natural attrition refers to the fact that workers in the SOE retired, resigned or died without being replaced by new workers. The remaining workers had to assume their role, so there was space for the SOE children to get in. Xuehua acknowledged that if a person's parents worked for EGC since the 1950s, when the parents retired, the industry would take care of their children. Whether the need for workforce replacement really existed at EGC after the centralised completion of the displacement of the children of workers in the late 1980s is open to question, but there is no doubt that "natural attrition" policy facilitated the children of workers.

In addition to care for the work allocation of workers' children, there was also care in education. Besides education from kindergarten

[8] The original Chinese text: *guoying qiye shishi laodong hetongzhi zanxing guiding*; *guoying qiye zhaoyong gongren zanxing guiding*; *guoying qiye chitui weiji zhigong zanxing guiding*; *guoying qiye zhigong daiye baoxian zanxing guiding*.

to high school, EGC also offered *zhigong zhongzhuan* (employees' technical secondary school for secondary school graduates), *jixiao* (technical school) for training technical workers, *yeda* (evening university) and *zhigong daxue* (employee university) for the development of educated professionals.[9]

Excellent benefits and provision of access to higher degrees, EGC was a very good employment opportunity for local residents until the 2000s, and it was very difficult for people not in the EGC system to get into the EGC. Chun (Interviewee 010) told me in 1986, only two positions to go to EGC's technical school were offered to high school graduates outside of EGC, and all the other places were allocated to the children of EGC's employees. So, the outsiders needed a good grade to have a chance to enter the SOE and get the iron rice bowl. University graduates from D city were assigned back to this city after graduation. Only those students who did well in high school had the opportunity to enter the enterprise's technical school for training and merit graduates from EGC's technical school were directly sent to EGC until the end of the 1980s. Once the person transferred to become a formal staff member in EGC, the person was guaranteed a permanent job position and all the welfare and benefits. Jobs that are considered to be much better than a blue-collar worker in the 2010s in the opinion of some interviewees, such as nurse, teacher, doctor, were much easier to access to by entering vocational training after secondary school until the early 1990s.

4.3 Research into SOEs and Economic Reforms

In general, the state was still in charge of the economy during the post-Mao period. The national economic reforms were bound to affect SOEs. In this stage, the situation of international confrontation had slowed

[9] Evening University required workers' leisure time, for instance, weekends and evenings for further education, and the workers needed to pass the Adult University Entrance Examination to get in. This was a second option if the workers could not pass the test to enter Employee University.

Employee University allowed the workers to be released from production. One interviewee told me that it was just like "real" university and could lead to promotion opportunities if you graduated from it with a degree certification (Interviewee 010). EGC's Employee University was established in 1958 as EGC's part-time university. It closed due to the Cultural Revolution and reopened in 1975 as *Qi Eryi Daxue* (Qi Eryi University). In 1980, it changed its name to Employee University.

down,[10] and policy bias no longer needed to sacrifice agriculture to prepare for war and industrial development. Moreover, in the past three decades of development, SOEs have shown problems.

The publication of the Reform and Opening Up policy in 1978 led to the beginning of China's economic reforms. There are different interpretations on the reasons for 1978 economic reform. Shirk (1993, p. 37) argued that the cause of the 1978 initiatives was the succession contest between Deng Xiaoping and Hua Guofeng.[11] Deng functioned as a political entrepreneur, using innovations in economic policy to attract support among groups in the CCP Central Committee and Politburo. The 1978 policies were intended to recentralise industrial financial and administrative authority after the chaos of the Cultural Revolution. Lee Peter (Nam Seok) (1987, p. 128) believed that the reason for reform is the post-Mao leaders' intention to return industrial finance and management to the golden age of the 1950s instead of creating something new. Lee mentioned that the most important 1978 document on industrial management, the *Thirty Articles* (or *guanyu jiakuai gongye fazhan ruogan wenti de jueding*, Decisions Concerning Some Problems on the Acceleration of Industrial Development,) drafted by the State Planning Commission, took the restoration line. The focus of the state had shifted to the development of the national economy in post-Mao era.

Research pointed to the revival of reforms of SOEs as the main target and vehicle of economic reform (Huang, 2003) and analysed the reasons for reform of Chinese SOEs. Lardy (1998) suggested the average SOEs' sum of bank debt, unpaid taxes, unfunded pension liabilities and net indebtedness to non-state firms far exceeded the value of SOEs' assets. Yan (2012, p. 362) believed that when personalisation and privatisation became necessary for development, CCP and the state used their power to initiate a reform of the system. Garnaut et al. (2005) disagreed with this idea by stating that the government's original idea was to change the internal governance of the market in which SOEs operated and improve the internal governance of SOEs but not privatisation. However, their

[10] Refer to PRC obtained China's Representation in the United Nations in 1971; US President—Richard Nixon visited China in February 1972; and the diplomatic relation between China and Japan was normalised in September 1972.

[11] Hua Guofeng was Party Chairman after Mao Zedong, Prime Minister and the Chairman of the Central Military Commission.

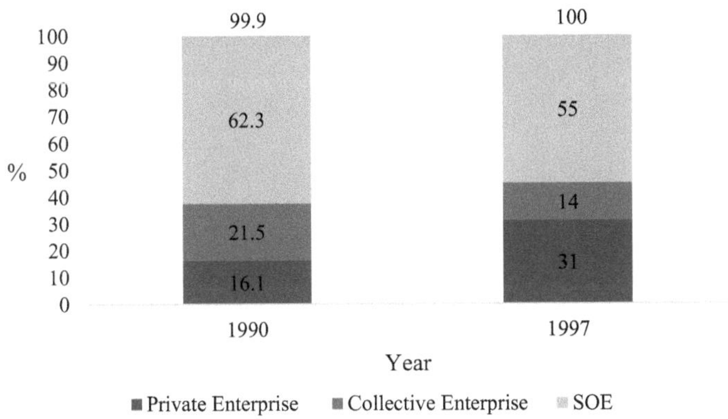

Fig. 4.1 Percentage of non-agricultuarl employment in three sectors, 1990 versus 1997 (*Data Source* Zweig, 2001, pp. 231–247; Bai, Li & Wang, 2003, pp. 97–121; Scalapino, 1999)

ideas do not touch the key issue that the party and state leaders in post-Mao period actually wanted to solve and rationalised, that is the issue of fairness and efficiency (*gongping he xiaolv*).

The inefficiency of SOEs can be reflected in the following statistical tables. On the one hand, to protect employment, SOE workers accounted for a considerable number in the non-agricultural population till the end of 1990s; On the other hand, SOEs' contribution in national industrial output and industrial growth had been a significant drop (Figs. 4.1, 4.2 and 4.3).

Party and State leaders, such as Deng Xiaoping, Zhao Ziyang, Hu Yaobang, Zhu Rongji and Jiang Zemin, polices include solving the inefficiency of SOEs, while at the same time, in fact, needs to be at the expense of fairness[12]; The full employment and the fairness in income is no longer

[12] Hu Yaobang, General Secretary of the Central Committee of the CCP between 1982–1987; President of the Central Committee of CCP between 1981–1982. Refer to Hu presided over the drafting of the "Decision of the Central Committee of the Communist Party of China on Economic System Reform" (*zhonggong Zhongyang guanyu jingji tizhi gaige de jueding*): "the most important issue is to moblise the internal vitality of enterprises and create higher labour productivity" (Gao Shangquan, 2015). Available on 12th September, 2022, *vide:* http://www.reformdata.org/2015/1231/26501.shtml.

Zhu Rongji, Premier of State Council from 1998 to 2003. In Zhu's reform program, SOEs reform became the fulcrum (Zweig, 2001, pp. 231–247). In 1998, "*sannian*

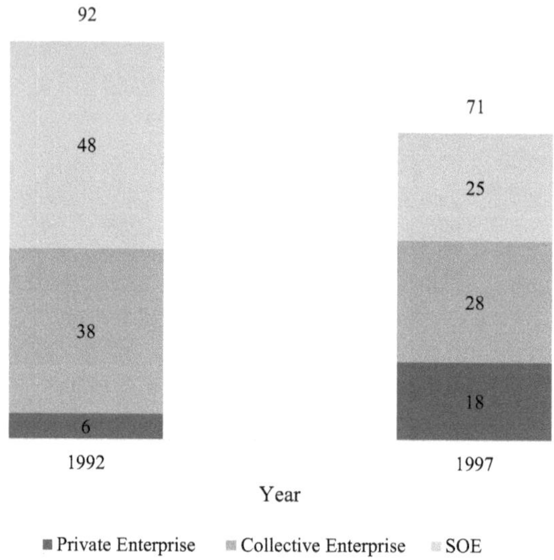

Fig. 4.2 The shares of national industrial output, 1992 versus 1997 (*Data Source* Zweig, 2001, pp. 231–247; Bai, Li & Wang, 2003, pp. 97–121; Scalapino, 1999)

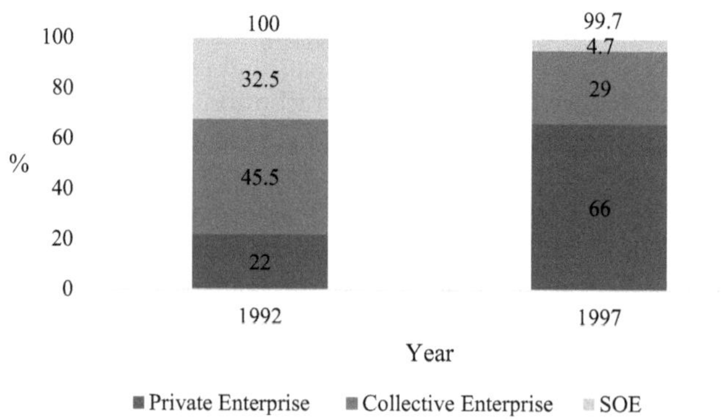

Fig. 4.3 The shares of the contribution to industrial growth, 1992 versus 1997 (*Data Source* Zweig, 2001, pp. 231–247; Bai, Li & Wang, 2003, pp. 97–121; Scalapino, 1999)

ensured. For instance, Deng's famous remark "enabling some areas where conditions permit and some people to get rich first, so as to lead and help underdeveloped areas and their people and ultimately achieve common prosperity" (Deng Xiaoping, 1993, pp. 110–111, 172, 373–374; Jian Xinhua, 2016, pp. 10–16).[13] Although Deng's policy was not designed to cause polarisation and new classes, we can see from the changes in the Total Factor Productivity and China's Gini coefficient (an international accepted measure of inequality) that production efficiency after economic reforms has indeed improved and has been accompanied by a significant gap between the rich and the poor, which is at the expense of socialist fairness.[14] This issue has not been as studied as it deserves.

Existing studies made some judgements on the SOE reforms. China Labour Bulletin (2007) summarised three stages of SOE reforms. The "management reforms" (more market autonomy for SOEs) between 1978–1984, the "dual track reforms" (*shuanggui*) (state ownership versus private ownership) between 1984 and 1992 and the "ownership reforms" (moving towards state capitalism) post 1992.[15] In addition to giving enterprises more autonomy, using bonuses to incentivise the managers,

tuokun" (all SOEs had three years to become profitable) was announced and set as a target by Zhu (Garnaut et al., 2005, pp. 35–63).

Jiang Zemin, General Secretary of the Central Committee of the CCP between 1989 and 2002; President of the PRC between 1993 and 2003. He accelerated the pace of SOE reform by making it politically legitimate (Yang Yiqun, 2002, p. 235). Regarding the restructuring of SOEs, Jiang stated that it was necessary to, "encourage mergers and acquisitions, standardise bankruptcy, redistribute laid-off workers, increase efficiency by reducing their number, carrying out reemployment projects, and form a competitive mechanism in which enterprises that survive are the fittest (*guli jianbing, guifan pochan, xiagang fenliu, jianyuan zhengxiao, shishi zaijiuye gongcheng, xingcheng qiye youshenglietai de jinzheng jizhi*)" (Hurst, 2009a, 2009b, p. 16).

[13] The original Chinese text: *Rang yi bufen you tiaojian de diqu, yi bufen ren xian fu qilai, daidong he bangzu luohou de diqu he renmin, zuizhong shixian gongtong fuyu.*

[14] Total Factor Productivity (TFP) is a measure of the output of economy and can tell the growth of economy (Yi Gang et al., 2003, pp. 25–33). The overall TFP growth rate of China's manufacturing industry is between 2 and 6%, with an average annual growth rate of 3.83% (Yang Rudai, 2015, pp. 61–74).

The Gini coefficient is a measure of inequality, the smaller the number, the more equal the society. It was 0.15 in Mao's China and increased and stood at 0.462 in the 1990s (Wright, 2010). It reached the peak at 0.491 in 2008 and currently, it is 0.468 in 2020 (National Bureau of Statistics, 2021). Available on 12th September, 2022, *vide:* http://www.stats.gov.cn/tjsj/zxfb/202109/t20210929_1822623.html

[15] More details of state capitalism will be discussed in Chapter 6.

and "*zhuada fangxiao*" (grasping the large and releasing the small) campaign to restructure SOEs,[16] SOE reforms had caused six in ten SOE workers to be laid off between 1998 and 2004 and the proportion of SOEs employees in all employment also dropped from 16 per cent in 1994 to eight per cent in 2005. Naughton (2003, 2014, 2016a and 2016b) stated that SOE reform is in fact moving towards a system of mixed ownership of which the government would manage enterprises as a wealth-owner, rather than as a direct executive. After SOE reforms, these enterprises are still owned and controlled by specific government bodies. Naughton also raised an unresolved debate about economic reforms and SOEs reforms. Some reformists believed that loose credit conditions and increase government debt can be sustained by China. By the contract, a different group believes that the state must gain control over credit and limit its growth, impose hard budget constraints on SOE and the rising debt endangers China's economy stability, and the investment should only be in profitable projects. These studies looked at SOE reforms from the perspective of the overall Chinese economy and hinted at a problem that workers became vulnerable in this period, and even formed an opposition to the professional managers, who are the representatives of the state's management of SOEs.

A theme that cannot be ignored in the study of SOEs during the reform period are laid-off workers (*xiagang gongren*). From the mid-1990s to the end of 2001, there was a 40% reduction in the number of workers in the state sector, which meant that the number of workers dropped from 113 to 67 million, 46 million workers lost their jobs (Cai, 2006; Giles et al., 2006, pp. 61–95; Lardy, 1998). 4.1 million state sector workers were registered as laid-off workers in 2001 (China Statistical Year-book 2001). Many studies have researched on this theme. Research into laid-off workers suggests regional differences. For instance, Hurst (2004, 2009a, 2009b) found that different regions of China had its own political economy and faced its own dilemmas regarding SOE labour reform and its effects. He found that the protests of laid-off workers in the eastern coastal region and the old industrial base in northeast China were more

16 "*Zhuada Fangxiao*" was released in 1995, aiming at restructuring SOEs. Small SOEs were denationalised while the state still controlled enterprises which related to national defence and security, important and special monopoly industries and enterprises that provide important public products and service pillar industries, and key enterprises in high-tech industries (Xiao Donglian, 2014, pp. 9–19).

effective, while laid-off workers' protests in the central region were not so effective. He pointed out that the local government's financial capacity and its relationship with the central government had a decisive influence on the outcome of laid-off workers' protests. O'Brien (2009) agreed on this by stating that the regional political economy has an influence on workers. Research into laid-off workers is focused on Northeast China to explore SOE workers' struggle and resistance in the reform era (Lee Ching Kwan, 2006; Mun Young Cho, 2013), while research focused on Pearl River Delta; Southeast China, interests in migrant workers' labour conditions and resistance to discrimination (Lee Ching Kwan, 2007; Ngai Pan, 2005).

Secondly, research shows that the workers' group have diverged due to the different interests (Cai, 2011, pp. 71–93; Chen Xi, 2019, p. 63; Perry, 1993; Solinger, 2009; Wu Qingjun, 2010, pp. 65–89), therefore, there were different demands at the time of protests and struggles. As a result of the fragmentation of SOE workers' identity, Chen Xi (2019) explained that if the claim focuses on resources or benefits for which workers may have to compete, they tend to have difficulty maintaining broad solidarity. Chen explained the fragmentation by stating workers' choice of narrow group through four mechanisms: segmentation, particularisation, competition, and co-optation/defection. The purpose of these four mechanisms is to maximise the satisfaction of workers' needs. Lee (2007, p. 237) also observed the cellular characteristic of workers' activism. Walder (1988) argued that the workers' resistance is not for opposing the central Party-state but pray for leaders to meet their material needs. As long as they could enjoy social welfare protection and benefits, the activism directed towards the central regime will be limited.

Thirdly, research into SOEs' laid-off workers is an analysis of Chinese socialism and reflects a very important change in Chinese social classes; SOE workers from the privilege class to the new urban poor (Chen Feng, 2009; Cho, 2013; Lee, 2007; Li Peilin, 2004; Li Qiang, 2002; Solinger, 2006, pp. 177–193; Thornton, 2017, p. 257; Wright, 2010; Yan, 2012, p. 50). Studies on China's social structure will be discussed in the next section.

Existing research illustrated that the market-oriented reform of SOEs is the result of state-led. The privatisation, bankruptcy, sale, transfer and even the stripping of the social functions of SOEs do not change the real owners or managers of SOEs[17]; Various levels of governments or institutions like SASAC, which means the changes are under state management (2016b; Naughton, 2003, 2014; Yan, 2012). The means of production are no longer owned by the whole people (SOE workers). Research also elaborated on a large number of SOE workers who had been laid off due to SOE reforms and their struggles and resistance. The factories want to improve efficiency and need workers to work harder, but the fact is superfluous and inefficient. Therefore, the primary task of SOEs' reform is to improve workers' productivity by reducing redundant personnel. However, reforms took away the benefits they had before, and from the workers' point of view, their efforts to increase productivity are disproportionate to their pay. These make them want to go back to the socialist fairness (Yan, 2012, p. 50). Laid-off workers must face the harsh reality: compete with unskilled rural migrant workers (whom most city dwellers view as social inferiors, or second-class citizens) (Lee, 2007) for jobs with low and often delayed pay, extremely long hours and draconian working conditions. In the reform era, on the one hand, they are still politically motivated by the state to encourage dedication. On the other hand, their material needs could not be met. This contradiction made the workers very frustrated.

Huang (2003) argued in *Selling China* that although SOEs shrunk through the reform period, there was always a political pecking order (the large SOEs over small and medium SOEs), where they enjoyed continuing privileges and status. A similar argument can be applied to the SOE working class. Although SOE workers' privileges politically did not translate to particularly good treatment, they continued to have access to better resources than others in the working class. Even so, SOE workers have often had to bear harsh and difficult treatment after reforms as Solinger's work (2006) shows.

However, there are some points that have not been pointed out to show the essence of the problem and could be studied deeper. Firstly, the SOE reforms illustrate the failure of building a utopian socialist enterprise. The reform in fact transferred the socialist characteristics of SOEs (eg. income equality and job security) close to capitalist characteristics (e.g.,

[17] See State council's documents and documents announced by SASAC and the Ministry of Finance (SASAC and the Ministry of Finance, 2017a, 2017b and 2017c). Available on 12th September, 2022, *vide*: http://www.gov.cn/zhengce/content/2016-06/22/content_5084288.htm.

pursue efficiency and promote competition), which further illustrates the aforementioned "reconciliation with the West". China has also withdrawn from the polar opposition between capitalism and socialism.

Secondly, Party's technocrats took over the leadership of SOEs, making them transferred from red bureaucrats to capitalists under Marx's class theory. They are separated from the workers. Before SOE reforms, the means of production were owned by the party and government, while the means of production can be privately owned by the management personnel after the reforms. Workers had never owned the means of production. In this top-down management system, SOE workers were in a passive and silent situation. Once the economic reforms come and policies impact on SOEs' parenting care and protection of workers, it is easy to eliminate SOE workers. Reforms have weakened or even taken away the interests of workers.

Thirdly, though researcher such as Jaeyoun Won (2009, pp. 185–201) argued that the socialist work benefits in China had gone due to economic reforms. Research did not point out that the improvement of efficiency will come at the expense of fairness, that is, the leadership status of the workers cannot be preserved. The socialist fairness pursued by workers is a privileged benefit. The contradiction between fairness and efficiency is an economy problem. Reform pursues efficiency, while workers pursue socialist fairness. The top-down reform on SOE is not initiated by workers. Workers do not care about the loss of state-owned assets. They are concerned about their own interests. SOE workers want to enjoy fairness without paying for efficiency. Before reforms, the policy bias towards the heavy and military industry with supporting their workers' life and service facilities makes this group of workers more profitable than others. However, SOEs were inefficient, and the shortage of economy made personal resources scarce. At the same time, the agricultural industry cannot continue to be sacrificed for industrial development. These SOEs dragged down the development of the entire society.

Fourth, Deng Xiaoping's reform allowed some people to get rich first, creating a new class division. Fairness is limited in efficient socialism. The protest of workers for wages after the reforms implies that state-owned assets have deteriorated, and therefore have class divisions and confrontations. The demands of workers, no matter if they are laid-off workers or in-service workers, SOE workers or migrant workers, are based on wages and benefits, which means that workers have admitted that they are in a lower position, and they care more about economic status rather than political one. Meanwhile, after the managers took over SOEs, the party led the economic development towards marketisation and capitalisation. After reforms, the managers can no longer be part of the working class. They have become the leaders of the working class. In fact, workers, whether within the state sector or not, have become wage labour. This is an obvious process of establishing Marxist capitalism. The studies on using Marx's class theory to explain China's new class structure will be discussed in the next section. Then, what measures will Chinese SOEs take to ensure their development is still in line with the value of socialism and for "the people" instead of becoming a capitalist enterprise? Although lay-off is the main strategy adopted in SOEs to control costs and increase labour productivity, are there any exceptions for enterprises to use other methods to achieve the purpose of reforms? These two issues are not well explained in the existing literature referred in this section.

Fifth, SOE reforms have revealed that in the reform period of pursing efficiency, there is no corrective mechanism to ensure fairness. Policies did not take workers' interests into account. Industrial reform policies proposed by Zhao Ziyang, Hu Yaobang, Zhu Rongji are based on economic judgements to improve efficiency, while workers have no say in the value judgements about the fairness issues. The top-down reforms have exploited workers and led to class problems.

Lastly, SOE reforms are neither perfect nor completed. Radical reforms have not lasted long (e.g., "sannian tuopin" policy mentioned above), and subsequent reforms have slowed down, and there are even signs of repetition. SOE reforms have always been exploring a way to balance between market dominance and state dominance. Some conciliatory measures for SOE workers dragged SOEs in the market back to their traditional paternalistic focus on workers. However, this kind of attention to workers is not earned by the workers themselves but determined by the priorities of production and development. For example, it can be seen that the emphasis on industrial workers, such as "skilled craftsmen" (*jineng gongjiang*) was proposed, and the restoration of SOEs welfare encouraged industrial workers to work more. The purpose of this is still for achieving better production. If SOE reforms go for a linear way, workers changed from privileged to no privileges, instead of reversals, workers are more receptive.

EGC's case and EGC workers' status in the 2010s China will help to understand the working class in SOEs a from different perspective.

4.4 Workers' Status in E Group Company After SOE Reforms

I previously mentioned the limitations of development of the heavy industrial built for a wartime economy at the expense of agriculture and light industry. EGC, like other heavy machinery enterprises, the inevitable decline can be expected when the policies shift, and the direction of national development changes.

Olson ([2000] 2014) pointed out in *Power and Prosperity*, the centralised planned economic system chosen by the Soviet-type communist states allowed the state to control national resources through the nationalisation of industry and collectivisation of agriculture, as a result, society produced a state of inefficiency. Murrell and Olson's (1991) theory explains the rise and fall of centrally planned economies states that there is a "take-it-or-leave-it" mentality towards the existence of state assets and that people behave in a way that takes a piece of the existing "cake" rather than trying to make it bigger. Since the introduction of the market economy has left SOEs with no ability to generate their own income in a competitive market, workers in SOEs are opposed to privatisation because their livelihoods are not as good as they were before economic reforms.

SOE reforms began with the 1978 economic reform (or even before), and the results or effects of SOE reforms were evident after the mid-1990s when the nationwide lay-offs of workers occurred. In EGC case, it maintained the privileges of SOEs and provided benefits to workers until the late 1980s, and it was only in the late 1990s, when large-scale national SOE reforms began, EGC gradually developed policies, e.g., "holidays" and "breaks" in response to unsaturated production tasks. SOE reforms before the 2010s did not have a significant influence on EGC's workforce or workers' income. EGC's SOE reforms were concentrated in the 2000s–2010s, in the late stage of national SOE reform.

Even in such an enterprise that strives to perpetuate the welfare features of state enterprises for as long as possible, there was no way to meet the conditions for a socialist enterprise to provide full employment in the economic reform period, not to mention protecting workers' welfare.

Loss of SOE Advantages and the Failure of Socialist Enterprises

Chun (Interviewee 010) gave an example of how difficult it is for the factory to become profitable. He mentioned that the sub-company's target was to have 180 million RMB in profit in 2019; however, he said that:

> We have a 300 million RMB order quantity plan for the next year; however, a very good annual profit could only be expected at 15-20% [of the order quantity]. Then, you need to minus the cost of raw materials, equipment, machines, the rent, the cost of human resources, financial costs, occupation of funds, loans, official costs, depreciation, utilities, and many other kinds of costs. In fact, we should complete the order quantity to 400 million RMB to ensure all these costs are covered and workers can get their salaries on time every month. 300 million RMB is the minimum that we must have for next year's order quantity. (Interviewee 010)

His statements were agreed by Xu (Interviewee 015) who was based in a different factory. His factory experienced a merger and restructuring with China Aviation Industry in 2016. He suggested that the products of machines and equipment for space module segments are not for profit but for the design and production autonomy.

> Nowadays, we have a production value of 100 million [RMB] every month, but it is impossible to achieve 10 million gross profits. Only by selling drugs can you make profits of 10–15% [of the production value] ...The best gross profit we can make monthly is a few million and then you should minus the energy costs, depreciation, raw material, equipment, pay. The retained profit is very little. However, as an SOE, if it can have a small retained profit, that is a good thing. Many SOEs don't have any at all and have to turn to the bank for loans. (Interviewee 015)

The financial problems of SOEs were a common phenomenon across the country and having to cover the welfare of workers was an even heavier burden. I discussed the functions of SOEs, especially for workers' welfare, have changed profoundly during the deepening reform period (2015–2017), with SOEs performing only corporate functions, while functions related to workers' livelihoods have been carved out. This means that while the workers' wages were numerically up in comparison to pre-economic reform era, the removal of SOE benefits left them with the need to pay for all aspects of their lives, which were originally over-provided to them by a socialist SOE. Once the enterprise no longer provided health care, education, housing, etc., free of charge, workers have had to bear more of the cost of living and took on debt to buy commercial housing. EGC's former attractiveness of wages and benefits for workers was no longer an advantage.

In other words, EGC's "iron rice bowl" was no longer tempting. Before the 2000s, EGC provided better care of its employees than the city government. However, in 2018 when I conducted the fieldwork research, "work in the city" as civil servants at government departments means good welfare, high pay, a lifelong job and access to the "golden rice bowl" (*jin fanwan*) from workers' perspective (Interviewee 008 and 009), which is obviously better than the iron rice bowl. Even in the private sector, better welfare can be offered than EGC. Xiaotian (Interviewee 004), who worked in a private company in Guangzhou City for a few years before he returned to Sichuan Province and joined EGC in 2012, mentioned that the welfare advantages that EGC offers are shrinking, while the private companies are caring more about their employees. He mentioned that the private company that he worked for has a tearoom where employees can take breaks and it provides breakfast and refreshments on workdays, none of which is provided at EGC. He suggested that "currently the welfare in SOEs is more like what private enterprises provided [in the past], and the private enterprises are more and more like the old time SOEs".

Apart from the financial difficulties, the units no longer recruited new employees but instead found ways to reduce the workforce, which contradicted the originally conceived socialist enterprise, i.e., the incapability to ensure socialist equality; employment for all, meant the inability of the construction of a socialist society in SOEs. Interviewees (003 and 006) pointed out that their factories have stopped recruiting new employees since 2012 or 2015 after the labour activism. EGC has implemented a hiring freeze (Interviewees 016, 018, 019 and 020).

At the same time, EGC no longer had the capacity to unite its workers in a unitary society, and the identification with the SOE culture has been decreasing. As a result of market reform and open recruitment, the composition of EGC's workers was no longer singularly concentrated in factory children or a group of alumni who graduated from EGC's technical school. From the announcement of *Provisional Regulations on State-owned Enterprises Recruiting Workers* in 1986 onwards, young university graduates have been continuously joining. The differences in education background, the obvious age gap and the comparative value placed on the young and old employees reduces the small society characteristic that EGC had. This has caused the collapse of the closed society. Yujia (Interviewee 002) noted that he is not friends with his colleagues, a more common occurrence.

> I don't even have my leader's WeChat account. I have few friends here. And after work, I really have little contact with my leaders. For my other colleagues, we sometimes arrange to play *majiang* (mahjong) together. The SOE is not the image [it was] in the past, the intrigue against each other is not less than in the 'outside'. I have been in the office (a group in the sector) for three years. We have only organised one dinner together and the whole Technical and Quantity Sector has only arranged three dinners for the last three Chinese New Year's. Last year, due to the bad profit, we did not even have the dinner party. (Interviewee 002)

He agreed that this is because the two generations have different life focuses and interests. It is very difficult for the young to engage in the traditional SOE culture.

> We are young people and most of the employees in SOEs are over 40 [years old]. In my office, only one other and I are in our 20s, basically the whole office is over 40 and the leaders are over 50. When you come to this enterprise, you feel lifeless. I prefer to see my leaders younger than me rather than seeing my leaders like my parents. The gap is big. If people are around the same age, it is easy to organise a dinner or a karaoke after work. However, they all have their families and children, they won't go out for fun. You cannot build contacts with them. The 10-year age gap can make many differences, [for example] the cognition and version. (Interviewee 002)

Xiaotian (Interviewee 004) shared the same opinion and said the eight-hour work shift is enough for him, he does not want to spend more time with work-related people after work.

> I want to control my free time. For example, many people used to gather for a dinner or a drink after work. I won't get used to this. I am not saying I do not belong to the workers, but I think [these activities are] a waste of time. [If I join the activities] I don't have much time for exercising, painting and listening to music. (Interviewee 004)

That sense of the first generation of EGC workers distinguishing between EGC workers as "us" and people outside of the enterprise as "others", work in EGC as "in the factory" and outside of the system as "in the city", is disappearing, and the unit society is gradually losing its function of providing support for workers and their families.

Loss of SOE Workers' Superiority

The previous section discussed that being a EGC worker before the 1990s asked for family relationship or good education background. However, it was no longer a difficulty to get a worker job role in EGC after economic and SOE reforms. The recruitment criteria are lower and SOE workers are no longer competitive in terms of education degree.

Feng (Interviewee 021) said, "if you graduated from university, will you be willing to be a worker?" Her belief was echoed by other interviewees (Interviewee 011, 014 and 022). The attraction of becoming an SOE worker is generally low to young university graduates. As Xiang (Interviewee 013) mentioned, "nowadays, young people don't learn this (workers' skills). The youngest front-line workers are over 30. I am quite young compared to my team group. The average age is over 40". The change of needing to compete to get into the EGC has caused workers to lose their sense of superiority in society. In their eyes, becoming an EGC worker has become a no-brainer, and they would not have come if they had a better option. Kai (interviewee 006) said after he started dealing with mechanics and machine construction, "I regretted that I did not apply for the master's program". Xuehua (Interviewee 009) said the lack of university education is the main reason why she chose to stay in the same company for over 30 years. EGC is not the best choice for people with good education degree.

EGC workers' children also no longer enjoy the privilege of education or job assignment. In 2003, the EGC Employee University merged with Sichuan College of Architectural Technology. In the same year, the EGC's Employee University system was cancelled. Since then, all graduates from this college need to meet the recruitment requirements to get jobs at EGC.

The loss of rights made workers question why SOE reforms in the 2000s and 2010s has to solve the enterprise's financial problem by reducing the number of workers and taking their benefits back. SOE reform in EGC is therefore not just an economic concept, but one that has involved social and cultural issues that are harder to track and more complex to conceptualise. Workers began to realise that they were no longer the masters of the country, but a group that could be easily eliminated just as what Marx's class theory described about the proletariat (Marx, [1844] 1932). The identity as SOE workers once can ensure workers' goods and benefits devalued after reforms. SOE workers are becoming more and more like other ordinary workers in the working class. As I discussed in the Chapter 1, SOE workers are frustrated by SOE reform because they were rhetorically glorified in pre-reform era but feel betrayed and abandoned by the socialist state (Chen Feng, 2006, pp. 42–60; Hurst & O'Brien, 2002, pp. 345–360). EGC workers' experiences examined this claim. The awareness of class consciousness (Marx [1844] 1932; Marx & Engels [1848] 2009) and the entitlements (Sen, 2002, [1983] 2016) and power (Foucault, 1999) that they tried to keep led to the subsequent strike and protest, which I will discuss in Chapter 5.

Status of Employed Workers

SOE workers have become China's new urban poor (Chen Feng, 2009; Cho, 2013; Lee, 2007; Li Peilin, 2004; Li Qiang 2002; Solinger, 2006, pp. 177–193; Thornton, 2017, p. 257; Wright, 2010; Wu Qingjun, 2008, p. 64; Yan, 2012, p. 50). The most obvious change in their status can be found from economic aspect, which I applied Bourdieu's economic capital concept to analysis it. According to Bourdieu's arguments in *Distinction*, the indicators of economic capital are variables such as income, the ownership of expensive cars and leisure boats and the habit of spending holidays at a hotel. Economic capital comprises money (wages, dividends, and financial investments), real estate and fine art products, as well as access to the means of production, such as machines, patents and factories (Bourdieu, [1979] 1984, p. 130). It reflects the ability to achieve the immediate satisfaction of people's material needs. In EGC, workers' economic capital can be classified as financial income and privileged access to resources to meet their living needs. Either can be kept as the same level as in the pre-SOE reform era.

For workers in employment, the difference between becoming "*zhengshi zhigong*" (official employees) or "*laowu gong/hetong gong*" (contract employees) is significant.[18] Only the official employees are in the state sector system. It will influence the person's welfare through the "*wuxian yijin*" (Five Insurances and One Housing Fund), pay and further career development within the SOE system.[19] Only the official employees can get housing fund support. Although both the official employees and contract employees are offered social insurances, the level is different. As the social insurance payment base is according to the employees' previous year's average income, the highest level is 300% and the lowest level is 50% (D City's Bureau of Human Resources and Social Security and Bureau of Finance, 2018); the enterprise thus has a flexible ability to differentiate between official employees and contract employees. Moreover, the contract is signed with the employment agency, which means the contract length is shorter than with an official employee. A contract employee also only has a temporary job at EGC, which means that if EGC is lacking labour, it will employ contract employees, but it does not guarantee them a permanent position. However, an official employee signs the labour contract with the SOE directly and the length of the contract is longer. For an official employee, the person signs the labour contract with EGC, and the contract is automatically renewed until the person's retirement age (if there is no early retirement). Only if the official employee breaks the rules or misbehaves, for example, embezzling money, engaging in corrupt activities, disclosing national secrets, or flighting and brawling that causes a colleagues' death in the enterprise, will the person's contract be ended. Compared to the official employees, the labour contractors earn less compensation if their labour contracts are cancelled and are more likely to end the labour contracts when EGC underwent reforms.

That is to say that after SOE reform, the traditional Chinese SOE workers in the true sense of word were whose who are in employment and official employees in the state sector system, while other types of

[18] University graduates enter EGC via university employment fairs will become official employees, while those from employment agencies (means they do not have a degree or who worked in other sectors before applying to EGC and are not eligible for the university employment fairs) will become contract labour. Contract labour can become official employees after passing the Regular Employee Examination.

[19] The Five Insurances refers to endowment insurance, medical insurance, unemployment insurance, employment injury insurance and maternity insurance. The Housing Fund refers to the housing provident fund.

workers were certainly not treated as well as this group of people, though all of them are in a poor financial position.

Kai (Interviewee 006) said that his average monthly pay in 2012 was below 2,000 RMB and his average pay in 2017 was below 3,000 RMB per month. Compared to a state sector worker's income in 2008 and the increased price of commodities, EGC workers' incomes had grown very slowly. Xie (Interviewee 011) said that:

> 2014–2015, my monthly pay was around 1,500–1,600 [Yuan]. I told my friend outside of EGC; they didn't believe me. They think we must have other types of income. I said, 'not at all'. Before the supervisor institute took over EGC, we regularly had cash bonuses, for instance, every month we had 440 [Yuan] for the telephone bursary. Now, in order to have the standard management, there is no cash bonus. If there is any bonus, it should be put on the pay and recorded. (Interviewee 011)

Although stopping cash bonuses could reduce the levels of corruption and make the management system stricter and more formal (Interviewees 006 and 011), it also directly influences workers' access to disposable economic capital and their quality of life. Compared to what they earned and the commodity price level, EGC workers' living standard has decreased. This became more serious for couples who both worked at EGC.

> Previously, the commodity price was not so high. We, each person had 1,700–1,800 [Yuan] monthly pay, the total was over 3,000 [Yuan], vegetables were only a few cents. We could use a small part of our income to live a decent life. However, now the commodity price has increased so much and the industry cannot make profits, nor do our salaries show big changes. Rice costs 2–3 RMB [per kg] now. The influence on us is huge. (Interviewee 018)

Jobs as SOE workers could no longer provide them with an advantaged socio-economic position in D city. Thus, their sense of status declined. EGC transformed from a socialist state enterprise into a company in the market economy, where it no longer provided benefits for workers, and instead workers had to rely on selling their labour for wages to buy what they needed to live, while workers' jobs were controlled by the cadres who had been given new status; the enterprise's management, who became Marx's "capitalists" (Marx, [1844] 1932), who satisfied the reformed

SOE's goal of profitability by pushing workers to create more surplus labour value. This was reflected in workers' workloads.

> Before my maternity leave, my working team had 12 people, and the other team had 20 people. After I returned to work [in 2015], the total number was 12 people. And then after the sub-companies' reorganisation, we had two more people. However, we had 14 people to not only do our original work, but also extend our work range. We cover the electrician work within a radius of 2 kilometres. The industry keeps losing benefits, and many workers have retired early or taken a buying-off. Some industries do not have electricians anymore or the remaining ones cannot do the job. So they outsource these jobs to others. The original 40 people's work is now on 14 people. And there are many things we need to operate to fix; the workload has more than doubled. (Interviewee 018)

EGC has undertaken stricter regulation in terms of managing workers made the workers in socialist state enterprise more like proletariat in capitalist society. First, the company closely controls the cost of parts. Interviewee 011 said that the official procedure is more complicated than before. He complained that:

> Currently, even [for] a 1 Yuan thing, you should write a report and wait for approval.[20] After this, there is bidding on the price and so many other procedures. The effectiveness is lower. The fastest procedure costs 3-4 days. (Interviewee 011)

Similar experience was shared by others. Interviewee 018, she said that if a worker wants to buy essential machine parts, they need to ask for four to five cadres' signatures. She suggested that this kind of invisible work added to her work burden. Interviewee 015 said that, in his work unit, if he wanted to buy something, he needed to answer questions:

> Why do you need to buy this? What is the usage amount in the factory and does the usage amount vary in a year? Which months need more, and which months require less? How long do you think this could be used and

[20] I later found that the report of 1 Yuan is highly exaggerated. Workers are allowed to buy machines parts that break constantly. Machine parts that cost less than 3,000 Yuan can apply the official bidding price orally. The oral bidding ensures the production process runs smoothly. However, although the control of product cost helps EGC to set up a more standard procurement process, it has increased and slowed down workers' work.

> when is the next purchase time? Did you compare different categories and know the advantages for the one that you want to buy? Plus, the superior will also ask to compare the prices online to the supplier to save on cost. (Interviewee 015)

The other regulation is the stricter commuter times and the control of entrances and exits. Since SINOMACH merged and reorganised with EGC in 2013, the control of the working hours has been stricter than before. All the employees are requested to keep to 8 am–6 pm working hours (with a two-hour break from midday-2 pm). Before the merger, all the employees could enter EGC freely at any time without a work ID, but now they are requested to bring their ID with them to enter and exit the industrial base during out-of-work hours.

These formerly privileged SOE workers, who were the aristocratic workers, found themselves having to work more to get the same or even less pay than before, and received stricter control. Middle-aged workers who had worked in pre and after SOE reform eras felt the changes more directly.

Particularly noteworthy are those workers who are employed but experiencing "break" (as I discussed as "*xigong*"), they are in a worse economic status. They could not gain the monthly bonus (Interviewee 009), only received 200 RMB per month in 1997 (Interviewee 010); or 70% of the basic pay per month in 2001–2002 (Interview 008).

Status of Workers in Early Retirement or Internal Retirement

China has a social insurance system for SOE retirees. Their endowment insurance funding is contributed by the enterprise and themselves. The state will provide appropriate subsidies when the funding is insufficient. However, for the early retirement and internal retirement workers, the enterprise has the autonomy to determine the treatment according to the business situation of the enterprise. According to **ST EGC: 2014 Annual Report*, EGC and its sub-companies had 8,779 retirees (including all types of retirees) (EGC, 2014). After EGC's 2015 labour activism, another 5,000 workers taking early retirement and internal retirement or end of contracts. As I discussed, people chose early retirement or internal retirement, as their labour relations with the enterprise will still be kept. In this sense, they are still workers in state enterprises.

Workers who opted for early retirement or internal retirement after SOE reforms, many chose to find a new job as they were not yet old enough to retire (one of my interviewees, Qiong [Interviewee 008], retired at the age of 45). Their reemployment options in D City are very limited, mainly in the service sector, for instance, after internal retirement from EGC, Xuehua (Interviewee 009) began to work several jobs, from a hot-pot restaurant waitress, to a cleaner, and then she began an e-commerce selling groceries in her residential area. With few having the opportunity to find work in the private industry, if they were skilled workers, for example, one of my interviewees was an electrician who worked as the electrician consultant in a private factory after taking early retirement (Interviewee 017). However, it is rare that these workers can re-enter employment in other SOEs in D city. Although the EGC does not mandate the type of workers who need to leave early, most of the workers who leave are fringe workers and are eliminated because they do not have the core skills. Their economic situation is made worse by the fact that they are not in the workforce and are not of full pensionable age.

Qiong (Interviewee 008) described her husband's case. Her husband had to retire early from his job in 2013. She noted that:

> He was just around 50, early retirement by five years, which is so *quede* [wicked]. He could only get 2,100 yuan a month. The next year was worse, only around 1,000 yuan [a month]. You must find a new job in the private sector to make a living. So, we had no choice but to find a job. (Interviewee 008)

Her husband has been a technician at EGC, but then found a reception job at a hotel. According to EGC's early retirement policy, her husband had left five years before the retirement age, which meant that he was going to receive steadily less "early retirement" pay until he reached 55 years old. To supplement her family's income, Qiong took on a service job at a tea house, though she worked as a chemist in EGC before.

A general look at the enterprise itself and EGC workers' status, the advantages are decreasing in value. The identity as SOE workers once brought workers actual benefits. Workers focus on what is behind the identity, which are Sen's "entitlement" (Sen, [1983] 2009, p. 58; Zou Libing, 2011, pp. 24, 27) and Foucault's "power" (Li Jing, 2013, pp. 60–68; Wang Xizong, 2013, pp. 5–6), but their grasp of the entitlement and power is limited, and they have to passively acknowledge the desperate situation they find themselves in.

4.5 Changes in the Composition of the Working Class in EGC

In Mao's China, the working class contained the symbol of progressive and revolutionary class attribute. It included not only the production workers, but also enterprise managers, state cadres and intellectuals (Xu & Shi, 2006). However, the market economy produces a complex stratification system (Zhou, 1993, pp. 54–73). When SOEs no longer held socialist characteristics but replaced by the market-oriented management system, workers' status changed and the division of positions became clearer. State cadres and enterprise managers were divided out of the ranks of the working class. Although SOEs managers (cadres) were worse off (to some extent) than before the SOE reform (Guan Qingyou, 2007, pp. 105–112), for instance, interviewees mentioned that SOE cadres had the right to allocate resources and the authority to decide the production plan in the pre-reform era, but they do not have exclusive power after SOE reform, they are not as easily eliminated from the enterprise as the workers. From EGC case, the cadres (or enterprise administrator in the capital market) face more pressure to perform in their new managerial capacity, such as targets for sales and profitability, but they are no longer part of the working class.[21] Meanwhile, the technicians, who had been on the same side as the workers, had a higher status than workers when I contacted the fieldwork research in 2018. Workers call them "sit in the office (*zuo bangongshi de*)". The pathways for workers to get promotions have been compressed, while the educated youth entering EGC with the identity of cadres had become the reserve of the management. The working class in EGC refers to Marx's working class, those at the bottom of the hierarchy, "the wage labour" (Marx, [1865] 1898), though EGC still generally refers to all employees who are not in management positions as workers (Figs. 3.9 and 3.11 on pp. 69–70). My analysis of the changing composition of the working class from the perspective of the individual, i.e., the interviewees' perception of their own identity, is an application of Weber's sociology ([1922] 1978): understanding the complex social

[21] This will also be proved in Chapter 5 when discuss workers' strike and protest.

structure from the perspective of the individual. Under this analytical method, both cadres (managers) and the technicians are excluded from the working class.

Workers: Returning to the Traditional Working Class

Just as the traditional working class, EGC workers returned to the bottom of the hierarchy in EGC. They realised they were no longer given privilege but were immersed in the afterglow of privilege. They did not fall into an absolute desperate situation of being absolutely oppressed and exploited, but the difference between them and the proletariat in class theory is small, i.e., limited control of all types of capital and power.

"The interest group" (Li Zenggang, 2002, pp. 77–81; Olson, [1965] 2012) of the working class in EGC can be concentrated in the group of workers who set their status as at the bottom in EGC. The workers' poor economic status can be told from their statements. They have been only able to sell their labour for barely subsistence wages, like Marx ([1844] 1932) speaking of the proletariat receiving the exploitation of the bourgeoisie, workers feel they are exploited by those further up the hierarchy in EGC. Learnt from the empirical research, workers used the term "white hat" (*bai maozi*) and "yellow hat" (*huang maozi*) to refer to the differences between the workers and the others (technicians and cadres). In the industries and workshops, front-line workers wear white hats during work for protection and for safety purposes, while the cadres wear yellow hats. This naturally differentiates workers as another interest group.

Moreover, as discussed, EGC workers' advantages that their SOE identity could bring them gradually disappeared, in other words, they became no different from the working class in the traditional sense. Their SOE identity used to be a symbolic capital (Bourdieu, 1991), which refers to the prestige or authority a person may have, or as a result of socially defined "signs of distinction". Differences or distinctions between people that are recognised as legitimate become symbolic capital, thereby yielding a "profit of distinction" (Bourdieu & Wacquant, 2013, p. 297). However, this identity no longer generated practical benefits, and became an outdated concept. The appeal of political mobilisation worked for the first generation of EGC workers, but in the interviews, my respondents were concerned about topics, such as the allocation of housing, free medical treatment, free education for children, cheap labour protection products, the work unit's organised trips and the increasing price of commodities in relation to the low pay rather than their SOE workers' identity. The identity itself has been devalued. "If I have opportunities to approach other units, I will go for it. (Interview 015)", "I will think about changing jobs after reaching the threshold to acquire a pension. (Interviewee 002)". Furthermore, even mentioning political rewards, such as "*sanba hongqishou*" (March Eighth Red Banner Pacesetter), for female workers who are role models in their work units; and "*jineng gongjiang*" (skilled artisan) or "*daguo gongjiang*" (great artisan), for skill masters who contribute to the country's technical skills.[22] The respondent addressed the economic benefits associated with the political reward, such as, "the monthly bonus for the first class is 8,000 RMB, the second class get 3,600 RMB and the third class get 1,500 RMB. In EGC, this reward lasts for two years (Interviewee 017)".

In general, their economic situation, social status and concerns and aspirations reflect the characteristics of the traditional working class. That is, the aura of socialist enterprise that this privileged SOE had brought to these aristocratic workers disappeared after economic and SOE reforms, and they became simply working class.

SOE Cadres

The cadres doing the labour work with the workers at the very beginning of the establishment of EGC (1950–1970s). Even the head of EGC joined in the establishment activities.[23] The difficult conditions at the time and the equalitarianism made the position of cadre not as good as it is now, but they were more like role models and a good example for the workers. However, I have made this reflection after reviewing SOEs and economic reforms that SOE cadres transferred from red bureaucrats to capitalists under Marx's class theory. These professional managers might not be opposed to the privatisation or marketisation of the enterprises, though they lost rights after reforms. They have formed a new interest group with new common interests to pursue and is apart from those of the SOE workers. They transformed from the level wage of cadres

[22] Most of the experienced workers are called "*shifu*" (master) with the apprenticeship in SOEs. *Shifu* also belongs to the workers' group as "*laobaixing*" (the common public). They work as teachers in the workshops to train and teach the young professionals in the practical technology.

[23] Narrative quoted from the interviewees, "*yi ba shou*".

to professional managers in the market. In this regard, the changes in the composition of the working class can be shown by discussing the transformation of SOE cadres as an opposing group.

In 1999, the Fourth Plenary Session of the 15th Central Committee published the *Decisions on Several Major Issues Concerning the Reform and Development of State-owned Enterprises* (Central Committee of CCP, 1999).[24] In this document, it was noted that SOE managers should be separated from the administrative level of the state sector. This document requested the deepened reform of SOEs' HR systems: neither the enterprise nor the cadres could have administrative hierarchy. The "abolition of the administrative hierarchy of SOEs" was addressed again in 2008 and 2009 when many SOEs sought Initial Public Offering (IPO). The administrative hierarchy was the key political power that differentiated the managers in SOEs from managers in the non-state sector. For example, they had the political power to review documents and the welfare right to enjoy cadres' medical treatment and housing. After the reform of cadre system, cadres became professional managers with the assessment system of capital market companies, such as more standard performance evaluation and more regulated hiring system.

The stereotype of an SOE cadre, reading newspapers and drinking cups of tea all day for a high pay, has gone. A cadre (Interviewee 019) said, "can imagine the manager position is as bitter as this?" Moreover, their identity as cadres has required them to sacrifice their economic capital in the reforms as a model for workers. Interviewee 010, as the head of a sub-company, was requested to reach 300 million RMB marketing orders in 2018. If he could not achieve that target, he would face a deduction of 100,000 RMB from his annual income as a penalty. With the high pressure of such a large fine, he has had to work very hard to ensure he gets the full annual pay.

Furthermore, the age requirements for managers are also more stringent. 35 years old is the upper limit for a basic level cadre and 50 years old is the upper limit for a middle level cadre. They are otherwise able to get promoted before the age limit or else hold the same position until retirement and in the last 2–3 years before their retirement, they do not have actual authority even though they are still in the manager positions.

[24] The original Chinese text: *guanyu guoyou qiye gaige he fazhan ruogan zhongda wenti de jueding*.

Some cadres mentioned they are in the same group as the workers in the working class. For instance, Chun (Interviewee 010) suggested that he belonged to the working class, despite being a leader of the working class.

> I did the CCP secretary position, then the factory director, and then the department director. I do not regard myself as a regular worker... I am not a SOE worker but an SOE cadre. Referring to my identity, I am an SOE manager. Referring to my class, I am working class. (Interviewee 010)

Chun noted that identity refers to daily work and work position, while class status describes the class position and attributes. When asked about his self-identity, he differentiated the political identity and the economic identity, but also addressed his position within the group. Xu (Interviewee 015) made a similar point. While he holds a technology manger position, he suggested that he in the workers' group and not a cadre.

After the abolition of the administrative hierarchy of SOEs, these cadres in the factories were supposed to return to the working class, as they are part of the wage labour (both the managers and the ordinary production workers have no ownership of capital, in this sense, these two groups are no different, being wage labourers). However, in EGC's case, I found the cadres more inclined to be bourgeoisised, i.e., the division from the proletariat is more pronounced in the post-reform enterprise. As I mentioned in the previous section, the supervision of workers became stricter after SOE reforms. Cadres' supervision reinforced class antagonism, while this antagonism was previously masked by SOEs' good welfare benefits and became visible after these benefits were withdrawn; The cadres (managers) were not considered an emerging class, but rather a change in the internal composition of the proletariat.

From workers' side, they thought that the cadres who represented the enterprise's benefits were taking an opposite position. For example, workers mention felt angry about their superiors' unfair allocation of work (Interviewee 001), the forcing of certain job contents (Interviewee 002), and the corruption gossip and negative impacts on workers' requirements (Interviewee 008). Meanwhile, the gap between cadres and workers is clear from the daily work, "the higher [the position], the easier [the job] (Interviewee 015)". Xu (Interviewee 015) further mentioned cadres' meeting is exclusive.

> They have meetings and deliver information within the meetings. You cannot approach that. The main director of each department, [such as] equipment department, general management department and procurement department. The directors have regular meetings every month. They will summarise last month's work and make the development plan for the next month. The meetings are only for them. The others cannot attend, and the contents of the meetings are closed. The department superior will allocate the work. You do your own work, but you do not know others' work. (Interviewee 015)

More so in terms of economic income, workers have kept the cadres out of their circle. Yujia (Interviewee 002) said:

> The regular employee gets 60,000 RMB annually, the factory unit cadre can get 80,000–90,000 RMB annually, and for the department director, they can get [at least] 100,000 RMB and above [annually]. (Interviewee 002)

Furthermore, workers pointed out the corruption and bribery of EGC cadres by suggesting that EGC invested a lot in the construction of the design centre in Chengdu and the new industry base in Jiangsu in the 2000s were simply excuses for cadres to seek personal benefits during the construction process. In general, EGC's cadres no longer belong to the working class, either ideologically or in terms of their economic status.

Technicians

Technicians with better cultural capital (education degree) became white-collar workers in EGC. Although these white-collar workers used more mental than physical labour, they are still indirectly involved in the process of production, i.e., the surplus value created by industrial workers (manual workers in the field of production), employed by the national capital. However, EGC case shows that both by technicians themselves and from the workers' point of view, the group of technicians were excluded from the traditional working class.

As technicians, they solve the technical problems that front-line workers cannot deal with, and they oversee and maintain the machines. They do not have to operate the machines themselves but manage the operation. Workers suggested that EGC should hire more workers, not technicians. From their perspective, the technicians do not do the practical jobs, nor do they help in the product process. The front-line workers experienced an increase in workload after EGC lost half of its employees. However, at the same time, with the enterprise's transformation, the number of educated technicians increased compared to the actual number of rank-and-file workers. Learnt from the empirical research, the front-line workers expressed their ideas online through *Baidu Tieba* (an internet discussion platform) in September 2014 by saying:

> "They [technicians] just stay in the office and propose unrealistic ideas for industry development".
>
> "(They) totally do not understand the hard work of the workers, only known for themselves in front of the leadership to patronize, seek benefits. A group of nerds, paper talk, not only harsh exploitation of workers, no benefit to the workshop. All day long only think about how to patronize, how to get promotions... If you want to get a good reputation, you should help the furnace (workers) to send samples, help the ingot maker to pass a few bricks, give a hand to open the wind, and so on, instead of coming out (from the offices) to get some air to find the feeling of being a cadre".
>
> "It is better to recruit workers than college students who can work".
>
> "There are a dozen people in the operating room (technicians), only 4–5 workers work".
>
> "Workers' labour is getting more and more intense, the number of workers is getting less and less, but your number (technicians) remains the same and your positions are not reduced, so you really have the face to come out and shout your grievances and say you don't understand?"
>
> "You (technicians) want to keep your income, you take advantage of the workers and exploit us by all means: working extra hours, extra work shifts and days ... Workers are so tired and sweaty that they have no place to rest, but you (technicians) gather together to talk and laugh so comfortable. What a magnificent picture: a few people are working while a group of people watch...It's always the workers who are deducted from the money ... and you can't satisfy your perverted and disgusting ugly nature without fixing the workers?"
>
> "The workers have been lost time and time again, treated like guinea pigs, and which of you (technicians) have seen it? Who has stood up and spoken out? ... We just want to stop being exploited for no good reason! ... We don't want to take your(technicians) jobs, do we? Our interests are gone, we are getting tired and hard at work, you have never been workers or spent time in the workshop, can you understand?"

For them, the technicians who are expected to solve problems in the production process in fact do not help them to address their work burden or pressure but join the exploiting group. For the sake of anonymous, the original text and link of the online discussions will not be released.

Workers think technicians only have better degrees but do not know or understand the industry at all. They feel it was unfair when they see the young graduates become technicians in a short time as they think technicians should be people who have substantial work experience and are selected from front-line workers. They clearly recognise that these technicians were not in the same interest group as them, and even deepened the exploitation and oppression of the workers in the factory, making their labour more intense and their wages less. Although, technicians are workers in the statistical sense of the enterprise, from the workers' view, only those who operate the machines with their hands are the real workers. These young educated technicians are not in the same camp as workers from the beginning but try to find ways to join in the group of supervisory workers. Thus, workers think that the technicians' priorities at work related to getting promotions rather than learning techniques. They think that the educated young people are not working steadily, suggesting that the young graduates who become technicians and cadres easily are not good for the enterprise's development due to their lack of experience and knowledge of practical work.

Both the workers and technicians know, the young graduates' internships in the factories are temporary. After technicians complete the internships, they can "*shanglou*" (go upstairs) and "*sit in the office*", no longer doing the actual operation work.[25] A degree allows the educated young people to thus avoid the heavy labour work. The different possession of capital (educational/cultural) differentiates the two groups of people. For the front-line workers, they realise that they do not have academic advantage, and this will limit their promotion opportunities, and thus they differentiate themselves from the technicians.

Xu (Interviewee 015) proved this claim and pointed out "the nature of the job position is a 'manager job role'". When he entered EGC, he and his co-workers did job rotation in the first year to get familiar with the

[25] Interviewees used these terms to describe the difference between cadres and workers. Workers work with machines in the workshop, while cadres stay upstairs, sitting in a bright office in their daily work.

industry production process. However, as a technician, his job content was more like that of an agent.

> My job is a management position; in other words, I manage the group of electricians and other workers. For instance, if a machine is broken, I am responsible for calling the maintenance personnel to repair, but I don't fix it myself. As a new graduate, we enter EGC without much practical knowledge. Basically, what we do in the workshop is: learn from electricians for two months, learn from bench workers for two months, learn from the technical group for another two months. Then, for the next half a year, I began to have my own job content. The work plant has many furnaces. I was in charge of managing the electric furnaces. After completing the internship, I was assigned to 'sit in the office'. (Interviewee 015)

Some technicians do not want to differentiate themselves from the workers (Interviewee 012, 003, 014), regarding themselves as the enterprise's employees in the market economy to weaken the divergence introduced by the class identity. They focus on economic status, which has close relationship to the material benefits. In this way, they recognise the distinction within the working class, but in order to avoid the contradictions caused by this distinction, and because they are not really part of the management in the official statistics, they use this way to keep themselves from being caught up in the struggle between the capitalists and the proletariat in the state enterprise. As can be seen in the next chapter on the workers' strike, even though the range of demands of the workers' strike and protest covered all the workers in the statistical sense, including the technicians, and the concerns expressed by the technicians in their interviews are one of the demands of the workers; the improvement of the economic status, the technicians were not involved in the workers' strike and are a separate interest group from the workers.

EGC's technicians are in a hierarchy between workers and cadres (as interviews mentioned that technicians are not workers nor do they in the management group). They belonged to workers' group in the theoretical and statistical sense of the enterprise, but they have better access to management, and they are in the upper class among the workers, and they are not thoroughly poor compared to manual workers. In terms of data, they have not been a large part of EGC, as can be seen from Figs. 3.9 and 3.11 (pp. 69–70), technicians accounted for 4.4% in 1997 and 1.5% in 2014 of the total number of the workers. So even if this small group is excluded from the analysis of the working class in EGC, the impact is statistically negligible.

References

Bai, C. E., Li, D. D., & Wang, Y. J. (2003). *Thriving on a tilted playing field: China's nonstate enterprises in the reform era*. Available on 12th September, 2022, *vide:* https://www.researchgate.net/profile/Chong-En-Bai/publication/254341382_Thriving_on_a_Tilted_Playing_Field_China's_Non-State_Enterprises_in_the_Reform_Era/links/5540a6b50cf2320416ed0f6d/Thriving-on-a-Tilted-Playing-Field-Chinas-Non-State-Enterprises-in-the-Reform-Era.pdf

Bourdieu, P. ([1979] 1984). *Distinction: A social critique of the judgment of taste* [*La distinction: Critique sociale du jugement*]. Translated by R. Nice. Harvard University Press.

———. (1991). *Language and symbolic power.* Edited by J. B. Thompson and Translated by G. Raymond & M. Adamson. Harvard University Press.

Bourdieu, P., & Wacquant, L. (2013). Symbolic capital and social classes. *Journal of Classical Sociology, 13*(2), 292–302.

Cai, Y. (2006). *State and laid-off workers in reform China: The silence and collective action of the retrenched*. Routledge.

Cai, Y. S. (2011). Distinguishing between losers: Institutionalizing inequality in China's corporate restructuring. *Going private in China: The politics of corporate restructuring and system reform* (pp. 71–93). Walter H. Shorenstein Asia-Pacific Research Center Books.

Chen, F. (2006). Privatization and its discontents in Chinese factories. *The China Quarterly, 185*, 42–60.

———. (2009). Guojia, Zhidu Yu Gongren Jiji De Xingcheng—Xifang Wenxian Jiqi Dui Zhongguo Laogong Wenti Yanjiu De Yiiyi [The state, institutions and the formation of the working class—Western literature and its implications for the study of labour issues in China]. *Sociological Studies,* 5(1).

Chen, G. Q. (2000). Qianxi Gongheguo Dizaozhe Jianguo Chuqi Guanyu Zhongguo Xiandaihua De Ruogan Sixiang [An analysis of PRC founders' ideas on China's industrial modernisation in the early years]. *Journal of Wuhan University of Water Resources and Electricity: Social Science Edition, 20*(1), 7–10.

Chen, X. (2019). The logic of fragmented activism among Chinese state-owned enterprise workers. *The China Journal, 81*(1), 58–80.

Central Committee of CCP. (1999). *Zhonggong Zhongyang Guanyu Guoyou Qiye Gaige He Fazhan Ruogan Zhongda Wenti De Jueding* [*Decisions on several major issues concerning the reform and development of SOEs*]. Available on

12th September, 2022, *vide*: https://www.chinanews.com.cn/2002-05-16/26/186031.html

Cho, M. Y. (2013). *The specter of "the people": Urban poverty in Northeast China*. Cornell University Press.

D City's Bureau of Human Resources and Social Security and Bureau of Finance. (2018). *Data of Social Insurance Payment*.

Deng, X. P. (1993). *Deng Xiaoping Wenxuan* [*Selected writings of Deng Xiaoping*] (Vol. 3, pp. 110–111, 172, 373–374). People's Publishing House. 1993 Edition.

Dong, B. X. (2001). Yingxiang Sanxian Jianshe Juece Xiangguan Yinsu De Lishi Touxi [An historical analysis of the associated factors of the policy marking of the third line construction]. *Shandong University Journal (shandong Daxue Xuebao), 1*, 89.

E Group Company (EGC). (2014). *EGC annual year report 2014*.

Foucault, M. (1999). *Guixun Yu Chengfa* [*Discipline and punish: The birth of the prison*]. Translated by B. C. Liu & Y. Y. Yang. Joint Publishing.

Gao, S. Q. (2015). *Hu Yaobang Zhuchi Qicao Zhonggong Zhongyang Guanyu Jingji Tizhi Gaige De Jueding* [*Hu's decision on economic system reform in central committee of CCP*]. Available on 12th September, 2022, *vide*: http://www.reformdata.org/2015/1231/26501.shtml

Garnaut, R., Song, L., Tenev, S., & Yao, Y. (2005). *China's ownership transformation: Process, outcomes, prospects*. International Finance Corporation and The World Bank.

Giles, J., Park, A., & Cai, F. (2006). How has economic restructuring affected China's urban workers? *The China Quarterly, 185*, 61–95.

Guan, Q. Y. (2007). Mancur Olson Jingji Sixiang Shupin [A review of Mancur Olson's economic thoughts]. *Shanghai Economic Research, 8*, 105–112.

He, D. C. (1990). *Dangdai Zhongguo de Laodongli Guanli* [The management of workforce in Contemporary China] (p. 152). China Social Science Press (Zhongguo Shehui Kexue Chubanshe).

Hurst, W., & O'Brien, K. J. (2002). China's contentious pensioners. *The China Quarterly, 170*, 345–360.

Hurst, W. (2004). Understanding contentious collective action by Chinese laid-off workers: The importance of regional political economy. *Studies in Comparative International Development, 39*(2), 94–120.

———. (2009a). *The Chinese worker after socialism*. Cambridge University Press.

———. (2009b). The power of the past: Nostalgia and popular discontent in contemporary China. In T. Gold, W. Hurst, J. Won, & Q. Li (Eds.), *Laid-off workers in a workers' state* (pp. 115–132). Palgrave Macmillan.

Huang, Y. S. (2003). *Selling China: Foreign direct investment during the reform era*. Cambridge University Press.

Jian, X. H. (2016). Quanmian Zhunque Lijie Deng Xiaoping Lilun Tuidong Sanda Zhanlue Zhanbian [A comprehensive understanding of Deng Xiaoping's theory to promote three strategic shifts]. *Deng Xiaoping Studies, 1*, 10–16.

Lardy, N. R. (1998). *China's unfinished economic revolution*. Brookings Institution.

Lee, C. K. (2006). *Working in China: Ethnographies of labour and workplace transformation*. Routledge.

———. (2007). *Against the law: Labour protests in China's rustbelt and sunbelt*. University of California Press.

Lee, P. N. (1987). *Industrial management and economic reform in China, 1949–1984*. Oxford University Press.

Lenin, V. (1916). *Diguo Zhuyi Shi Ziben Zhuyi De Zuigao Jieduan* [*Imperialism: The highest stage of capitalism*]. Available on 12th September, 2022, *vide*: https://www.marxists.org/chinese/lenin/15.htm

Li, J. (2013). Chuanboxue Shiyu Zhong De Foucault: Quanli, Zhishi Yu Jiaowang Guanxi [Foucault in communication: Power, knowledge and relations of communication]. *International Journalism, 2*, 60–68.

Li, P. L. (2004). *Huashuo Shehui Fenceng* [*Talking about social stratification*]. China Social Science Literature Press.

Li, Q. (2002). Zhongguo Shehui De Fenceng [Chinese social stratification]. *Ai Sixiang (Thinking)*. 23rd October, 2002. Available on 12th September, 2022, *vide*: http://www.aisixiang.com/data/1894-2.html

Li, Z. G. (2002). Olson Jingji Sixiang Shuping [A review of Olson's economic thoughts]. *Economic Review, 5*, 77–81.

Marx, K. ([1844] 1932). *1844 Economic and philosophic manuscripts*. Available on 12th September, 2022, *vide*: https://www.marxists.org/chinese/marx/marxist.org-chinese-marx-1844.htm. Also Available on 28th March, 2022, *vide* in *Collections of Marx*. Translated by Bureau for the Compilation and Translation of the Works of Marx and Engels, Lenin and Stalin, Central Committee of the CCP. People's Press. 2000 Edition.

———. ([1865] 1898). Gongzi, Lirun He Jiage [Value, price and profit], 25–78. *Marx and Engels collection* (Vol. 3, 1864–1883). Translated by Bureau for the Compilation and Translation of the Works of Marx and Engels, Lenin and Stalin, Central Committee of the CCP. People's Publishing House.

Marx, K., & Engels, F. ([1848] 2009). Gongchandang Xuanyan [The Communist Manifesto], 3–67. *Marx and Engels collection* (Vol. 2, 1848–1859). Translated by Bureau for the Compilation and Translation of the Works of Marx and Engels, Lenin and Stalin, Central Committee of the CCP. People's Publishing House.

Murrell, P., & Olson, M. (1991). The devolution of centrally planned economies. *Journal of Comparative Economics, 15*(2), 239–265.

National Bureau of Statistics. (2021a). *2020 Nian Zhongguo Tongji Nianjian* [*China statistical yearbook 2020*]. Available on 12th September, 2022, *vide*: http://www.stats.gov.cn/tjsj/ndsj/2020/indexch.htm

———. (2021b). *Zhongguo De Quanmian Xiaokang Baipi Shu Xinwen Fabuhui Da Jizhe Wen* [*Q&A at the Press Conference of the White Paper "China's Comprehensive Well-being"*]. Available on 12th September, 2022, *vide*: http://www.stats.gov.cn/tjsj/zxfb/202109/t20210929_1822623.html

Naughton, B. (2003). The state asset commission: A powerful new government body. *China Leadership Monitor, 8*, 1–10.

———. (2014). After the third plenum: Economic reform revival moves toward implementation. *China Leadership Monitor, 43*(1), 23–36.

———. (2016a). Supply-side structural reform: Policy-makers look for a way out. *China Leadership Monitor, 49*(1).

———. (2016b). Two trains running: Supply-side reform, SOE reform and the authoritative personage. *China Leadership Monitor, 50*(19).

O'Brien, K. J. (Ed.). (2009). *Popular protest in China*. Harvard University Press.

Olson, M. ([1965]2012). The logic of collective action. *Contemporary Sociological Theory, 124*.

———. ([2000] 2014). *Power and prosperity: Outgrowing communist and capitalist dictatorships*. Basic Books.

Pan, N. (2005). Jieji De Shiyu Yu Fasheng—Zhongguo Dagong Mei Yanjiu De Yizhong Lilun Shijiao [Disappearance and emergency of class—A theoretical perspective on the study of Chinese working girls]. *Open times, 2*, 95–107.

Perry, E. J. (1993). *Shanghai on strike: The politics of Chinese labor*. Stanford University Press.

State State-owned Assets Supervision and Administration Commission of the State Council (SASAC) and the Ministry of Finance. (2017a). *Guanyu Guoyou Qiye Zhigong Jiashuqu "Sangongyiye" Fenli Yijiao Gongzuo De Zhidao Yijian* [*Guiding opinions on the separation and transfer of the workers' family dependency areas in state-owned enterprise*]. Available on 12th September, 2022, *vide*: http://www.gov.cn/zhengce/content/2016-06/22/content_5084288.htm

———. (2017b). *Guanyu Guoyou Qiye Ban Shizheng Shequ Guanli Deng Zhineng Fenli Yijiao De Zhidao Yijian* [*Guidelines on the separation and transfer of functions such as municipal community management by state-owned enterprises*]. Available on 12th September, 2022, *vide*: http://www.gov.cn/zhengce/content/2016-06/22/content_5084288.htm

———. (2017c). *Guanyu Guoyou Qiye Ban Jiaoyu Yiliao Jigou Shehui Gaige De Zhidao Yijian* [*Guidance on the deepening reform of educational and medical institutions run by state-owned enterprises*]. Available on 12th September, 2022, *vide*: http://www.gov.cn/zhengce/content/2016-06/22/content_5084288.htm

Scalapino, R. A. (1999). *The people's republic of China at fifty.* National Bureau of Asian Research.

Sen, A. K. (1983). *Poverty and famines: An essay on entitlement and deprivation.* 2009 Edition, 38 and/or 2016 Edition, 191–192, 202. Commercial Press.

———. (2002). *Yi Ziyou Kandai Fazhan* [*Development as freedom*]. Translated by J. Ren & Z. Y. Yu. 2002 Edition, 62, 85. Renmin University Press.

Shirk, S. L. (1993). *The political logic of economic reform in China.* University of California Press.

Solinger, D. J. (2006). The creation of a new underclass in China and its implications. *Environment and Urbanization, 18*(1), 177–193.

———. (2009). *Contesting citizenship in urban China.* Translated by C. G. Wang & L. Q. Shan. Zhejiang People's Publishing Houses.

Song, S. C., & Li, R. H. (2001). Globalization and the construction of socialism with Chinese characteristics. *Social Science in China,* (06), 4–13, 204.

State Council. (1978). *Guowuyuan Guanyu Banfa 'Guowuyuan Guanyu Anzhi Lao Ruo Bing Can Ganbu De Zanxing Banfa' He 'Guowuyuan Guanyu Gongren Tuixiu、Tuizhi De Zanxing Banfa' De Tongzh*i [*State council circular on issuing state council temporary measures on providing for old, weak, sick and handicapped cadres and state council temporary measures on workers' retirement resignation*]. Available on 12th September, 2022, *vide*: https://www.cecc.gov/resources/legal-provisions/state-council-circular-on-issuing-state-council-temporary-measures-on

———. (1981). *Guowuyuan Guanyu Yange Zhixing Gongren Tuixiu Tuizhi Zanxing Banfa De Tongzhi* [*State council circular on strict implementation of the interim measures on workers' retirement and resignation to limit and restrict retirees and from finding new employment*]. Available on 12th September, 2022, *vide*: http://www.law-lib.com/law/law_view.asp?id=2322

———. (1986a). *Guoying Qiye Shixing Laodong Hetongzhi Zanxing Guiding* [*Provisional regulations on the institution of the labour contract system in SOEs*]. Available on 12th September, 2022, *vide*: ibidem.

———. (1986b). *Guoying Qiye Zhaoyong Gongren Zanxing Guiding* [*Provisional regulations on SOEs recruiting workers*]. Available on 12th September, 2022, *vide*: ibidem.

———. (1986c). *Guoying Qiye Chitui Weiji Zhigong Zanxing Guiding* [*Provisional regulations on SOEs to dismiss and discipline employees*]. Available on 12th September, 2022, *vide*: ibidem.

———. (1986d). *Guoying Qiye Zhigong Daiye Baoxian Zanxing Guiding* [*Provisional regulations on unemployment insurance for employees at SOEs*]. Available on 12th September, 2022, *vide*: ibidem.

Thornton, P. M. (2017). A new urban underclass? Making and managing "vulnerable groups" in contemporary China. *To Govern China: Evolving Practices of Power*, 257–281.

Walder, A. G. (1988). *Communist neo-traditionalism: Work and authority in Chinese industry*. University of California Press.
Wang, H. S. (1989). Jianguo Chuqi Gongye Jianshe Daolu De Huigu Yu Sikao [A review on the indurtsial construction development in the early stage of PRC]. *Journal of Henan University: Social Science Edition, 6*, 45–50.
Wang, X. Z. (2013). Lun Gongchang Changyu Zhong De Guixun Quanli [The discipline of power in the factory field]. *Modern Communication: THe Second Half of the Month, 8*, 5–6.
Weber, M. ([1922] 1978). *Economy and society: An outline of interpretive sociology* (Vol. 1, p. 4). University of California Press.
Won, J. (2009). Farewell to socialist labor in China. In T. Gold, W. Hurst, J. Won, & Q. Li (Eds.), *Laid-off workers in a workers' state* (pp. 185–201). Palgrave Macmillan.
Wright, T. (2010). *Accepting authoritarianism: State-society relations in China's reform era*. Stanford University Press.
Wu, L., & Wen, R. (2006). *1949 Nian Yilai Zhongguo Gongyehua De "Qin Zhong" Zhi Bian [The "light, heavy" discourse of industrialization in China since 1949]*. Available on 12th September, 2022, *vide*: http://www.erj.cn/UploadFiles/1949%E5%B9%B4%E4%BB%A5%E6%9D%A5%E4%B8%AD%E5%9B%BD%E5%B7%A5%E4%B8%9A%E5%8C%96%E7%9A%84_%E8%BD%BB_%E9%87%8D_%E4%B9%8B%E8%BE%A8.pdf
Wu, Q. J. (2008). Shichang Zhuanxing Shiqi Guoqi Gongren De Qunti Renting Yu Jieji Yishi [Group identity and class consciousness of SOE workers in the market transition period]. *Sociological Research, 6*, 58–79.
———. (2010). Guoqi Gaizhi Zhong Gongren De Neibu Fenhua Jiqi Xingdong Celue [The internal division of workers in SOEs refrom and workers' action strategies]. *Society, 30*(6), 65–89.
Xiao, L. (1990). Qiye Youchang Zhuanrang, Jianbing yu Zichan Cunliang de Tiaozheng (Corporate transfer for compensation, mergers and asset stock adjustment). *Economic Studies, 9*.
Xiao, D. L. (2014). The Road of SOE Restructuring: from "Decentralization of Power and Transfer of Profits" to "Institutional Innovation". *Studies of the History of Chinese Communist Party* (Zhonggong Dangshi Yanjiu), *3*, 9–19.
Xu, C. W. (2010). Mao Zedong Dui Shihe Zhongguo Guoqing De Shehui Zhuyi Jianshe Daolu De Tansuo [Mao Zedong's exploration of sinicization of the constructions of socialism]. *Marxism and Reality*, 133–141.
Xu, J. Z. (2008). Waiguo Xuezhe Lun Zhongguo Tese Shehui Zhuyi [Foreign scholars' studies on socialism with Chinese characteristics]. *Studies on Socialism with Chinese Characteristics, 3*, 39–51.
Xu, Y. P., & Shi, X. Y. (2006). Gongren Jieji Xingcheng: Tizhi Nei Yu Tizhi Wai De Zhuanhuan [The formation of the working class: Transitions within and outside the system]. *Xuehai (studies), 4*, 27–39.

Yan, Y. Q. (2002). Zhong Su Lunzhan Yu Mao Zedong Guanyu Shehui Zhuyi Shehui Jieji Douzheng Lilun Xing [An analysis of the Sino-Soviet War and the formation of Mao Zedong's Theory on class struggle in socialist society]. *Party History Research and Teaching, 3*, 30–34.

Yan, Y. X. (2012). *The individualization of Chinese society*. Translated and published by Shanghai Translation Publishing House.

Yang, R. D. (2015). Study on the total factor productivity of Chinese manufacturing enterprises. *Economic Research Journal, 2*, 61–74.

Yang, Y. Q. (2002). *Touzi Licai De Xinxing Lilun, Fangfa Yu Shiwu [New theories, methods and practices of investment and financial management]*. Tsinghua University Press.

Ye, S. Z. (2010). Kaige Kaifang: Po Sidalin Moshi Fanli Chuang Zhongguo Tese Shehui Zhuyi [Reform and opening up: Breaking the barriers of the Stalinist Model to create socialism with Chinese characteristics]. *Exploration and Controversy, 1*(5), 29.

Yi, G., Fan, G., & Li, Y. (2003). A theoretical analysis on economic growth in China and total factor productivity. *Economic Research Journal, 8*(1), 25–33.

Zhou, X. (1993). Unorganized interests and collective action in communist China. *American Sociological Review*, 54–73.

Zou, L. B. (2011). Pinkun De Ling Yizhong Quanshi: Quanli De Huode Yu Boduo- Jianpin Amartya Sen Pinkun Lilun [Another interpretation of poverty: The acquisition and deprivation of rights: A review of Amartya Sen's Theory of poverty]. *Neijiang Science and Technology, 32*(2), 24, 27.

Zweig, D. (2001). China's stalled "fifth wave": Zhu Rongji's reform package of 1998–2000. *Asian Survey, 41*(2), 231–247.

CHAPTER 5

"Nostalgia" and "Protests": Class Consciousness and *Class-For-Itself*

The working-class resistance I want to discuss is that of workers. EGC's cadres and technicians, as different interest groups excluded from the working class, are used as comparative references to understand the workers' resistance movement.

EGC workers' declined status in SOE reform era and the following strike and protest proved that a major factor of SOE workers' mobilisation is the nostalgia for the pre-reform era (Lee, 1999, 2000, 2002, 2003). After economic and SOE reforms, the illusion of SOE workers (privileged position and advantaged benefits) was removed, SOE workers' consciousness has had a shift. This chapter analyses the workers' group in EGC from their nostalgia, labour activism and resistance through "individual's understanding" (Weber, [1922] 1978). EGC workers as an "interest group" (Olson, [1982] 2008) found their hold on all types of capital, both "material and symbolic capital" (Neveu, 2018) declining, reverting to the proletariat, the object controlled by capitalists in the capital market. EGC workers' nostalgia is linked to the pursuit of power and benefits that are held by this interest group.

Although their resistance has different aims, interviews show that whether workers concern about material or symbolic capital, i.e., a direct appeal to economic status or an attempt to evoke and return to SOE workers' identity as the political identity of the privileged class, their

S. S. Huang, *The Political Economy of Reforms and the Remaking of the Proletarian Class in China, 1980s–2010s*, Palgrave Studies in Economic History, https://doi.org/10.1007/978-3-031-20455-5_5

Table 5.1 NVivo nodes and memos used in Chapter 5

Nodes	Chinese Communist Party (CCP)
	Changes in state workers' identity
	Classification
	Family background
	Female promotion
	New blood
	Movement (labour activism)
	Peer workers' stories
	Relationship
	Job and unit allocation
	Opportunities to promote or change
	SOE reform
	Self-identity
Memos	Family influence
	Female in industry
	Lies and cheatings
	Institute versus people
	Power
	The importance of obtaining the official employment
	The ways to get into SOE
	The unit as a society
	Welfare
	Work pressure
	Workers concerns

Data Source Fieldwork research

nostalgia and the demands of the labour activism, are all anchored in "entitlements". The most intuitive and most important change for workers was related to their immediate interests—the material benefits they could obtain. Even in the abstract of the loss of the superiority of the status of SOE workers, they were concerned with the privileges provided to them under the constructed socialist enterprise, and when this right was taken away, they ceased to be a privileged class in terms of both ideologically and materially.

In this chapter, I divide EGC workers' protests into two categories: the explicit protest via labour activism which is also the way Marxian believed workers could escape exploitation; and the implicit protest that only some workers are able to resist their dissatisfaction with the status quo through "relationship". Nodes and memos created in NVivo and used in this chapter are summarised in Table 5.1.

5.1 Nostalgia: The Socio-Political Condition of Working-Class Protest

Nostalgia is a common phenomenon among SOE workers. The deep logic behind it is class consciousness, the recognition that SOE workers' class-given rights have been reclaimed. Nostalgia is also a broad basis for the revolt of the SOE workers. In contrast to those workers, who entered private or foreign-owned factories after the Reform and Opening Up were exposed to the capital market from the outset and recognised their class affiliation from day one. These non-state sector workers are controlled by the capitalists, the dichotomy between wage labourer and capitalist is more visible and easily identified by these workers. However, workers in SOEs were constructed from the outset to have the attributes of "aristocracy" among workers, especially in the period of Cultural Revolution (1966–1976), as Joel Andreas (2019) discussed when workers were literally given the right to run the enterprise as true "masters".[1] SOE workers in the privileged class constructed a status that they were willing to accept, and this ideological upper class gave workers more rights. When this privilege was broken down by a change in state policy (the Reform and Opening Up), workers developed a widespread shared nostalgia, hence the subsequent protest. This means workers' nostalgia for the pre-economic reform period applied only to workers in SOEs. Within the group of all workers, the consciousness of SOE workers emerged later than that of those who had worked in private or foreign-owned enterprises from the beginning.

Furthermore, what SOE workers perceive as a good past refers specifically to Mao's era. No one in the interviews, either joined EGC before or after the Reform and Opening Up, was nostalgic about the situation of the working class before the PRC was established, or compared to the situation of workers before 1949, even though the workers' resistance and class struggle were more in line with Marx's statement about the awakening of class consciousness and the transformation of *class-in-itself* to *class-for-itself*. SOE workers missed the privileges granted to

[1] "The industrial citizenship" as Andreas (2019) discussed in the period of Cultural Revolution was not evident in the interviews due to most of the interviewees joined EGC after the Reform and Opening Up. However, as I mentioned when discussing EGC workers' status in the pre-reform era, workers were paid as usual even during the production downtime within the 10 years revolution, which in another way confirms workers' privilege.

them by the CCP and the socialist state, because the workers were by nature seeking more entitlements (material benefits) and less work. The pre-reform period of "*daguo fan*" was more in their interests and that their status is tantamount to a return to a status without privileges.

Nostalgia and collective action are tightly linked. Many empirical studies on SOEs and workers have pointed out the theme of workers' resistance and protest in the reform era. When exploring the reasons, they have inevitably mentioned the nostalgia of the past, especially Maoist period. The iron rice bowl has created a certain nostalgia for people who have or even have not experienced it (Hurst, 2009; Yang, 2017). A case in 2014 reported that a mother was cheated out of 2.6 million Yuan (Chinese Currency, RMB) by an employer in exchange for a position for her son in the state sector, more than the entire salary of a man until retirement (Dong Bihui, 2014). This case illustrates the significance of securing a job and the attraction of welfare in the state sector and the traumatic effect of laid-off workers (Solinger, 2006, pp. 177–193; Yang, 2007, pp. 77–105).

Hurst (2009, p. 117) summarised previous studies on nostalgia in China. In Hurst's idea, nostalgia should be treated as framework not a claim which most of the previous studies explained. Yang Guobin's (2003, pp. 267–296) studies of nostalgia during the 1990s for the Cultural Revolution period reflected the people's maintaining and continuing sense of identity. Other scholars, such as Kevin O'Brien and Li Lianjiang (1999, pp. 375–393), Li Lianjiang (2001, pp. 573–586) and Geremie Barme' (1999) viewed nostalgia as an influence on a broad number of Chinese population's behaviour. Ching Kwan Lee (1998, pp. 3–33, 2000, pp. 217–237, 2002, pp. 189–228, 2003, pp. 87–109) pointed out that in some degree, nostalgia of the Maoist past is a major factor behind laid-off workers' mobilisation. From Hurst's thoughts (2009), there are three dimensions of nostalgia that can be observed in contemporary Chinese society: political, economic and cultural. He then uses more specific categories: relational, material and ideational nostalgia.[2] Even people who

[2] Hurst's (2009, pp. 117–118) definitions on the three dimensions of nostalgia: "Relational nostalgia refers to the perception that power relations between a given person and other individuals or groups have changed to his or her disadvantage". "Material nostalgia is quite simple: an individual or group perceives that their material situation has deteriorated when compared with some time in the past, often in absolute terms, but sometimes in relative terms versus some other person or group". "Ideational nostalgia entails a perception- somewhat more difficult to observe or measure than material or relational

have not experience the past can feel all these dimensions of nostalgia. Meanwhile, in Hurst's study, Chinese SOE workers' nostalgia can use geographical regions as the basis of classification. For example, in *Laid-off workers in a workers' state: Unemployment with Chinese characteristics* (Hurst, 2009), a table of nostalgia dimensions observed in recent Chinese academics mentioned that ideational nostalgia did not exist in the upper Yangzi area.

However, if a case can be found to refute this type of division, additional information can be added to the existing conclusion or might further emphasise that workers only have nostalgia for material benefits and the nostalgia for the political reputation is not real. Workers' interest might have never changed, which is the accreditation of entitlements behind politics.[3] It was given during Mao's period and taken away during Deng's reform period. At the same time, SOE workers are part of a broader change in national policy, they are relatively stable and do not resist if they are guaranteed the interest. Hurst's research is typographical and divides both SOEs and SOE workers into geographical types and he used qualitative research method, interviews, to explore Chinese laid-off workers. This is a revelation that when studying big questions, it can derive conclusions from studying the individuals. A case study can provide new data to see how SOEs reflect political trends in the context of China's macroeconomic reform and development, for example, the transformation between industries and the changes in management and monopoly. It can also provide new data on the impact of reforms on SOEs and SOEs' responses. Furthermore, the nature of workers' resistance and nostalgia can be reflected from a case study, and the regional division can also be confirmed or falsified from it.

After studied EGC's case, I found all the three categories can be found from the interviews:

1. Respondent has nostalgia for the simple interpersonal relationships of the past unit society and the mutual help of the workers. Feng (Interviewee 021) felt she was looked after by her colleagues and

nostalgia, that ideological, moral, ethical, or spiritual aspects of life were better in some earlier era".

[3] See Amartya Kumar Sen (1976, pp. 1273–1280; 1986; 1987, pp. 7–10), an entitlement is a right for the individual to get material benefits and services. Sen argued entitlements from a socio-economic perspective.

the cadres in a familiar cultural environment and social network. She stated how close the social network in the work unit society was. She said, "it is more relaxing to deal with the interpersonal relationships within SOE".

2. The economic and material level of the past can be more easily read into the conversations of the interviewees. In Chapter 4, I discussed the stable and well-paid SOE workers' jobs. Here, to address workers' good material life before SOE reform again:

> All the housing, medical treatment and children's education were free. We were assigned a house and the house was equipped with a registered permanent residence. All the furniture, like beds, chairs, and desks, all these were free. The hospital only cost 0.05 RMB for a registration fee, and then you got the medicines for free. (Interviewee 017)

3. Interviewees also mentioned the feeling of the glory of being SOE workers. The kind of spiritual or ideological nostalgia for SOEs and SOE workers in Mao's era, which they consider better. Zhang (Interviewee 017) told me that, for him, in the 1990s EGC was the module of a communist society. He suggested that society was more equal before. It was the working age and not the job position that decided a person's income and welfare. The difference between the rank-and-file workers and the cadres was small. Everybody was assigned a house and people who had worked longer were first in line.

Zhang said because of the Maoist political education he had, he holds the view that the most important thing is to complete your own work as capably as you can and then your leader will notice that and promote you. He did not have strong feelings about competition or promotion after showing his skills and techniques, even though he was a secondary fitter, which was rare in EGC at that time. Further analysing his discourses, it is a classic thought (ideology) in the era of Mao Zedong when SOE workers were encouraged to undertake hard work at low pay and dedicate themselves to industry development as a sacrifice to the country. They considered work for SOEs to be meaningful, contributing to the development of the country. Working for SOEs was thus working for the state. People who held the same belief as Zhang have nostalgia for the constructed socialist enterprise where workers were guaranteed a privileged political status. This thought continues to impact EGC workers in 2018, even though the person has not experienced Mao's SOEs. Rong (Interviewee 018) said,

> When I went to the secondary school classmates' party, I told my classmates what kind of products our factory made, and I am proud of that. At least I made contributions to the development of the country. (Interviewee 018)

Political motivation—how glorious and honourable it was to be SOE workers—still works for Interviewees 017 and 018. Such workers think highly of themselves, believing that they were contributing to the state. The more they believe in the Maoist era, the heavier the nostalgia they have, and the harder it is to acknowledge and accept their status, such workers may choose not to resist in the face of their declining status, having the illusion that the SOE can return to its former glory era, or as Xin (Interviewee 019) said, "As an SOE, even if it is not profitable, the state will undertake it (*guojia hui guan*)". The three interviewees make up a small percentage of my respondents, while the rest of the workers acknowledge their current reality and want to assert their rights by fighting against the class that exploits them.

EGC workers' three types of nostalgia are very closely linked, even cross-covered, in this sense, I refer to the nostalgia of EGC workers as a composite type. The essence is a nostalgia for the loss of privileged class identity that cannot be singularly attributed to ideational nostalgia because workers care about the materiality that privilege represents and that feeling of superiority in the socio-economic structure. Their nostalgia even with imaginary feelings appears as an imaginary deviation, allowing it to compensate for today's dissatisfactions. A status that was once fictionalised as a very stable, harmonious, humane and even enjoyable working state of its own. A status that is not necessarily real, but an imaginary one that even people who did not experience that period would use to comfort their present dissatisfactions.

5.2 Explicit Protest: Labour Activism in EGC

In sociological terms, the traditional sociological view, represented by Durkheim (1893), sees non-institutionalised resistance such as strikes as social disorder, a social phenomenon used to explain social disintegration. The other school of sociology, represented by Charles Tilly, argues that resistance is a disorganisation rather than a disintegration of society, and that collective action is the main driver of structural change (Chen Zhouwang, 2012, pp. 102–112; Li Pingju, 2010, p. 236). In this research, I applied the latter interpretation. The resistance of EGC workers validates my analysis in the last chapter: the change in the composition of the working class in EGC. By taking labour activism, EGC workers want to reassert their identity.

Workers' protest in China is not a new thing that emerged because of economic reform. It was already historically important and was an important part of the democratic movement (Perry, 1993). EGC workers' labour activism was not an isolated case in the 2010s. According to Xuehua (Interviewee 009), "There was a lot of labour activism in D city, the strike, the protest and the demonstration, but those always ended up with nothing definite". Another SOE in D city experienced labour activism when announced the laying-off policy and workers even petitioned the city government to solve their problems. A wider view at the national data on Chinese workers' labour activism over a ten-year period (2011–2021) is summarised in the following charts.

Figure 5.1 shows SOE workers' protests accounted for 12.24% in the total number of Chinese workers' protests between 2011–2021.

Figure 5.2 shows 85.1% of the protests demanded for meeting the financial requirements, including wage arrears, pay increase, compensation, social insurance, housing fund and others.

Figure 5.3 reflects the quantitative trend of SOE workers and all types of workers' resistance in China. The peaks were in 2015 and 2016 separately for Chinese workers and workers in SOEs.

In the introduction to case fieldwork in Chapter 3, I discussed some facts about EGC workers' 2015 labour activism, which serves as an important marker in the history of EGC, distinguishing between the moderate reform policies and radical reform policies for employees before and after 2015. The root of the workers' protest is their dissatisfaction about the decreased economic status. The resistance is for sustaining their status not against SOE reforms. This explains why since economic reforms started

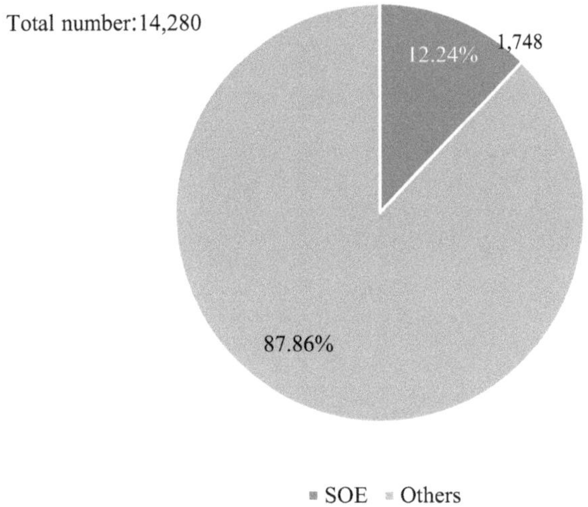

Fig. 5.1 2011–2021 Chinese workers' protests (ownership) (*Data Source* China Labour Bulletin[4])

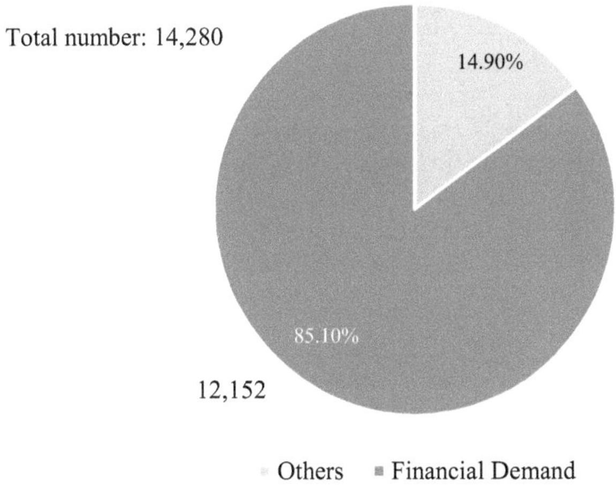

Fig. 5.2 2011–2021 Chinese workers' protests (Financial demand) (*Data Source* China Labour Bulletin[5])

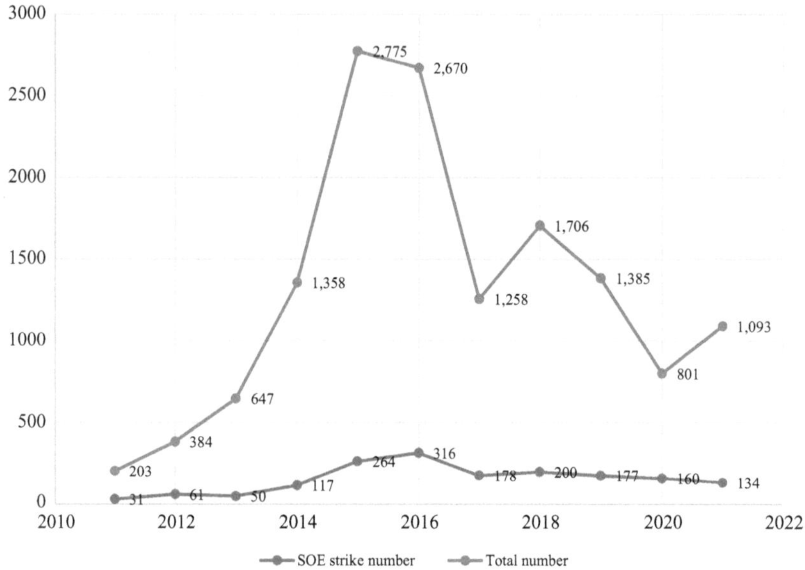

Fig. 5.3 2011–2021 Number of Chinese SOE workers' protests and all workers' protests (*Data Source* China Labour Bulletin[6])

in 1978 and EGC's SOE reforms started since the 1990s, workers did not care much or have held a massive strike before 2015.[7] If workers' rights could be guaranteed, they were not at all in concern about the reform nor did they relate themselves to the reform. However, in the 2010s, EGC's reform could not maintain the same welfare for workers

[4] China Labour Bulletin. Earliest statistics from 2011. Available on 12th Sep, 2022, *vide*: https://maps.clb.org.hk/?i18n_language=en_US&map=1&startDate=2018-01&endDate=2018-12&eventId=&keyword=&addressId=&parentAddressId=&address=&parentAddress=&industry=&parentIndustry=&industryName=

[5] Ibid.

[6] Ibid.

[7] Xuehua (Interviewee 009) mentioned there was another workers' protest at EGC in 2014 when the enterprise asked workers to retire early but did not offer a proper policy. According to the fieldwork study, there was also a strike organised by crane workers in 2013 in EGC. However, these two events were not mentioned by many other interviewees due to the event's scale and the number of people who were involved.

and had to reduce the number of workers and workers' benefits. The 11 of May 2015 labour activism is an expression of EGC workers' dissatisfaction in public as a group. Workers found they were eliminated by the SOE. It is an awakening of consciousness, a revolt for their own benefit, and a pathway to secure their economic benefits. Through EGC's case, the interest group in the collective action and how labour activism can reflect workers' construction of class within the SOE can be understood.

Interest Group and Collective Action

EGC's strike and protest on 11th May 2015 were organised and planned by a dozen workers requesting better wages. It was a factory protest and then gradually became enterprise-wide collective activism. The trigger for workers to act was the low wages for months and the enterprise did not offer enough compensation when workers had chosen to leave. This protest finally attracted thousands of workers, including retirees. Xiaotian (Interviewee 004) described the details of this strike and protest,

> "I was in a night slot that night and then received a text message saying: go to the East Gate on Monday morning for a gathering. We all understand that the gathering is a strike... It was led by some 40 [years old] '*shifu*' [experienced workers] and supported by other young professionals. (Interviewee 004)"

According to Xiaotian, the enterprise knew the details about the leaders of this collective action, scholars and organisations that supported EGC's workers as the information was shared in the Youth League Committee's meeting. However, among the workers, specific details about the organisation of the movement were not available from the interviews, but only rumours they had heard, for example, EGC workers' strike and protest were supported by the same group which had had a similar labour activism few months earlier in Guangdong province (the Citizen-Watch Factory).

Interviews reflect that most of the participants are manual workers and not the entire workers' group resorted to this explicit protest (labour activism) in face of the declined status. Since individuals pursue their own interests and the working class in EGC which constructed by the state's ideology is a fractured group, members who are likely to benefit more from collective action are more active in participating in collective action and contributing greater to it (Jiang Wenneng, 2009, pp. 75–79;

Li Zenggang, 2002, pp. 77–81; Olson, 1965). The larger the collective is, the stronger the incentive to "hitchhike" and the harder it is to detect "hitchhiking" (Guan Qingyou, 2007, pp. 105–112; Wang Jingxian, 2010; Zheng Zifeng, 2011, pp. 42–66). EGC workers could not unite and fight together because they have different interests. Yujia (Interviewee 002) and Weng (Interviewee 012) proved the above statements. They did not participate in the labour activism because they thought the protest was for people who had decided to leave and wanted to ask for a better early retirement policy, and they thought they did not suffer from the same burden and pressure in the enterprise. Although the protest aimed to change the overall situation of the workers, they thought it was not related to them. However, it does not mean that those workers who did not participate in the strike would not protest in their daily work. This point will be discussed later.

Feng (Interviewee 021), who was the only one to clearly reveal that she participated in the 11 of May 2015 workers' strike and protest in the interviews, said she believed that only a few people had not joined in. She said she heard at that time that cadres from different units were all there to "catch the troublemakers".

> "Catch who? Everyone was there and many people invited their old grandfather and grandmother [who worked for EGC before] to come… I think we are together. If the cold working industries do not have enough production orders, then the next are our thermal working industries. We are the same, you cannot help thinking about the future. We finally got the solution: ensuring the lowest pay is 1,200 [Yuan] per month when there has not enough work to do. (Interviewee 021)"

Although SOE reform caused all the employees at EGC to experience economic deprivation, just as the cadres (managers) and technicians are excluded from the working class, among my interviewees, neither the cadres nor the technicians participated in the 11th of May strike or joined in the protest. Applying Olson's individual analysis research methods to the study of collective action, the construct of different interest groups in EGC can be understood. As a different interest group, on the contrary, cadres needed to do ideological work (*sixiang gongzuo*) for workers to stop such activities. While the workers considered this protest a reasonable way for them to request a fair pay, the cadres regarded it as a protest raised by workers that influenced the proper production process.

Chun (Interviewee 010), who was working as the director of an industry at EGC in 2015, said that most of the people actively and aggressively involved in the workers' protest did not belong to EGC, nor were they good workers.

> "I was not against this protest. It is a very normal thing to ask for fair payment. I think this protest reflected EGC's management problem very deeply - many job positions were created because of people [not because of demand]. This protest had a very negative impact on people who were actually good at their jobs. They resigned because they did not see any hope and were influenced by the rumours. There were also many people who joined in this event without a clear understanding of the purpose. They were just idle at [their] work units. They felt the gap between the incomes and then raised their hopes. (Interviewee 010)"

Instead of pointing out the workers' financial demand, Chun suggested that the lack of communication between the workers and the enterprise caused the collective action. From the cadres' side, instead of protest and strike, workers were suggested to express their requirements at the Employees Congress. The labour activism had a very negative impact on the enterprise's business development.

Young technicians did not take part in the strike and protest either because they have a long career ahead of them. If the leaders knew that technicians were involved in such activities, the negative impression could affect technicians' future promotions. As Kai (Interviewee 006) said,

> "I never thought about participating in an event like this. I received a message the day before, asking us to arrive at our units earlier to avoid the crowds. I was earlier by more than 10 minutes but there were already many patrol wagons around the North Gate. I didn't know what happened because EGC never had any large collective events. Then I saw people pull out the banners. I passed by and thought this must be the gathering. I heard from my colleagues that many people had participated in it, but the leaders told us 'Do not go', so I didn't go."

Although Kai felt guilty because of his absence and was sympathetic to the workers, considering this an event where people pursue the same interests; "if you do not go, then next time, when you request something, people will not support you in return", he thought his participation could not change anything. To some extent, his thought is right as I mentioned in Chapter 4, the number of technicians was only about 5% of the total number of workers' group in EGC in 2010s.

EGC workers' labour activism wanted to get a widespread support. Different from the larger the collective action, the more difficult to unite people together (Olson, 1965); the greater the number of participants, the more EGC realised that workers were not confined to a small workshop, or a factory, but were the grievances of the workers as a whole. So, when there are different interest groups in EGC (cadres, technicians, among workers' group there are very few workers who do not acknowledge their status and still believe that SOE workers are privileged), workers united with retirees with shared nostalgia to arouse wider indignation at the loss of SOE workers' aristocratic and privileged position, with a view to meet the economic requirements they were proposing at that moment.

The Demand for Protest: Economic Satisfaction and Political Slogan

Although the root of the revolt was due to economic reasons, the workers were demanding much more than economic satisfaction. EGC workers used the target of "*fanfu changlian*" (combatting corruption and upholding integrity), which was aimed at finding the one person or a group of people that had made EGC unprofitable. From EGC's statistics which I presented in Fig. 3.1 (p. 58); the profits of the enterprise had been declining since the year 2010. From interviews, workers argued that EGC cadres took profits from the construction of the design centre in 2008 and the new manufacturing base in 2009, which led to the 2010s reform. In EGC workers' protest, they emphasised the importance of the working class, especially using the status given to the working class during Mao's era to emphasise the contribution of SOE workers to national construction from the level of ideology. Although most of the striking and protesting workers were not involved in the production of EGC during the Third Line construction at all, they raised the goal of their protests to the level of ideology to seek support. In this way, they were already at the *class-for-itself* level (Chen Zhouwang, 2015, pp. 142–147; Marx, [1844] 2000, [1847] 1920). They represented not just workers as individuals, limited to workshop, a factory or just EGC as an SOE, but recognised their working-class attributes, i.e., as Marx described the proletariat, the wage labour and went into revolt on behalf of the class as a whole. They wanted their important political and social value to be affirmed and raised their collective action for meeting economic and wage demands to political demands in order to have their legitimacy recognised and gain wider attention, practising what Marx saw as a key to the victory of the proletariat's struggle, which is to have a clear class consciousness and to know what they are fighting for.

EGC workers' strike and protest reflect the desperation of workers under a double downward of economic contradictions and socio-political tensions. EGC case shows that the lowest level of workers' demands is economic and when economic demands are met, they have no other resources to support them to achieve more, for example, combatting corruption and upholding integrity and the advancement of the working class. However, this does not mean that the working class will not engage in similar activities afterwards. The picketing of enterprise's cadres and managers is due to the workers' realisation that the SOE has become a company under state capital and that these managerial cadres are managing them on behalf of state capital, essentially a perception of the bourgeoisification of cadres under state capitalism.

The Characteristics of the Chinese Workers' Activism, Class Consciousness and the Transformation of Class in the Light of EGC Workers' Restricted Explicit Protest

EGC workers' strike and protest were concentrated within a week. The collective action ceased a month and a half later when documents (*2015 EGC Measures for the Termination of Labour Contracts* and *2015 EGC Worker Absences Cultivation Measures for its Implementation*) (EGC, 2015a; 2015b) on workers' demands were issued. Learnt from the interviews, some did not participate in the labour activism at all, and some returned to job positions a week or a month later after the 11th of May protest. EGC's production did not completely stop because of the labour activism. The collective actions stopped in such a short time and according to a speech by the Chair of SINOMACH said at the first forum on Reform and Development of Chinese Enterprise (*zhongguo qiye gaige fazhan luntan*) in 2017, there was no workers' petition in EGC (Sina Finance, 2017). From EGC's case, the restriction of workers' collective protests can be told. As interviewees mentioned in the previous section, leaders from different units were at the workers' rally to "catch the troublemakers" and leaders from D city and police officers were also there to prevent the labour activism form worsening, such as personal injury to

EGC's leaders or violent conflict between workers and managers' groups (Interviewee 004 and 021).

The legitimacy of EGC workers' collective protest had been questioned by the leadership group due to the restrictions on freedom of assembly. Furthermore, workers' discussions about the 11 of May strike and protest on online platform were also under restrictions. Leaders would ask the workers to delete them. EGC workers' situation is the same one that Chinese workers have to face. Learnt from China Labour Bulletin's research into SOEs workers in 2008,[8] Chinese workers' collective protests can easily be labelled as criminal, for instance, "gathering a crowd to disrupt social order", gathering a crowd with "disruptive intent", and "having serious impacts on work, production, management, training and research activities, resulting in significant (economic) damage", even charges such as "subversion of state power"—an essentially political crime—is one of the most serious crimes in China. Once the collective protests are criminalised, workers who deemed to be troublemakers can be subjected to "administrative punishment" (*xingzheng chufa*), detention and "re-educated" (*zai jiaoyu*), making workers more apprehensive about whether to choose to protest openly when their entitlements are infringed.

A review of the history of Chinese workers' resistance reveals that at different stages of history, Chinese workers have taken collective action for different purposes. Prior to the establishment of the P. R. China in 1949, according to *The Basic Theory of Trade Unions* (All-China Federation of Trade Unions, 2006) and *A Brief History of Chinese Trade Unions* (Writing Group of China Institution of Labour Movement, 2020),[9] workers' strike movement was mainly an economic struggle for better living conditions, followed by a conscious and organised political struggle. The working class existed before the CCP was founded. Before the World War One (1914–1918), there were one million industrial workers in China in 1914 and before the "May 4th movement" in 1919, China had over 2.6 million industrial workers. If all the manual workers

[8] China Labour Bulletin. (2008). "No Way Out: Worker Activism in China's State-Owned Enterprise Reforms", pp. 14-15. Available on 12th Sep, 2022, *vide*: https://clb.org.hk/sites/default/files/archive/en/File/research_reports/no_way_out.pdf

[9] Edited by All-China Federation of Trade Unions (*zhonghua quanguo zong gonghui*) and Writing group of China Institute of Labour Movement (*zhongguo gongyun yajiusuo bianxiezu*).

were included, the total number reached between 18 to 20 million.[10] The trade unions set up by the CCP promoted the whole working class group to transform from a "*class-in-itself*" to a "*class-for-itself*" phase through the propagation of class ideology. In this phase, communist movement needed the support of the workers, the trade unions formed by the CCP were more class-oriented than those formed by the industrial workers themselves. During Mao Zedong's period, the identity of the working class as masters of the state could be well reflected in its participation in movements such as the suppression of counter-revolution, particularly prominent in the protests during the Cultural Revolution (1966–1976) when workers really took control of power and were able to subvert the factory regime through the activism. The workers' activism was inseparable from the political movement.

As China Labour Bulletin's 2008 report on SOE workers (China Labour Bulletin, 2008), in the post-economic reform China, the conditions for workers' public protests are harsh, and there is a lack of support from independent trade union organisations. Besides the high possibility that workers' collective protests will be criminalised, the main function of trade unions was no longer to organise workers' activism, but to maintain coordination and stabilise labour relations (Wang Jianping, 2021, pp. 57–62). The trade unions are apolitical and instead they became workers' clubs, organising cultural and recreational activities such as events for International Women's Day, workers' sporting, Spring Festival parties, etc., enriching workers' lives. The trade union in EGC was a "decorative organisation" in the 2015 workers' labour activism and did not perform the function of fighting for workers' rights as it should have done. Instead, during the strike and protest, workers mentioned in their demands that the trade union should have 80% of workers' representatives and that they should be chosen by a vote of all workers rather than appointed by the leadership.

In a rapidly changing society, the relative changes in people's socio-economic status make them particularly sensitive to their gains and losses and may therefore generate a clear consciousness of class stratification (Liu Xin, 2002, p. 81–90). Analysing the resistance of the EGC workers, after SOE reforms, the so-called socialist enterprise were unable to protect their entitlements in the competitive market economy or even diminish

[10] Statistics from All-China Federation of Trade Unions, *The Basic Theory of Trade Unions (2006)*.

their rights and interests, and in the absence of an independent organisation to help them defend their entitlements in difficult circumstances, EGC workers have a sense of organising collective resistance, a sense of fighting for their rights, a sense of demanding fairness and justice in terms of income, and at the same time claiming their rightful but now lost economic and social status as a working class, it can reflect that the EGC workers have become a self-conscious class (*class-for-itself*).

The formation of class consciousness and the transformation of the class phases among EGC workers occurred throughout the Chinese working class. From reports on Chinese workers' labour activism over the period 2000–2017 (China Labour Bulletin, 2000–2004, p. 35; 2005–2006, pp. 47–48; 2007–2008, p. 2; 2009–2010, p. 18; 2011a, statistics from 2011; 2011–2012, p. 36; 2013–2014, p. 2; 2015–2017, pp. 11, 24), workers were aware that they have not reasonably shared the fruits of economic development after the Reform and Opening Up but are caught in a situation where their rights and interests are being compromised. The restructuring of SOEs has subverted the political and social status of the working class, and the privileges of SOE workers have been stripped away, bringing the interests of the working class as a whole very close. Workers' class consciousness is in a state of constant clarification, and a new generation of working-class identity is being formed. The reconstructed working class is not an ideological "leading class" or "master of the country" (a given label), but an identity and consensus of interests based on reality, generated in the factory; that is, wage labourers. This creates a "sense of rights", which makes workers aware of the justice and legitimacy of their actions (Chen Bulei, 2009). The collective action of workers practices their social and political rights, and the sense of organisation (the power of solidarity) is demonstrated. There is greater clarity about the rights they are seeking and greater practicality in negotiations with management, with a clear path from disorderly action to orderly strikes to rational collective bargaining.

The existing studies (China Labour Bulletin's research and observations up to 2017) have argued that the working class in China is in a phase of transition, with the growing number of workers' strikes across the country reflecting the transition from "*class-in-itself*" to "*class-for-itself*". However, the EGC case study furthers the conclusion by stating that this group of workers, who chose to fight openly despite the constraints, have already made the transition to the "*class-for-itself*" level. As discussed in Chapter 1, SOEs are experiments in the artificial construction of socialist enterprises in China, and in a supposedly classless socialist society (if indeed it is socialist), the completion of the transformation of the SOE workers' identity heralds the transformation of the working class in society as a whole. Because in this privileged enterprise, this group of privileged people are class-conscious, the situation of those workers who are not privileged and are not in a privileged enterprise can be imaged.

5.3 Implicit Protests and Practices of "Relationship"

If workers are allowed to assemble freely, then mainland workers should realise their rights through trade union organisation in the same way as workers in Hong Kong, or even in the Western countries, where legal strikes and protests are more direct and more clearly targeted. However, due to restricted conditions, EGC workers can only express their long pent-up grievances through occasional acts of strike. Nevertheless, the end of EGC workers' labour strike and protest in 2015 does not mean the cessation of workers' resistance. Due to the restrictions on explicit protest and the great risk that workers had to take, workers turned to individual resistances.

When workers recognised their disadvantaged position and that there was little hope of change, workers resorted to passive rebellion, besides the engagement of an explicit protest. For example, using relationship (social network) to get easier jobs, slack off at work, join their opponents—the management, join the political club, especially the ruling party (CCP), to gain another form of political identity, to grasp SOE workers' new status as unprivileged workers. Whatever the form of resistance, the reasons and motives for it all point to the class consciousness and the formation of a "*class-for-itself*" status because the logic behind these actions is that workers seek to use as much of their power as possible to maximise their entitlements through existing or constructed relationship, though this may not be justified.

"Relationship" is generally seen as a means for workers to improve their situation within the power structure of the factory. Walder (1988) argues that the power structure in the traditional Chinese factory is manifested in a patron-client network, a network of patronage relationships that contains personal emotional elements and impersonal moral beliefs. There are two important mechanisms within this power structure, one is "organised dependence", and the other is "principled particularism".

Organised dependence means the extent and manner in which workers are economically dependent on the enterprise, politically dependent on the (communist) party leadership of the factory, and personally dependent on the direct leadership of the workshop. Principled particularism means that, in the context of organised dependence, in order to control the factory, the decision-makers intended to create an impersonal "political incentive system" in the factory aimed at stimulating political beliefs and moral qualities, but in unit practice, the leaders, in pursuit of self-interest, transformed it into a personalised reward system aimed at encouraging close and long-term relationships between workers and leaders (Li Lulu et al., 2009, pp. 1–25). In this research, more than taking relationship as a tool, I see the application of relationship as a practice of workers' resistance to their existing status, i.e., the application of relationship is a form of resistance to the loss of privileges of the SOE workers and a confrontation with the bourgeois SOE cadres. The using of relationships is a resistance and confrontation that milder than the explicit protest described in the previous section, and therefore I call it implicit protest.

Using Bourdieu's concept of capital to understand relationship (Bourdieu, 1980, p. 3; Bourdieu & Wacquant, 1992, p. 95), the relationship applied by EGC workers are a network of resources and rights that they can mobilise, an institutionalised network of acquaintanceship or recognition. Workers' resistance under the table has always existed in the daily work. However, those who are able to satisfy their needs through relationships are in the minority. Whether it is the extent to which family relationship can play a role in EGC, whether the relationships can be transferred from parents to children, or whether workers join in a political group to acquire a new political identity to meet a need, from this research, workers are not equally entitled to such rights. No matter how well they use the relationships to protest and express their dissatisfaction with the status quo, the oppression of workers remains.[11]

Implicit Protests in Daily Jobs

The Utilisation and Possession of State-Owned Assets

If making personal profits does not harm the state property too seriously, workers can use their positions of appropriate authority to make

[11] Again, this proves Marx's thoughts on the working class that they should still choose explicit protest—labour activism—to satisfy their demands.

personal profits without receiving punishments. Even though workers in the rear services sector, they can maximise their own benefits by doing so. Cases can be found in the interviews (interviewee 008 and 009), for example, charging a fee for outsiders using EGC facilities, such as the public bath house; stealing steel and other mechanical materials to sell; selling labour protection supplies and summer beverages for internal workers to outsiders.

Although stealing state property is always strictly prohibited in EGC, it is impossible for the mangers to control every detail in a large SOE like EGC and hand down severe punishments every time. Qiong (Interviewee 008) mentioned her team leader's case. The leader's sister was caught stealing steel from the industry and then her mother begged the superior's forgiveness; her brother attempted to make money by selling the industry's cable but was caught by the superior, etc. None of them have been dismissed from EGC for illegally taking possession of state property.

Rejecting Leadership Requests

Workers who do not want their time or labour to be squeezed more in their daily work choose to refuse the demands of their leaders. Yujia (Interviewee 002) refused to do the year-end report even though his leader was trying to convince him that it was a good opportunity to showcase his abilities in front of the leaders. He saw it as the leader forcing him to do works that were not within his capabilities. Kai (Interviewee 006) rejected the requests of overtime work, "I received calls after 10 pm during the week about solving machine problems. I refused sometimes by saying I will look into it for you tomorrow morning".

Part-Time Jobs

The decline in economic status has resulted in workers not earning enough to meet their living needs. Therefore, the dissatisfaction with the income makes workers turn to other jobs. Xiang (Interviewee 013) owns a tailoring shop alongside the manual work at EGC. If he has a night shift at EGC, he will spend the daytime at the tailoring shop. For him, it is more accurate to describe that the job at EGC is a part-time job. Kai (Interviewee 006) took part-time jobs time to time during weekends to earn more money, even though sometimes the factory requests the whole group of workers to do overtime works (without payment) during the weekends.

Using Relationships to Reduce Workload

There are two ways to reduce a worker's workload, either by making more workers available in their department, or by slacking off at work through relationships with leaders and passing the workload on to other workers.

The first way is out of the control of the workers, who can only expressly or implicitly tell their leaders that the workload is more than the workers can handle, so that they can expect to recruit more people for their units. In this case, their leaders need to keep a good relationship with the director of the Human Resources (HR) department to get a new workforce out of the limited number of new employees. The impact that workers can make is very limited.

For example, after the labour activism on the 11th of May 2015, there were a vast number of early retirees and buyouts workers. The Chair of SINOMACH stated that the number of employees had reduced from 15,000 to 7,500 after the enterprise restructuring in a conference in 2017. Many interviewees noted that EGC is suffering from the fact that it does not have enough skilled rank-and-file workers for production purposes. They undertake the same amount of work with fewer people and experience the increasing work pressure (Interviewee 003 and 006). In this circumstance, if their units' leaders maintain good relationships with the HR department, their work burden can be shared.

> "The HR department will refer to the last year's vacancy of different sub-companies, if they could recruit enough employees, then the HR [department] will allocate the employees according to the record number; if they cannot recruit enough employees, then the allocation is based on the relationship with the HR director. (Interviewee 011)"

The second way, slacking off at work through relationships with leaders, though can be manipulated by the workers themselves, only a very small number of EGC workers can achieve more money with less work. Two cases (Interviewee 002 and 008) are found among my respondents. Yujia (Interviewee 002) who joined in EGC and got the official employment in 2014 through family relationship. Although his work group reduced from over 30 people to 12 people after the 2015's labour activism, his workload remains easy.

> "My job is sitting in the office every day, drawing some pictures and reading some materials for techniques. Sometimes the workers might come

> upstairs to ask questions... I hold this card (staff ID) every day but I haven't punched the clock for over a month. We have the working hours 8am-12pm and 2pm-6pm. However, as long as you complete your work and are in position when your leader needs you, you will not get any punishments. Unless you are absent from work every day. The leaders are humanistic, they will not force you to work... After the [2015] reform, during the peak time, in a half day you can finish your daily work; during the off-peak time, usually you only work three hours per day. Then you know how we fooled around before. (Interviewee 002)"

Qiong's (Interviewee 008) husband had a very good relationship with her monitor, as a second-line worker managing storage and distributing materials, she always left earlier in the afternoon. The monitor addressed the absenteeism problem at group regular meetings, but she did not pay much attention, nor did she get any punishments. She can even argue openly with her direct team leader.

> "She said, 'if you do a bad job, I will deduct your money'. She does not know how to talk nicely. I got mad and said, 'if it is not my fault, do not even think about deducting a penny from me.' She does not know how to get along well with people. (Interviewee 008)"

These workers, who are looked after by the leaders, "would not leave as long as they could enjoy relaxing work and still get the money (Interviewee 017)". They slack off at work, making them less work but getting the same wages as the other workers. The use of relationships by this minority group of workers deepens the proletarianisation of other workers. Those who do not have relationships with leaders can only work honestly and do extra work that this minority group of workers do not do. They are more deeply exploited in their daily work to produce more surplus value without corresponding pay. When workers who can apply relationships to slack off at work and carry out this practice, they exploit other workers in disguise. Therefore, as I noted at the beginning of this section, the majority of workers' group should opt for explicit protest as their way out for entitlements as Marxian suggested. Only then are they fighting against the capital that exploit their labour and the root that cause their poverty, rather than creating more divided interest groups or competing rivalries within the workers' group.

Practices of Relationship in Employment

Obtaining Better Employment

Workers have tacitly accepted that working as SOE workers does not guarantee them privileges, therefore, workers rely on relationships to obtain relatively better treatment within the manual workers' group (the working class). The first way is to obtain an official employment to maximise the welfare package, which I discussed the differences between the regular employees and labour contractors, and I mentioned how family relationship can help workers' children to get the employment in Chapter 4. Further discussion here on how relationships help workers gain access to the official employment.

Xiang (Interviewee 013) worked for a private company as a seller for many years after graduating from college before he made the decision to return to D city. He said it was quite difficult to get into EGC and get a regular staff position without the help of relationship.

> "After the recruitment, there is a Regular Employee Examination. It tests lots of professional knowledge as well as practical technology [knowledge]... The Regular Employee Examination is not the only way for a labour contractor to become a regular SOE employee. Besides the tests, [the cadres] will evaluate your working performance." (Interviewee 013)"

According to Xiang, the Regular Employee Examination for contract workers to become regular workers in fact entails two aspects: the examination results, which reflect a person's knowledge; and the evaluation of superiors, which might go beyond a person's work capability and account more for how good the person is at building relationships with cadres. When Xiang took the examination in 2008, only 2 out of 10 people could pass the Regular Employee Examination. As superiors have the power to make final decisions, good relationships with the leaders can help the contract workers get regular job positions when competing with others with similar cultural capital.

In the late 1990s, Xuehua (Interviewee 009) experienced "*xigong*" (break) when a large number of workers had to take long breaks at home due to the enterprise's low profits. Although job training was given to those workers affected based on the demands of the industry's development, there were cases where people were not eligible for the new job positions and had to leave EGC after completing the training. Xuehua used relationship to get a new job (regular employee) at EGC after attending job training for around four months.

Obtaining Easy Job Positions

This research found that new employees will be allocated to the workplace in response to a lack of labour rather than their willingness if they do not have relationships. Many graduates who entered EGC through university careers fairs did not know what they were going to do or which sub-company they would be allocated to before they officially started the job. Before starting, they only knew that they had got job offers from EGC, but they were given no specific description of the position or work content. After the job allocation, the actual role is decided by the cadres at the basic level. The decision, as with the job assignment process, is made quite crudely: the HR director checks the vacancies and the demand of each unit and then decides the allocation. In most cases, the HR officer reads the person's academic qualifications in a very simple way. For instance, an interviewee who studied painting at university was allocated to paint the wall (Interviewee 004) and a graduate who majored in Industrial Design at university was assigned to the Quality Inspection Department (Interviewee 003).

Those who have relationships are more likely to be assigned to a relaxing position in the factory. HR officers read applicants' resumes to see whether they have an EGC background, for example, if any of their family members work at EGC. Applicants' families will also "*da zhaohu*" (contact the interviewer in advance to discuss their jobs and cases) if they have the contacts, making the interview a "*zou guochang*" (mere formality) (Interviewees 009 and 022). Xuehua (Interviewee 009) pointed out her classmate's father was a cadre in EGC, so when the allocation work began, with the family's help, her classmate found a profitable and relaxing position. As this is the industry sector, a lot of jobs involve heavy labour; her classmate got a job in the support department as a liaison. She said that if a person's family has a good relationship with their superiors and those who make decisions, then they will be given a good position. Xuehua herself entered EGC as an electric welder. The work environment was very difficult and had a bad influence on physical health. She later depended on relationships to change to a rear service position. She said, "If you are the cadres' family relatives, your leader might be quite lenient to you. But to the ordinary workers, the leaders will be very strict". The other example is provided by Xu (Interviewee

015). He said he had a clear idea about which sub-company he wanted to be at in the final year of university. He noted that both of his parents were EGC employees and "*zuo bangongshi*" (sit in the offices), meaning that both of his parents were cadres. He agreed that only people with strong social network could choose their positions as new employees.

For people who do not have strong social relationships, they have very little choice in whether they end up in a profitable sub-company or manage to avoid the sub-industries which adverse working conditions (Interviewee 003, 004 and 019).

Promotion as a Means of Protest and Practices of Relationship

EGC workers acknowledge the desperate proletarian situation but are resigned to it and manifest the working class's dissatisfaction with the status quo by joining the antagonistic group, which seems to be a contradictory interpretation. The working class should fight against the antagonistic bourgeoisie to win rather than join the antagonistic group to escape the workers' status. However, the reality is that those workers who have no way of relying on relationships to alleviate the exploitation and oppression in their daily work and job position selection, joining the antagonistic class is a rational choice of resistance to avoid the fate of being the most miserable and underprivileged workers in EGC. The underlying logic is the same as the protests that mentioned previously: workers seek to gain more entitlements, which can be translated into higher positions, better wages and easier work. Through promotion, workers change their subordination to their leaders, so that the source of their oppression no longer exists or is alleviated, which means that workers can gain more freedom.

However, the promotion pathways for workers have reduced. The university-educated technicians are regarded as a backup to managers as I discussed in Chapter 4 when analysing the changes in the composition of the working class in EGC. Meanwhile, the number of cadres (managers) in the reformed SOE has been reduced as well. This research found that in EGC's 2019 spring recruitment campaign, half of the middle managers did not pass the job interview. The promotion opportunities were only possible when there were vacancies in management positions (Interviewee 003 and 008). Qiong (Interviewee 008) said her husband had waited a long time for a junior manager position, his supervisor was supposed to move to another position but never did, so the manager position was not vacant and there was no way to promote her husband until his early retirement. Yujia (Interviewee 002) gave an example from his work section. This technical department has around 60–70 people; many are older and have more work experience than him. "They graduated from Harbin Institute of Technology and so, and they are still doing the basic technical service work. Unless they leave the unit, otherwise, the [promotion] opportunities are theirs". Kai (Interviewee 006) also thought he had no chance of promotion. He said, "Firstly, I think I don't have the opportunity... Another reason is that I think they will select from their cadres' group. 80%, I cannot get the position, so I gave up, I don't want to be cannon fodder".

Due to the opportunities for promotion being compressed, workers who want to achieve a change of status need to first endure deeper labour exploitation voluntarily in order to demonstrate their enthusiasm for their work with a view to gain the appreciation of their leaders (Interviewee 006, 014 and 016). Weng (Interviewee 012) once went to the work plant at 3 am to ensure the machine could operate properly. By doing so, the workers appear to have given up resistance and willingly accept the control of the cadres, but in fact they are trying to achieve a break from the roots of oppression.

There are very few cases of successful promotion through workers' own efforts, such as self-study for certification or on-the-job study for diploma. Interviewee 014 got the financial certificate through self-study, and he changed from a front-line job (a blue-collar worker) to a purchase specialist position (a white-collar worker). He said, "At least I don't have to come to the worksite to operate my work. I do contact (contact people to assign work), more flexible". However, Rong (Interviewee 018) who also obtained qualifications and got a higher diploma still worked as an electrician.

Most worker promotions, especially beyond the category of workers (blue-collar workers and white-collar workers), rely on relationships to achieve the transition from workers' group to cadres and managers' group. The relationships can be divided into two kinds, one is the relationship with the leaders, the other is the relationship network gained through joining the political party, especially CCP.

Relationship with Leaders[12]

Workers try to maintain good relationships with their superiors for accessing promotion opportunities. To the workers, it is normal that they please the leaders (Interviewees 004, 006, 008 and 015). Xu (Interviewee 015) said,

> "The most important thing is to maintain a good relationship. As a young professional, to be honest, I would like to go upper [manage level] ... unless you are in a private company or a foreign capital company, they regard the working capacity more importantly, [because] you earn the money for the boss... the capacity to maintain good relationships is more essential than working capacity [in SOEs]. Unless you are the only expert, no one can complete the work as you do [this situation is rare]. [However,] in most common situation, if you don't want to do it, the boss can always find somebody [with the same working capacity] to do it. (Interviewee 015)"

Xu's opinion was agreed by Xin (Interviewee 019), who said that the reason why he got promoted was because he was obedient, "listen to the leaders' words and act quickly"; a similar opinion was provided by Weng (Interviewee 012), who said, "the superiors will select their favourite people. You should be obedient and get on well with them". When a worker is appreciated by the leadership, the worker's career development can be helped and supported by the leadership, otherwise, there is no chance of promotion once the worker reaches the age line of promotion to the cadre.

Joining a Party to Build New Relationships

I see the choice of EGC workers to join a party, particularly the CCP to gain a new political identity, as a way for workers to gain a new social network. Some workers used this as a way of obtaining a degree of comfort and seeking possible future improvements of their status through this new network. It is an implicit dissatisfaction with their status. As it is

[12] Interviewees pointed to promotions in factories in exchange for sexuality. The gossips in the workshop about the female worker got team leader position by having an affair with a manager. However, I do not have solid data to prove these gossips or further explore the promotion topic from this perspective, so I will not discuss this in this research. The gossips details are summarised in Appendix E, where I summary the annotations of the interviews in NVivo.

difficult to change their economic situation, therefore, they turned to a search for political identity.

SOE workers in the period of Mao Zedong were already part of a privileged group without having to specifically seek membership of a party. EGC workers lived well as SOE workers. The ruling party (CCP) encouraged a wider group of workers to join them in order to strengthen their ranks. In my interviews, Li (Interviewee 005) mentioned that he was invited to join the CCP when he was an ordinary accountant. However, as I discussed, the class privilege and advantage as the working class was gone. EGC workers started to feel that joining a political party in the SOE would facilitate their survival, and thus compensate to some extent for the fact that they were totally oppressed by the managers and exploited by the capital market. When Chun (Interviewee 010) was a worker, he found his colleagues who were more easily admitted by the organisation (in his narrratives, *zuzhi*) and were able to show their abilities and capabilities, are CCP members. That was a main factor of what encouraged him to join the CCP.

It is not surprising that workers think it is essential to be a CCP member to secure a job promotion. Cases found in EGC are those young technicians, if their leaders are interested in grooming them to be their successors later, they will also be given some political duties first. They will hold posts related to the CCP and the Communist Youth League, such as secretary or deputy secretary. However, ordinary workers are hardly to be assigned to or access to these political positions as those reserve cadres, they must join the political party through applications if they want the political identity and the process is cumbersome and time-consuming. For example, if a worker wants to join the CCP, the person needs to first make an application and then the Party organisation will investigate the person, which will take about a month. If the worker passes the investigation, the person will become a "*rudang jiji fenzi*" (positive applicant for party membership). Then, the person will start taking courses learning about the CCP and participating in the party's activities. After a year, the organisation will select people they think are capable among the applicants and undertake a political investigation. The successful candidates will become "*yubei dangyuan*" (probationary party members). The CCP organisation investigation does not end here. It will then take another year for a probationary party member to become an official party member.

However, the status of a political party does not equate with the status of workers. This research found that some workers who gained a new political status did not benefit from changing their economic status as a result (Interview 006, 015, 017 and 018). As workers with communist party membership are still workers, their economic status will not change by obtaining the new political identity as CCP members. In other words, membership of political parties is no longer simply a choice of beliefs or values for EGC workers but has become a bargaining chip, especially the CCP membership (Walder, 1988), that can increase a person's chances in the competition to find a good job both within and outside of state enterprises.[13] As Rong (Interviewee 018) said, after she became a communist party member, she got to know more people and learnt that this social network, connected by the same political status, will help her in her career. Therefore, she actively participated in party meetings and study groups. When workers found that very few workers in reformed enterprises could get promoted or treated better through their own efforts or relationships with their leaders, they wanted to build new networks through party membership to improve their situation, but success was not easy and, as I mentioned earlier, becoming a party member did not guarantee that workers would be promoted.

Certainly, there are workers who choose to join the CCP because of their political beliefs, but the percentage is very low. In my interviews, only Zhang (Interviewee 017) mentioned that he joined the CCP because of his beliefs, and indeed the CCP membership did not guarantee Zhang a promotion in EGC, he has always worked as a bench worker in the workshop. He joined the CCP because "it is a conceptual difference", and "a sign of progressive thinking". The party membership is an honour to him and stimulates him to make more progress at work. From his perspective, the difference between him—a worker with party membership—and other workers is that he does not mind spending more time developing the technology to help EGC and he takes on more responsibilities at work.

> "If you are excellent, the organisation will find you and encourage you to join the [communist] party. It is a representation of progressive thought... I compared [party members and non-members] ... It is an honour to join the Party... There are many meetings in EGC [that] are only open to [communist] party members. After joining the [communist] party, my

[13] Evidence outside of SOEs: a study found that 30% of college students in China openly state that they joined the communist party to find good jobs (Rosen 2004).

thoughts changed. No matter whether I am in the manager position or not, I will be strict with myself. (Interviewee 017)"

For Interviewee 017, the party membership reflects his political status and his loyalty to the CCP. He suggested that it is a good way to prove one's ability to some extent and show his desire for progress.

According to the fieldwork research, workers discussed that for the cadres (managers), it is much easier to join a party, and even more diverse in their choice of party affiliation, than for the majority of workers who expect to rely on having a communist party affiliation to help them survive in the enterprise. For instance, Xiong (Interviewee 020) who was working as the head of communication in EGC in 2018 mentioned that the core cadre group has people who are democratic party members and nonpartisan.

"There are nonpartisan members. Our newspaper office's former chief editor is nonpartisan. Now, the vice president [of EGC] is [a member of] *Zhongguo Minzhu Tongmeng* (China Democratic League). The former minister of the financial department is [a member of] *Jiusan Xueshe* (Jiu San Society). A head of a sub-company is [a member of] the *Zhongguo guomindang gemin weiyuanhui* (Revolutionary Committee of the Chinese Koumintang). This is not saying that if you are other parties [members], [EGC] will not trust you... multi-party cooperation is also requested in the enterprise. It is a political arrangement. (Interviewee 020)"

In this reformed SOE, managers in the core cadre group were not promoted from workers but were mostly appointed by the supervisor unit. This means that they could not join the CCP as a means of promotion as the workers did but had more options. While other managers, who started out in junior cadre position in EGC before being promoted to higher ranks, when they reach a certain level of management, they will be encouraged and invited to join the CCP if they haven't already done so because the CCP want to ensure its leadership in the SOE (Interviewee 015 and 017).

"I know some cadres in my work unit were not [communist] party members when they entered EGC. Once they got promoted to a middle manager position, it was very easy for them to join the [communist] party. This is an SOE. Only if somebody promotes you, the process to become a [communist] party member is very quick. (Interviewee 015)"

Kai (Interviewee 006) and Yu (Interviewee 016) agreed with this opinion by suggesting that the higher the position is, the more important the consideration of political status. Being a CCP member can be an additional condition for EGC's management and might be requested in particular party-associated positions in EGC (Interviewee 020). This, again, illustrates why workers see building a new social network via joining a party as a way for them to resist their despairing situation in EGC.

Based on EGC workers' case, only a minority of workers succeeded in passive or implicit protests because only a small number of workers were able to reduce their job pressure or get job promotions on the basis of their own abilities or relationships. The majority of workers had to protest openly and explicitly if they want to reobtain their status and request the enterprise to meet their interests. However, I am not suggesting that open protest is a higher level than workers' private resistance; workers choose their own form of resistance according to their situation. Whether it is an explicit (open protest) or implicit (private, passive and on the basis of the individual situation) protest, protest in itself means that workers recognise their class, i.e., they have class consciousness, and they are conscious of protesting as a *class-for-itself*.

References

All-China Federation of Trade Unions. (Ed.). (2006). *Gonghui Jichu Lilun Gailun* [*The basic theory of trade unions*]. Zhongguo Gongren Chubanshe [Chinese Workers Press].

Andreas, J. (2019). *Disenfranchised: The rise and fall of industrial citizenship in China*. Oxford University Press.

Barme, G. (1999). *In the red: On contemporary Chinese culture*. Columbia University Press.

Bourdieu, P. (1980). Le Capital Social. *Actes De La Recherche En Sciences Sociales* (Vol. 31, pp. 2–3). Cited from: Neveu, E. (2018). *Bourdieu's Capital(s): Sociologizing an Economic Concept*. In T. Medvetz, & J. J. Sallaz (Eds.), *The Oxford Handbook of Pierre Bourdieu* (pp. 347–374). Oxford University Press.

Bourdieu, P., & Wacquant, L. (1992). *An invitation to reflexive sociology*. The University of Chicago Press.

Chen, B. L. (2009). *Labour rights and development: A multidimensional analysis of power theory and functional theory*. Law Press.

Chen, Z. W. (2012). Guojia Jianshe, Kangzheng Yu Minzhu- Charles Tilly Guojia Yu Zhengzhi Lilun Shupin [National construction, resistace and democracy: A review of Charles Tilly's Theory of the state and politics]. *Fudan Political Science Review, 1*, 102–112.

———. (2015). State, worker, and identity struggle: Look back on Marx. *Fudan Journal (social Sciences), 2*, 142–147.

China Labour Bulletin. (2005). *Zhongguo Gongren Yundong Guancha Baogao (2000–2004)* [*Observation report on the Chinese workers' movement 2000–2004*]. September 2005, 35. Available on 12th September, 2022, *vide*: https://www.clb.org.hk/sites/default/files/archive/en/File/No.4%20labourmovement%28S%29.pdf

———. (2007). *Zhongguo Gongren Yundong Guancha Baogao (2005–2006)* [*Observation report on the Chinese workers' movement 2005–2006*]. May 2005, 44–47. Available on 12th September, 2022, *vide*: https://www.clb.org.hk/sites/default/files/archive/schi/File/No9_labourmovement2006_SC.pdf.

———. (2008). *No way out: Worker activism in China's state-owned enterprise reforms*. September 2008, 14–15. Available on 12th September, 2022, *vide*: https://www.clb.org.hk/sites/default/files/archive/en/File/research_reports/no_way_out.pdf

———. (2009). *Zhongguo Gongren Yundong Guancha Baogao (2007–2008)* [*Observation report on the Chinese workers' movement 2007–2008*]. March 2009, 3. Available on 12th Sep, 2022, *vide*: https://www.clb.org.hk/sites/default/files/archive/schi/old_files/No.15%20labourmovementreport2008(PS).pdf

———. (2011a). *Workers' collective actions statistics.* [*Earliest statistics from 2011a*]. Available on 12th September, 2022, *vide*: https://maps.clb.org.hk/?i18n_language=en_US&map=1&startDate=2018-01&endDate=2018-12&eventId=&keyword=&addressId=&parentAddressId=&address=&parentAddress=&industry=&parentIndustry=&industryName=

———. (2011b). *Zhongguo Gongren Yundong Guancha Baogao (2009–2010)* [*Observation Report on the Chinese Workers' Movement 2009–2010*]. May 2011b, 18. Available on 12th September, 2022, *vide*: https://www.clb.org.hk/sites/default/files/archive/schi/old_files/No.19%20labourmovementreport(PS).pdf

———. (2013). *Zhongguo Gongren Yundong Guancha Baogao (2011–2012)* [*Observation report on the Chinese workers' movement 2011–2012*]. June 2013, 36. Available on 12th Sep, 2022, *vide*: https://www.clb.org.hk/sites/default/files/archive/schi/File/other/2011-2012%E5%B7%A5%E4%BA%BA%E8%BF%90%E5%8A%A8%E6%8A%A5%E5%91%8A.pdf

———. (2015). *Zhongguo Gongren Yundong Guancha Baogao (2013–2014)* [*Observation report on the Chinese workers' movement 2013–2014*]. April

2015, 2. Available on 12th September, 2022, *vide*: https://www.clb.org.hk/sites/default/files/archive/schi/File/other/%E4%B8%AD%E5%9B%BD%E5%B7%A5%E4%BA%BA%E8%BF%90%E5%8A%A8%E8%A7%82%E5%AF%9F%E6%8A%A5%E5%91%8A%EF%BC%882013%20%E2%80%93%202014%EF%BC%89.pdf.

———. (2018). *Zhongguo Gongren Yundong Guancha Baogao (2015–2017)* [*Observation report on the Chinese workers' movement 2015–2017*]. August 2018, 11 & 24. Available on 12th September, 2022, *vide*: https://clb.org.hk/sites/default/files/%E4%B8%AD%E5%9B%BD%E5%B7%A5%E4%BA%BA%E8%BF%90%E5%8A%A8%E8%A7%82%E5%AF%9F%E6%8A%A5%E5%91%8A%EF%BC%882015%E2%80%932017%EF%BC%89%2020181218_%E4%BF%AE%E6%94%B9%E7%89%88.pdf

Dong, B. H. (2014). Milian Tiefanwan Shizhongbing Dezhi Ah [Obsessed with iron rice bowl is kind of sick, need to rule]. *Qianjiang Evening News*. 19th November, 2014. Available on 12th September, 2022, *vide*: http://star.news.sohu.com/20141119/n406162537.shtml

E Group Company (EGC). (2015a). *EGC Jiechu Laodong Hetong Shishi Banfa* [*EGC measures for the termination of labour contracts*]. 30th June, 2015.

———. (2015b). *EGC Zhigong Ligang Xiuyang Shishi Banfa* [*EGC worker absences cultivation measures for its implementation*]. 30th June, 2015.

Guan, Q. Y. (2007). Mancur Olson Jingji Sixiang Shupin [A review of Mancur Olson's economic thoughts]. *Shanghai Economic Research, 8*, 105–112.

Hurst, W. (2009). *The Chinese worker after socialism.* Cambridge University Press.

Jiang, W. N. (2009). Da Bianche, Jiti Xingdong Yu Guojia Xingshuai- Olson Jiti Xingdong Lilun Shupin [Hitchhiking, collective action and the rise and fall of the state: A review of Olson's theory of collective action]. *Academic Forum, 11*, 75–79.

Lee, C. K. (1998). The labor politics of market socialism: Collective inaction and class experiences among state workers in Guangzhou. *Modern China, 24*(1), 3–33.

———. (1999). From organized dependence to disorganized despotism: Changing labour regimes in Chinese factories. *The China Quarterly*, 157, 44–71.

———. (2000). The revenge of history' collective memories and labor protests in North-Eastern China. *Ethnography, 1*(2), 217–237.

———. (2002). From the specter of Mao to the spirit of the law: Labor insurgency in China. *Theory and Society, 31*(2), 189–228.

———. (2003). Pathways of labour insurgency. *Chinese Society,* 87–109. Routledge.

Li, L. J. (2001). Support for anti-corruption campaigns in rural China. *Journal of Contemporary China, 10*(29), 573–586.

Li, L. L., Miao, D. L., & Wang, X. X. (2009). Shichang Zhuanxing Yu "Danwei" Bianqian [Market transformation and the change of "unit"]. *Society, 29*(4), 1–25.

Li, P. J. (2010). Qianxi Charles Tilly De Kangzheng Yu Minzhuhua Lilun- Jiyu Zhengzhi Shehuixue De Shijiao [A brief analysis of Charles Tilly's theory of resistance and democracy: A political sociology perspective]. *Journal of Economic Studies, 22*, 235–236.

Li, Z. G. (2002). Olson Jingji Sixiang Shuping [A review of Olson's economic thoughts]. *Economic Review, 5*, 77–81.

Liu, X. (2002). Relative deprivation status and class perceptions. *Sociology Research, 1*, 81–90.

Marx, K. ([1844] 1932). *1844 Economic and philosophic manuscripts.* Available on 12th September, 2022, *vide*: https://www.marxists.org/chinese/marx/marxist.org-chinese-marx-1844.htm. Also Available on 12th September, 2022, *vide* in *Collections of Marx.* Translated by Bureau for the Compilation and Translation of the Works of Marx and Engels, Lenin and Stalin, Central Committee of the CCP. People's Press. 2000 Edition.

———. ([1847] 1920). *The poverty of philosophy*, 194–195. Foreign Language Publishing House.

Neveu, E. (2018). Bourdieu's capital(s): Sociologizing an economic concept. In T. Medvetz & J. J. Sallaz (Eds.), *The Oxford handbook of Pierre Bourdieu* (pp. 347–374). Oxford University Press.

O'Brien, K. J., & Li, L. (1999). Campaign nostalgia in the Chinese countryside. *Asian Survey, 39*(3), 375–393.

Olson, M. ([1965] 2012). The logic of collective action. *Contemporary Sociological Theory, 124.*

———. ([1982] 2008). *The rise and decline of nations.* Yale University Press.

Perry, E. J. (1993). *Shanghai on strike: The politics of Chinese labor*. Stanford University Press.

Sen, A. K. (1976). Famines as failures of exchange entitlements. *Economic and Political Weekly*, 1273–1280.

Sina Finance. (2017). *EGC Chongzu Wu Yili Zhigong Shangfang Susong Shijian* [*Official report to summary EGC's status after the 2015 labour activism*]. 23rd February, 2017.

Solinger, D. J. (2006). The creation of a new underclass in China and its implications. *Environment and Urbanization, 18*(1), 177–193.

Walder, A. G. (1988). *Communist neo-traditionalism: Work and authority in Chinese industry.* University of California Press.

Wang, J. P. (2021). An experimental discussion on the relationship between the history of the communist party of China and the history of the workers' movement in China. *Journal of the Tianjin Gonghui Guanli Ganbu Xueyuan Xuebao, 38*(4), 57–62.

Wang, J. X. (2010). *Qiantan Olson De Jiti Xingdong Lilun—Jiti Xingdong De Luoji Dushu Biji* [*An introduction to Olson's theory of collective action—The logic of collective action*]. *Law and Society*, 15.

Weber, M. ([1922] 1978). *Economy and society: An outline of interpretive sociology* (Vol. 1, p. 4). University of California Press.

Writing Group of China Institution of Labour Movement. (Ed.). (2020). *A brief history of Chinese trade unions.*

Yang, G. B. (2003). China's "Zhiqing" generation: Nostalgia, identity, and cultural resistance in the 1990s. *Modern China, 29*(3), 267–296.

Yang, J. (2007). "Re-employment stars": Language, gender and neoliberal restructuring in China. *Language Power and Social Process, 19*, 77.

Yang, J. (2017). *Mental health in China: Change, tradition, and therapeutic governance.* John Wiley & Sons.

Zheng, Z. F. (2011). Jiti Xingdong Lilun De Kunjing Yu Chulu- Du Olson Jiti Xingdong De Luoji [The dilemma and solution collective action theory: Reading Olson's the logic of collective action]. *Southern Journal, 6*, 42–44.

CHAPTER 6

The Reconstruction of Classes and a Class Society in China

From the analysis in the last two chapters, the trigger for EGC workers' class consciousness and the return to proletarian status is SOE reform. EGC workers found that the afterglow of the identity as SOE workers could not comfort them in their real situation, could not hide the fact that their status is the lowest level in the factory and could not eliminate their contradictions with capital which is represented by managers and cadres (leaders) either. Therefore, they used a clear class discourse to fight for their interests. In such a context, the class consciousness and the reconstructed working class were no longer given by the party-state but grew out of the factory working routine. If classes exist in a privileged society (work unit society) such as the SOEs, meaning that classes exist in a constructed socialist enterprise (environment), then the wider existence of classes in Chinese society can be inferred.

Based on the case study of EGC and the research into the increasing frequency of workers' activism in China since the 2000s (see Figs. 5.1, 5.2 and 5.3 on pp. 110–111), I have found that Chinese workers as a class are becoming more and more class-conscious, and that the working class has reconstructed to the "*class-for-itself*" level. The significance of the reconstruction of a "*class-for-itself*" working class is, on the one hand, to prove that a class society has not been eradicated in post-economic reform China

S. S. Huang, *The Political Economy of Reforms and the Remaking of the Proletarian Class in China, 1980s–2010s*, Palgrave Studies in Economic History, https://doi.org/10.1007/978-3-031-20455-5_6

or in the constructed socialist China but exists, even deepening class divisions and contradictions in the context of economic development and the general growth of social wealth; on the other hand, the significance of the reconstruction of classes and a class society is that it allows for a better identification of groups that are encompassed in the working class but have essentially differentiated themselves from it, such as the management (cadre managers) I mentioned in the case of EGC.

The situation faced by SOE workers after the economic reforms is not absolutely desperate when compared with the working class as a whole, especially those who are not part of the aristocratic group within the working class in the first place, for example, migrant workers, or with the peasant class who depended on the weather for their livelihood.[1] This point has been proved by interviews. Interviewees (001, 002, 006, 010, 013, 016, 017, 018 and 021) mentioned that private companies in D city do not provide insurance and support workers' housing fund; contract workers, most of whom are migrant workers, are not provided the same welfare when comparing to regular (official) workers. However, besides the comparison with others, the reflection of EGC workers on their own situation is one of the keys to the formation of their class consciousness. In this chapter, I will first discuss the relationship between workers' relative deprivation (Merton, [1949] 1968; Runciman, 1966), multiple exploitation (Wright, 1985, 1997, pp. 41–72) and the formation of class consciousness, to further substantiate my research finding on the reconstruction of the working class, a class-conscious working class.

Secondly, according to official government accounts, in the early 1950s, there were four classes and one stratum in China: the working class, the peasant class, the petty bourgeoisie, the national bourgeoisie and a management stratum that was closely linked to the working class and independent of it by virtue of its particular social function. Later in 1956, the state declared the completion of the socialist transformation—the completion of transformation of the socialist means of production. The establishment of the economic system of public ownership (*gongyou*

[1] Migrant workers belong to the working class. According to a report by National Bureau of Statistics (2020), the total number of migrant workers reached 298 million in 2019, and among the entire non-agricultural workforce, after deducting party and government cadres, employees of institutions, employees of social organisations, etc., migrant workers account for 60% of the workforce and have become a major component of industrial workers.

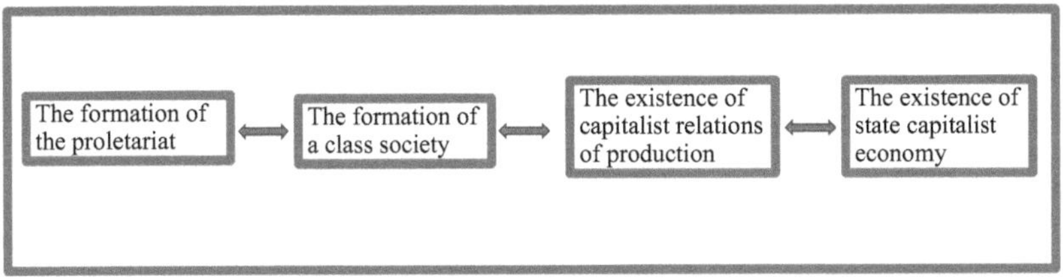

Fig. 6.1 Logical inference diagram (*Data Source* The author's original work)

zhi) means only two classes remained in Chinese society, i.e., the working class and the peasant class. There was a stratum, the intellectual stratum, but in the state leaders' definition, the intellectuals belonged to the working class. In other words, with the disappearance of old classes, China constructed a theoretically classless society, compatible with Marx's ideal of linear development in humanity, i.e., a successful transition from a capitalist to a socialist society. In this new socialist society, the workers and peasants are owners of capital (means of production) and there is no longer any economic exploitation. However, in Mao's China, allegedly socialist and equitable, the disappearance of social classes can be challenged. In post-Mao's China, especially in post-economic reform China, class (*jieji*) has been diluted in state discourse, replaced after the 2000s by a more politically neutral term—stratum (*jieceng*)—both in state discourse and in Chinese scholars' studies of social structure (Yuan Yinchun, 2015, pp. 99–106).

However, the narratives of "*jieceng*" in Chinese do not explain the social structure of China, because it circumvents the obvious contradictions between different interest groups that "*jieji*" represents. In this chapter, I separate class and stratification from "*gongren jieji*" (the working class) and "*gongxin jieceng*" (salariat or salaried stratum) in a discourse which is very from Chinese state claims. I analyse how the term stratum blurs the formation of class consciousness and the structure of classes. Moreover, through a discussion of labour-capital relations (relations of production), I redefine Chinese society as a society of classes and its economic development as state capitalism. Figure 6.1 shows my logical inference of this chapter.

Theoretical deduction: The return of the privileged working class under the socialist system to Marx's proletariat and the emergence of interest groups opposed to the workers implies the formation of a class society; the recognition of a class society means the recognition of capitalist relations of production because under socialist relations of production, there is no exploiting class due to the pursuit of socialist equality. In other words, China's contemporary labour-capital relations are capitalist; Moreover, the existence of capitalist relations of production deduces the existence of the capitalism form of economy, i.e., state capitalism, in China. The inverse of this theoretical logical also holds true. The existence of capitalist relations of production is evidence that China's artificially constructed socialist society has regressed (theoretically and logically, not in terms of economic development) to a stage that is consistent with the actual situation, i.e., transition stage from capitalism to socialism—the stage of state capitalism, as Lenin (1918 [1995]) put it.

6.1 Relative Deprivation, Multiple Exploitation, and Class Consciousness

Relative deprivation and multiple exploitation look at the "power" (Foucault, 1999) and "different forms of capital" (Bourdieu, 1977, [1979] 1984). Where workers of the same "interest group" (Olson, [1982] 2008) pursue the same "entitlements" (Sen, 1983), the oppression of some workers by others exists. When workers recognise their working-class identity and flight against the opposing class for the benefits that belong to the working class, then they exist as a class for themselves. This demonstrated in the case of the EGC.

Both state sector workers and non-state sector workers are working class. After the economic reforms, the shell of SOEs was gradually shattered, most evident in weakening or withdrawal of the socialist security guarantees given to SOE workers; the entitlements (Sen, [1983] 2016) that SOE workers had to fight for were very similar to those of other workers. As I discussed the economic status of EGC workers in Chapter 4, SOE workers were treated above the average material level of society in the pre-economic reform era, especially at the early stage of PRC establishment; the social status of the working class was fully recognised by the party and the state. However, when the economic reforms laid bare the nature of the capitalist market's pursuit of efficiency rather than socialist-style fairness, workers found that their production was not so much for the people and the state as it was for capital; that is, they felt a change in the relations of production. The economic form of state capitalism (I will discuss this concept later) still exists in China, so do the exploitation of people by capital and its representatives. This return of the working class to proletarians is a phenomenon that has been characteristic of the working class in countries that have undergone market reforms under the Soviet model of industrial development, where economic reforms have acted as a trigger for explicit (open) protests and implicit (private) protests (both have been discussed in Chapter 5 in EGC's case) to defend their rights and interests, which can be seen in historical cases such as Poland and the Czech Republic in Eastern European as examples (Li Zhengtu, 2016).

Having lost their vested interests under traditional socialist conditions and not receiving the expected benefits of economic reforms, workers in SOEs were reduced to a relatively deprived situation in the process of social transformation (Liu Xin, 2002, pp. 81–90), resulting in a sense of relative deprivation. The sociologists Robert K. Merton ([1949] 1968) and Walter Garrison Runciman (1966) discussed the concept of relative deprivation, whereby individuals feel deprived when they compare their situation to that of people in their reference group and find themselves at a disadvantage. This deprivation is relative because people are not compared to some absolute or eternal standard, but to a variable, which can be other people, other groups, or their own past. In the case of the EGC, the main source of deprivation for the SOE workers is comparison with the past and with the outside of the SOE, as can be seen in their nostalgia and in the workers' descriptions of the "city", where they gave good ratings and used the SOE as a reference, for example, by suggesting that "they are the SOEs of the past (Interviewee 004)". Moreover, I discussed EGC workers' protests in Chapter 5, that those workers who can use relationships to get easy works, slack off at job positions or leave their work to other workers, their actions are an exploitation of other workers who have no access to relationships. Workers with relationships, on the one hand, also sell their labour to the factory; on the other, although they do not have the power (Foucault, 1999) to dominate others in the organisation, they are exploiters, exploiting other workers, in a class structure analysis framework that Wright (1985, 1997, pp. 41–72) refers to as "multiple exploitation". This means, in addition to the opposition between the proletariat and bourgeoisie, there are also organisational and skill-based forms of exploitation. Through the increased dimensions of exploitation, groups that do not fully possess some exploitative capitals are placed in the position of both exploiting others and being exploited (Li Wei, 2004, pp. 80–95).

The relative deprivation and multiple exploitation of workers contribute to the emergence of class consciousness. Differing from "class awareness", which means that class members do not have an active self-group identification, nor a tendency to exclude others, "class consciousness" distinguishes "us" and "others", which has clear psychological boundaries of what a community (interest group as Olson put forward) is. According to Giddens (1973, pp. 111–113), class consciousness can be conceptualised as class identity, class conflict and revolutionary class consciousness. It is also what Marx called the formation of "*class-for-itself*", and an important criterion for judging the formation of "*class-for-itself*" is resistance (Ossowski, 1998), the class action driven by an explicit class consciousness. This point is agreed by another sociologist Michael Mann (1973, p. 13) in *Consciousness and Action among the Western Working Class*.

I have demonstrated the construction of a traditional working class (proletariat) from my case study on EGC workers. This section, again, proves that the emergence of protest represents the construction of a class and supports the first step of my logical inference. Not all factors in the emergence of this class consciousness are objectively conditions, but also subjectively feelings. This also justifies my application of Weber's ([1922] 1978) sociological approach to explore the reconstruction of working class from the individual micro-perspective.

6.2 Analysis on Transformation of China's Social Structure

Research into Chinese social stratification, Lu Xueyi (2002, p. 137) pointed out SOE workers as "aristocratic workers" (*guizu gongren*). SOE workers in the transform process keep the pre-transition political identity, which created a safe and tranquil harbour for workers. They pursue ease and comfort like aristocrats, become lazy and slack, unwilling to put in more effort, cannot tolerate high-intensity labour and are unwilling to learn and apply new skills. After the economic transformation, workers with more resources in physical strength and operational skills entered SOEs, excluding these "aristocratic workers".

However, in Lu's research, he did not mention that SOEs workers, the aristocratic workers, in the planned economy were more like the labour aristocracy occurred in Britain after the Industrial Revolution.[2] They had privileges while other workers did not have. They would not protest when they can guarantee their own interests and generate small groups due to different interests. This group of workers mastered the use of better resources and wanted to keep it to themselves. The aristocracy was embodied in their access to better welfares and treatments. They were in a privileged position but not a leisure class with absolute more wealth as Lu's definition of aristocratic class. This point again contradicts the core of socialist society, which should eliminate classes and eventually become a classless society. However, Chinese socialism has given a group of special rights from the beginning. Furthermore, the aristocratic workers (SOE workers) did not actually have political rights. After they were fed by agriculture surplus, they also needed to fight for citizenship. Researchers like Joel Andreas (2019) looked at SOE workers' citizenship and autonomy to understand workers' different situations in workplace. According to Andreas, workers enjoyed strong workplace citizenship under the work unit system, but their autonomy was weak. SOE workers' citizenship and autonomy are not static in China. For example, during the Cultural Revolution, the factory workers' autonomy and citizenship were relatively high, but the work unit system was never very democratic. The changes in the working class will undoubtedly cause changes in the class structure. As discussed previously, such changes are top-down rather than spontaneous. Their citizenship during the Cultural Revolution was a one-off right, just like the heavy industry, which is very affected by polices and passively accepts the power granted by the party and the state. Workers, along with peasants and soldiers, occupied the superstructure; however, the slogan "Grasp the revolution and promote production" (*zhua geming, cu shengchan*) in fact reflected that workers'

[2] See Wu Musheng's (1988) excerpt of Eric John Ernest Hobsbawan's discussion on British aristocratic workers in the nineteenth century, also see works of Wu Musheng (1982), Qian Chengdan et al. (2004) and Wang Lixin (1989). This term "labour aristocracy" refers to a group of workers who have higher salary, better treatment, more reputation in social status and more moderate politically than the ordinary workers. Workers from different industries established many opposing union organisations to protect their rights and interest. This had caused the organisational division of the working class. A few worker leaders betrayed the masses of workers. The status of workers was once only lower than their employers and much higher than others. However, between the "boss" and workers, there are aristocratic workers, technicians and independently recruited managers. The ordinary workers' promotion opportunities were limited and the gap between the ordinary and aristocratic workers was widening.

roles as leaders in the revolution and producers in the factories were not compatible.[3] Once they participated in the revolution, it was difficult for them to participate in production again. Conversely, once they participated in the production, their rights would be taken back, and they just played a role in the revolution.

Studies have shown that, Marx's class theory is still a useful tool for explaining class problems in contemporary Chinese society, especially with regard to contradictions between classes and working class's resistance. In the background of market system transformation, when SOE workers are finally cut off from the ownership of state assets, even if only theoretically, they tend to rise in protest and thus move in the direction of class formation. To understand the essence of class relations, the neo-Marxist Michael Burawoy brought out the concept of "factory regime" for explaining how migrant workers and the original SOE workers in the transitional period constructed a working class in the market economy (Shen Yuan, 2006, pp. 13–36). Michael Zhang and Huiqing Liu (2006, pp. 159–184) use Han Dongfang's data to conclude that the social marginalisation of the SOE workers is the root cause of the Chinese workers' collective actions.[4] Qiu Liping (2006, pp. 23–42) reiterated that the analysis of China's social structure should return to Marx's theory of class. It is precisely because of the contradictions between classes and the existence of working-class resistance that class studies are still meaningful in China.

Other researchers discussed China's social structure from the dual opposition between urban and rural areas and the gap between the rich and the poor. For instance, the different social insurance in urban and rural areas and the reform on the urban social insurance system caused the differences between enterprises' employees in the urban area and farmers in the rural area (Shi Hongwei, 2007). This has a negative impact on agriculture and farmers due to the prioritity of industrial development (Zhong Dajun, 2002).

[3] "Grasp Revolution and Promote Production" was officially proposed in 1966 by Mao Zedong. It aimed to ensure that cultural revolution is balanced with production and the cultural revolution must not be opposed to the development of production (Wang Junwei, 1996; Wang Xiangqing & Hu Dan, 2016; Wu Minxian & Sun Chengjun, 1994; Zheng Qian, 2011).

[4] Han Dongfang is the founder of China Labour Bulletin; he has had telephone interviews with workers in Dazhou, Sichuan Province and Fushun, Liaoning Province since 1998.

However, existing studies have not specifically pointed out the composition of the working class in the new social structure. For instance, when referring to the working class, whether it still includes intellectuals, non-state sector employees and even mangers, should be questioned. The relationship division between workers and managers in SOEs is not a simple binary opposition; the contradiction between labour and capital and the representative of the capital has not been fully explained. More research into the relationship between cadres and workers can be done.

6.3 Classes and the Perception of a Class Society

When analysing the contemporary China's social structure, there is a recent novel opinion which argues that *suzhi* (quality) can replace the concept of class. The original concept is called: "improvement of *suzhi*" *ex ante* which is documented in CCP manifestos.[5] As far as we can tell, this is the attempt to upgrade China's national educational level in science and technology. This strategy can loosely be related to Human Development Index (HDI) which has been the established quality of human capital. According to HDI, which was proposed by the United Nations Development Programme in 1990, years of education (including average years of education and expected years of education), average life expectancy at birth and per capita gross national income are the three indicators for calculating the value of HDI (Li Xiaoxi et al., 2014, pp. 69–95, 207–208; Yang Yongheng et al., 2005, pp. 4–7). Indeed, HDI readings are outcomes *ex post* of countries' educational developments over a period of

[5] See Notice of the State Council on Issuing the Outline of the National Scientific *Suzhi* Action Plan (2006–2010–2020) (*guowuyuan guanyu yinfa quanmin kexue suzhi xingdong jihua gangyao*). Available on 12th Sep, 2022, *vide*: http://www.gov.cn/zhengce/content/2008-03/28/content_5301.htm;

Notice of the General Office of the State Council on Issuing the Implementation Plan of the National Scientific *Suzhi* Action Plan (2016–2020) (*guowuyuan bangongting guanyu yinfa quanmin kexue suzhi xingdong jihua gangyao shishi fangan*). Available on 12th Sep, 2022, *vide*: http://www.gov.cn/zhengce/content/2016-03/14/content_5053247.htm;

and also see Notice of the State Council on Issuing the Outline of the National Scientific *Suzhi* Action Plan (2021–2035) (*guowuyuan guanyu yinfa quanmin kexue suzhi xingdong guihua gangyao*). Available on 12th Sep, 2022, *vide*: http://www.gov.cn/zhengce/content/2021-06/25/content_5620813.htm.

time, which relates to improving *suzhi*. But there is fundamental difference between HDI and the improvement of *suzhi*: Improvement of *suzhi* refers to education only, while HDI includes other things.

In addition, there is a spin-off by Andrew Kipnis who decides to use *suzhi* as a key criterion to separate individuals in society.[6] In other words, though the emergence of class differentiation and the inequality between people can be measured by *suzhi*, the two concepts: *suzhi* and class, are not interchangeable. Replacing class by *suzhi* in class division does not conform to Marxist class theory. Similarly, like party leaders used the loyalty to the party to classify people's class attributes and composition during Mao Zedong's era. This kind of classification deviates from Marxism. *Suzhi* has nothing to do with the means of production. In the end, *suzhi* blames and judges workers themselves. For instance, workers do not obtain higher education, do not have enough cultural capital or even do not work hard enough to obtain high *suzhi*, which could be the reason why they are in lower status. However, in fact, Marxism did not regard *suzhi* of the proletarians as a criterion when describing the conditions for the victory of the proletarians' revolution or the characteristics of proletarians. Meanwhile, when China uses Sinicised Marxism as the programme of revolution to unite the broader masses of the lower classes: workers and peasant, *suzhi* was not regarded as the standard. If we assume that cadres (managers of SOEs) and workers are divided by *suzhi*, then cadres at higher positions should have higher *suzhi*. However, they have indeed become the upper strata of the new social structure and the exploiters of workers. This violates Marx's original intention. Same as the way Mao used loyalty to the party to classify class attributes, Kipnis's classification of social structure by *suzhi* as a criterion is also revisionist. Kipnis's *suzhi* decides one's income and social standing (which are the basic indications of class), while from the state's policy, improving *suzhi* has nothing to do with individual's income and social standing but about

[6] For example, Andrew Kipnis (2006, pp. 295–313) believed that "*suzhi* justifies social and political hierarchies of all sorts". People with "high" *suzhi* deserve more income, power and status than those of "low" *suzhi* after the economic reforms. From Kipnis's statements, the meanings and uses of *suzhi* after the economic reforms in China can be summarised in three points. "*Suzhi* is limited to individually embodied" but "no longer connotes the natural in a nature/nurture dichotomy". "*Suzhi* has taken on sacred overtones and marks the hierarchical and moral distinction between the high and the low now and its improvement is a mission of national importance". In his opinion, therefore, *suzhi* can be a very important standard to evaluate the level of social development.

upgrading national human capital. The differences between Kipnis' use of *suzhi* and Chinese government's target of improving *suzhi* are obvious.

Using *suzhi* as the classification method can be very subjective. It attributes the nature of which class people belong through their own ability, efforts or even birth and genes. To improve personal *suzhi*, national *suzhi* or *suzhi* education, the state should aim at social development, which should be a requirement in the face of the future and not used as a standard for objective class divisions. If workers accept the definition of pseudo-class to divide their status, they are posed in the sacrificial role, which means they have to accept that their miserable situation is caused by their low *suzhi*, low efficiency, low education or other factors that are personal and subjective. However, efficiency is about the return of capital. Workers cannot completely solve efficiency issues by themselves, nor can they solve the fairness issues by their own efforts.

Except *suzhi*, the use of the two terms "social class" and "social stratum" in existing study is usually mixed. However, in further analysing the reconstruction of the class in Chinese society from the EGC case, I found the substitution of class (*jieji*) and stratum (*jieceng*) in state discourse has a particular meaning. Yuan Yinchun (2015, pp. 99–106) did word frequency analysis of "*jieji*" and "*jieceng*" in newspapers (the official paper of China—the People's daily) between 1950 and 2010. By using the formula:

The permillage of articles containing the specific keyword = Number of articles containing the specific keyword/Total number of articles for the year X 1000.

The research found that "*jieji*" was used more often when the country's politics was at the centre of national activities; for example, the highest and second highest peaks of class occurred in 1968 (380‰) and 1976 (300‰), both during the Cultural Revolution period; conversely, "*jieceng*" was used more frequently when the economy became the centre. The term stratum replaced the term class after the 2000s.

Marx's class division is based on the economy. Orthodox Marxism thus sees classes as a representative of social relations the economy. Marx sees contradictions and antagonisms between different groups, particularly between the proletariat and the bourgeoisie; "classes" capture the structure of society. However, as I discussed in Chapter 1 about this research's background, Mao Zedong's interpretation and application of the term class in China were based on political connotations. His emphasis on class struggle made the term politically charged. As a result, the term "class" has become a political taboo in China. Consequently, any discussions of Marx's classes are considered politically incorrect. Therefore, such a discussion is consciously avoided both by the government and by Chinese academics. Officials and Chinese scholars use other terms, such as stratum, to replace "class". For instance, Lu Xueyi (2002, 2003, 2006) defined "then major strata" in China rather than "ten major classes". Unlike class which is used by the state for political mobilisation and power struggle, the term stratum is politically neutral limited in engaging in economic discourses with, typically, incomes. This means that clashes between different interest groups are taken as problems within the same class, rather than between the proletariat and the bourgeoisie.

However, in the following analysis of the most fundamental labour-capital relations, relations of production and the appropriation of wealth, it reflects not a division within the same class, but between different classes. Therefore, my analysis rejects the use of stratum as it blurs the division of classes, misunderstands society and leads to misperception of China's social and economic structure.

The use and division of strata complicate the social structure of classes. In other words, if applying Marx's method of means of production relationship to view the social structure, society can be clearly divided into two classes, the proletariat without means of production and the proletariat with means of production. The introduction of stratum makes the classification of the salariat richer. It can include, in addition to industrial workers, craft workers, transport workers, construction workers, agricultural hirelings and ordinary workers in commerce and finance; cultural workers such as teachers, journalists and actors; professional and technical labourers such as engineers and technicians; and even officials in government departments. This means apart from the peasants and those who own their own business, all other wage labour, whether they are selling their physical labour or mental labour, as long as they have no means of production, they are wage labour (salariat). However, combined with Marx's definition of class, it is hard to include those who are highly paid to manage workers on behalf of capital to the same stratum as the workers. Thus, I argue that the use of the concept of stratum in China has made it easy for people to be misled in their perception of their class identity. Examined in EGC's case, the managers on behalf of the SOE or the state to manage workers are not included in workers' group, and even technicians (so-called white-collar workers) are excluded. Those who are divided into the working class oppressed the workers in their daily work production. There were even managers who considered themselves as working class; they spoke of considering themselves as leaders within the working class (Interview 009 and 020). However, it is important to note that the return to the proletariat must be only for workers, not for managers or technicians who are also in the salariat. Cadres (narratives in the interviews as "*dangguan de*"), learnt from the fieldwork study that both EGC managers and technicians are given the identity as cadre, are in opposition to the ordinary workers as holders of power. The dichotomy can also be found among political officials (as a new class with emerging power) and ordinary people in the socialist state (Djilas, [1957] 1983, p. 38). The concept of "*gongxin jieceng*" blurs the concept of the "*gongren jieji*" and has even been deliberately conflated to avoid knowledge and discussion of the formation of the class society in China.

If one were to distinguish between the existing studies of social stratification in China and Marx's class theory on the structure of social classes, I would argue that the image of social stratification is ladder-like; that is, mobility between strata is predictable or expected. Strata can be refined according to two main criteria: occupational income and social prestige. However, classes are more like separate and distinct groups, with contradictions and conflicts between them. It is difficult for people in different interest groups to change the attributes of classes and the class mobility lower than the strata form. Seeing the existing studies on social strata and social class structure in China (Goodman, 2014; Li, 2005, pp. 55–73; Lu, 2002, 2003 and 2006; Pan, 2007, pp. 35–37; Pang & Qiu, 1989, pp. 63–75; Zheng, 2002, pp. 5–9; Pan, 2007, pp. 35–37), I drew schematic diagrams of Chinese strata and classes in general terms, noting that legends do not (or accurately) reflect the percentage of each class or stratum in the total population.

Managers in the schematic diagrams include both cadres in SOEs and management in the non-state sector.

Label groups belong to the salariat in Fig. 6.2; I drew up Fig. 6.3.

Theoretically speaking, the class structure of an idealised socialist society should be classless (or more general speaking, at least free of class contradictions). Excluding unemployment (due to the national employment guarantee of a socialist society), the structure of society should be like Fig. 6.4. The salariat can be replaced by the working class. This is also a way of confusing the two concepts. Due to the economic reforms, private entrepreneurs (business owners) are allowed to exist.

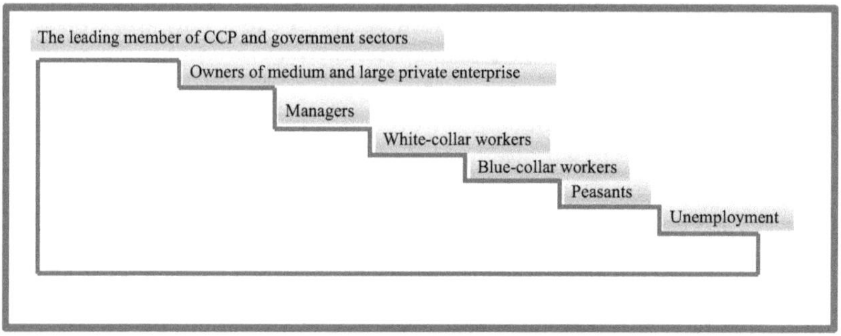

Fig. 6.2 Diagram of social stratification[7] (*Data Source* The author's original work)

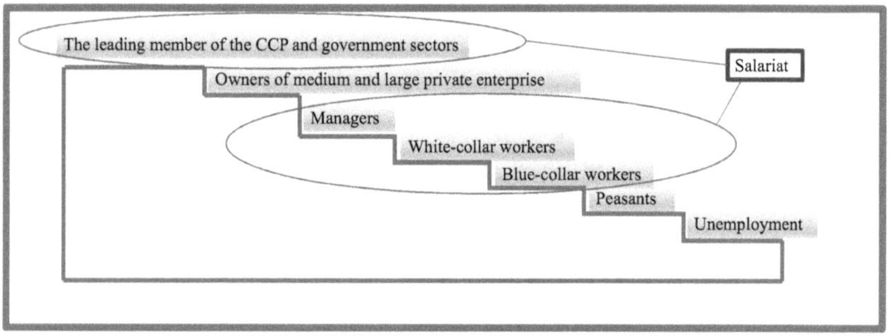

Fig. 6.3 Diagram of social stratification- salariat (*Data Source* The author's original work)

Furthermore, according to the 2019 National Economic and Social Development Statistical Bulletin, I made Table 6.1 and Table 6.2.[8]

[7] Certainly, the strata can be further refined to put those professionals such as doctors, lawyers and engineers between the managers and the white-collar workers, civil servants could also be excluded from the white-collar workers, and those small private business owners could also be placed above or below management. As my focus is on workers (manual workers), I will not go details.

[8] National Bureau of Statistics, Feb 28th, 2020, *P. R. China 2019 National Economic and Social Development Statistical Bulletin (zhonghua renmin gongheguo 2019 nian guomin jingji he shehui fazhan tongji gongbao)*. Available on 12th Sep, 2022, *vide*: http://www.stats.gov.cn/tjsj/zxfb/202002/t20200228_1728913.html.

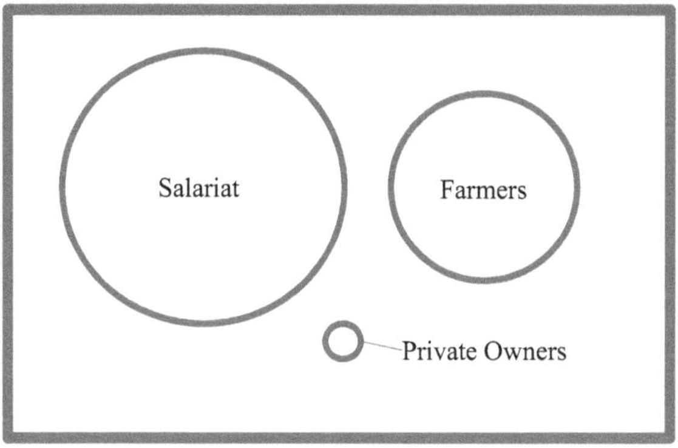

Fig. 6.4 An ideal classes diagram (*Data Source* The author's original work)

The official statistics define all those employed in the secondary and tertiary sectors as the working class. The data reflect an illusion of the ideal socialist social class composition, in which only two classifications are in the working population: workers and peasants. However, except for those employed in agriculture and private business owners, can we really classify all the employed population into the working class?

It is a very convenient approach to classify the majority of society as working class because statistically they make up the majority of China's employed population and are not a small proportion of the country's population. So, when it is declared that the working class is the leading class and that the alliance of workers and peasants is the basis of the people's democratic dictatorship of the socialist state, it covers almost everyone and gives everyone the equal status of power. Moreover, if owners, those petty bourgeoisie or big bourgeoisie are allowed to exist in Chinese society after the economic reforms, in statistically speaking (which is 0 in the official data) and theoretically speaking, they only account for a small part. So they should have little impact. However, this "small" group occupies the majority of the interests of the society. Referring to China Merchants Bank's (*zhaoshang yinhang*) 2018 report (pp. 55–56), I made Table 6.3.[9]

[9] China Merchants Bank, 22nd March 2019, Full text of China Merchants Bank Co., LTD 2018 Annual Report, (*zhaoshang yinhang gufen youxian gongsi 2018 niandu baogao quanwen*). Available on 12th Sep, 2022, *vide:*

Table 6.1 1978 versus 2019: Number and percentage of workers

Year	1978	2019
Number of Employees (million)	180	580
Percentage in the National Workforce (%)	29.5	74.9

Data Source National Bureau of Statistics, 2020

Table 6.2 2019 Number and percentage of employees in the three major industries

Industry	*Primary*	*Secondary*	*Tertiary*
Number of employees (million)	194	210	370
Percentage in the National Workforce (%)	25.1	27.5	47.4

Data Source National Bureau of Statistics, 2020

Table 6.3 Wealth possession in 2018

Customer Classification	*Number of Customers*	*Total Assets (Yuan)*	*Average Assets (Yuan)*
Retail Customers	12,541.44 million	6,802.105 billion	60,000
Golden Sunflower Customers[10]	2,362,600	5,508,235 million	2.33 million
Private Banking Customers	72,938	2,039,290 million	27.77 million

Data Source China Merchants Bank, 2019

The figures show that 0.05% of the population holds 30% of the wealth and 1.9% of the population holds 81% of the wealth. Such concentrated wealth holdings can hardly support a society free of class antagonism and class conflict.

https://file.cmbimg.com/cmbir/201903/fec83752-d517-4236-a04f-03b97a4cbf15.pdf

10 Golden Sunflower Customers (*jin kuihua kehu*) means retail customers with monthly average daily total assets of 500,000 Yuan and above.

As I have demonstrated in the case of EGC, among the same "*gongxin jiceng*" (or ideologically "*gongren jiji*"), workers clearly defined who are part of their class members, in which capital representatives—managerial cadres, and technicians—with managerial or supervisory rights over workers are not part of the working class. The division and opposition in the social class structure are presented in Fig. 6.5.

The above diagrams and tables demonstrate that it is inappropriate to replace the working class (*gongren jieji*) with the salaried stratum (*gongxin jieceng*). Moreover, it is also inappropriate not to recognise the formation of a class society. The salariat is divided into different interest groups, and they form different classes from the working class rather than different strata within the same group. Classes integrate the socio-economic, cultural and political elements that divide social stratification. Based on those, classes emphasise human action, change, conflict and response to conflict.

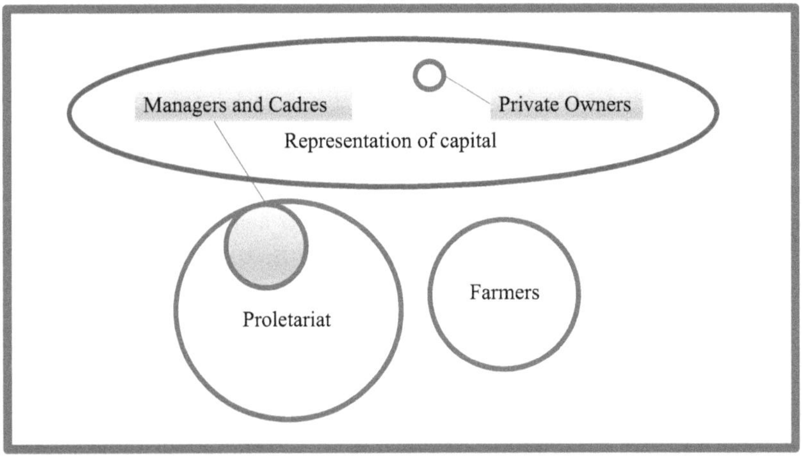

Fig. 6.5 Social classes diagram[11] (*Data Source* The author's original work)

[11] Certainly, same as Fig. 6.2, in Fig. 6.5, there could be more circles within the working class to represent subgroups, distinguishing between those who work for state enterprises or those who do not, or according to the EGC case, those who are technical professionals, doctors, engineers, accountants, lawyers, etc. These groups do not represent capital and are even controlled by it. However, their interests are certainly not common to those of workers.

When I apply Weber's sociological approach to the analysis of EGC workers in terms of capital (Bourdieu's capital), power, interest group and entitlements from the perspective of the individual, I found that the workers themselves use the term "class" (*jieji*) rather than "stratum" (*jieceng*). It is also the class that is formed within the framework of state enterprise of EGC. Their class consciousness can be viewed when workers face their new position in the socio-economy structure and their class consciousness can be reflected in their strike and protests. However, the language of class is still somewhat taboo in SOEs; for example, workers who have experienced the Cultural Revolution are very sensitive when asked questions about the working class and the contradictions between factory leaders and workers (Interviewee 005 and 007). This sensitivity makes them avoid speaking out as a class subject to prevent "settling scores afterwards" (*qiuhou suanzhang*). However, the SOE workers' perceptions of themselves were clear; for example, they mentioned in the interviews that "the working class is useless"(*gongren jieji meiyong*) and that "the working class is an outdated word" (*gongren jieji guoshi le*); it is clear that they noticed that this class, which had been given meaning and privilege by the party-state, had changed. The new working class that has been formed from the factories is a "proletariat" without privileged status.

In my opinion, there are several reasons why the reconstruction of class social structure in China has not been universally recognised: 1. The confusion between class and stratum is used to justify the great changes in Chinese society after the economic reforms, to rationalise the new bourgeoisie that has been stripped away from the working class, i.e., by explaining that they are the upper stratum of the salariat, but still belong to the working class, in order to hide the fact that their class has changed. This is a tactic to hide the fact that they have social privileges different from those of the working class (for instance, the occupation of a huge amount of wealth as I mentioned previously). The emphasis on individual effort, professional division of labour, equality of opportunity and the opening up of the market have led to the suppression of reflection on class (Pan Yi, 2007, pp. 35–37). From Figs. 5.1, 5.2 and 5.3 (pp. 110–111) on Chinese workers' activism in the last decade, the Reform and Opening Up and the introduction of the capitalist market have resulted in a clear class division, a wider awareness of which has led to class consciousness, contradictions and resistances.[12] If it were only a more refined strata, the conflicts between different interest groups would not have been so intense.

2. The generalised application of the concept of working class in China. In 2020s' China, many perceptions of the working-class identity, or the definition of working class, extend to the salariat. Everyone can call themselves "*dagong ren*" (salaried workers), selling their labour for wages just as Marx ([1844] 1932, [1865] 1898) described as wage labour (proletariat). However, it is a kind of self-degrading, reflecting the empathy for factory workers that extends to themselves. People find themselves in a period of history where "*dagong ren*" compete with each other; the sense of defect makes them empathise with the working class. However, the difference between real wage labour and those who claim to be salaried workers is significant in terms of discursive power, material rights and their value creation in the social evaluation system. Based on Fig. 6.5, I made Fig. 6.6.

Although all can be called incomes, there are different types. Using the criterion of earning income to generalise the concept of the working class blurs the existence of class.

3. To recognise a class society is to recognise the contradiction of classes and the reality of the working class as the proletariat exploited by capital, which is incompatible with the ideology of the socialist state. If everyone except the owners can be called working class,[13] then executives of multinational companies (if they don't own shares) and workers on the factory floor can be included, as can the president of the state and the farm labourers. They are mixed within a group and do not need to choose sides creating the illusion that they belong to the same interest group, which weakens the conflict between classes; however, if their different class attributes are recognised, they represent different interest groups. The case from EGC demonstrates that the relationship between workers and managers is not an intra-stratum but a class relationship. However,

[12] Liu Xin (2002, 81–90) did a survey about class consciousness in Wuhan City in 1996, having the sample of 754 respondents. 77% of the respondents had clear conscious and thought of society as stratified. Although Liu used the term "*jieceng*" (strata) in the title, the whole research mixed the class and stratum, thinking these two terms are interchangeable. That means I am right about the confusing use of class and stratum in China and the whole society's class consciousness was revoked after the economic reforms.

[13] Of course, I exclude the peasant class here unless they are farm labourers.

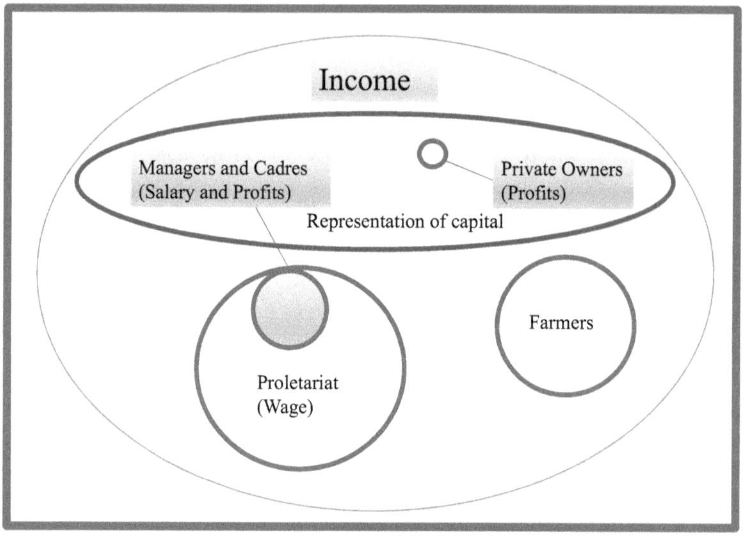

Fig. 6.6 Income concept map (*Data Source* The author's original work)

the recognition that workers and managers belong to different classes is a challenge to the party-state because as early as the completion of the socialist transformation in 1956, the state declared the non-existence of the bourgeoisie. Meanwhile, an important feature of the socialist state is that it is classless (free of class contradictions). Socialist fairness will not cause class opposition due to the large gap between the rich and the poor. It is true that in Maoist China there were equality and fairness, but not in post-economic reform China. As we can understand from the Gini-coefficient, which has risen from 0.15 before the Reforms and Opening Up to 0.468 in 2020, with the 10-year period from 2002 to 2012 exceeding the 0.4 threshold, indicating the income gap between

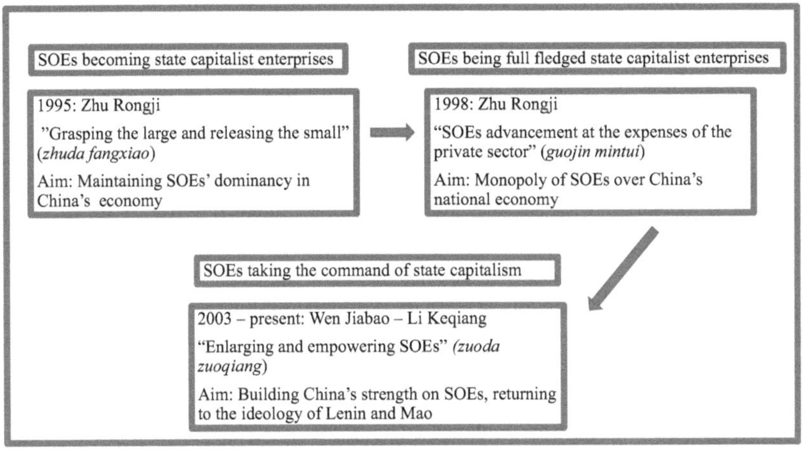

Fig. 6.7 Flow of SOE changes, 1995 to present day[14] (*Data Source* The author's original work)

[14] Premiers in PRC have been in charge of daily running of the economy, including economic reforms. Therefore, this study counts them directly responsible for changes to take place. Although Zhu Rongji (premiership: 1998–2003) was not the Premier of PRC in 1995, since his appointment as Vice-Premier in 1993, he had been in charge of China's economic policy-making. The other two Premiers' premierships: Wen Jiabao, 2003–2013; and Li Keqiang, 2013-present.

The idea *"fangxiao"* was proposed in 1993 and "*zhuda fangxiao*" was published in a central document in 1995. See Decision of the Central Committee of the CCP on Several Issues Concerning the Establishment of a Socialist Market Economy System (*Zhonggong Zhongyang guanyu jianshe shehui zhuyi shichang jingji ruogan wenti de jueding*) and Proposal of the Central Committee of the CCP on the Formulation of the Ninth Five-Year Plan for National Economic and Social Development and the Visionary Goals for 2010 (*Zhonggong Zhongyang guanyu zhiding guomin jingji he shehui fazhan "jiuwu" jihua he 2010 nian yuanjin mubiao de jianyi*). Available on 12th Sep, 2022, *vide*: http://www.people.com.cn/item/20years/newfiles/b1080.html and http://www.gov.cn/test/2008-04/21/content_950407.htm.

The ideas of *"guojin mintui"* and *"zuoda zuoqiang"*, see Wu Xianyun's (2018, p. 302) *History of China's Financial Industry* and government work reports by Wen Jiabao and Li Keqiang. Available on 12th Sep, 2022, *vide*: http://www.gov.cn/wszb/zhibo20070315/content_541977.htm; http://www.nhc.gov.cn/cms-search/xxgk/getManuscriptXxgk.htm?id=34939d870550475485425ebcbc640893 and http://www.xinhuanet.com/politics/2016-07/04/c_1119162333.htm.

the rich and the poor in China is widening.[15] The coefficient explains class differentiation rather than stratification.

In conclusion, Marxist theory clearly explains the problems that occurred in China during the social transformation period, especially the class problem. Returning to the Marxist class theory, the means of production are no longer owned by the whole people is a violation of the concept of socialism and communism. If the class had been eliminated after PRC established, workers should not be the upper strata of the class structure, nor should they be the masters of the society. At least, they should be the same as the peasants instead of having the peasants support the workers. It is still meaningful to discuss social structure and class in 2010s China, even though they no longer need to exploit agriculture to support the development of industry and industry can even support agriculture and accelerate the development of the tertiary industry. Workers are wage labourers in the capital market. Their means of production are held on behalf of cadres, party and the state. Is there any difference between this holding relationship and the capitalists' possession in a capitalist society? Is it possible that changes in labour-management relations will change the nature of China's society and China will begin to adopt a form of capitalism instead of Chinese characteristic socialism? These points are worth discussing.

6.4 State Capitalism and the Working Class

At the beginning of this chapter, I mentioned my logical inference (Fig. 6.1, p. 199), the reconstruction of the class society justifies capitalist relations of production (the existence of deprivation and exploitation), which further allows for the deduction that Chinese society is currently in the stage of state capitalism. On the argument of whether or not to recognise China as state capitalist, Chinese and Western views differ significantly.

[15] See National Bureau. (2021). Q&A at the press conference of the White Paper "China's Comprehensive Well-being (*Zhongguo de quanmian xiaokang baipi shu xinwen fabuhui da jizhe wen*). September 29th, 2021. Available on 12th Sep, 2022, *vide*: http://www.stats.gov.cn/tjsj/zxfb/202109/t20210929_1822623.html; also see Word Bank, Gini coefficient- China. Available on 12th Sep, 2022, *vide*: https://data.worldbank.org.cn/indicator/SI.POV.GINI?locations=CN.

Western scholars, for example, sociologist Manuel Castells's (1998, pp. 287–307) analysis of post-economic reform China, argued that although China remains a strong state-led state, it has been incorporated into the global capitalist system. Instead of viewing Chinese economic development as a new model with "Chinese characteristics", Yasheng Huang (2008) suggested that the Chinese model of development can find its parallels in Brazil in the 1960s–1970s. According to Huang, it is not a new economic development model, but rather a reinterpretation of an established state capitalist development model in a different country and at a different time. In addition to the two scholars mentioned above, many researchers have defined China's economic model as that of state capitalism when studying China's post-reform society (Kwok-bun Chan et al., 2008; Redding & Witt, 2007; Ten Brink, 2019; Wai-chung Yeung, 2004; Xiaoshuo Hou, 2013). They focus on explaining China's economic model in terms of path of business development, the links to globalisation or the characteristics of the capitalism established in China from the perspective of the urban–rural dichotomy. Although their research shows how the capitalism established in China links firms and the party-led state institutions, they did not analyse the formation of Chinese state capitalism from understanding the working class. Therefore, they did not pay attention to the important changes that the reconstruction of the working class and a class society in China due to a path of economic development had been applied.

In terms of the discourse of the Chinese official mainstream media, *Qiushi Wang*, the government has given a strong political logic to explain the difference between China's socialist market economy and state capitalism.[16] Certainly, under this discourse, the fruits of economic development are attributed to the superiority of the socialist system rather than capitalism, and state capitalism is a misinterpretation of Chinese model and even a target for attacks on the Chinese socialist system.

However, a theoretical analysis of the concept of state capitalism shows that state capitalism is an important intermediate form of transition from capitalism to socialism, as it is more visible in times of economic decline,

[16] *Qiushi* Wang, 2018, *Getting to the bottom of the problem of "state capitalism"* (*renqing guojia ziben zhuyi wenti de zhenxiang*). Available on 12th Sep, 2022, *vide*: http://www.qstheory.cn/dukan/qs/2018-09/01/c_1123362691.htm.

and as "one of the main features of social life during the decline of capitalism.[17] "However, my recognition that China is in a state capitalist society is not an economic or social regression, but theoretically, more logical to describe the class relations (relations of production) in China in the 2010s. State capitalism is a concept introduced by Lenin ([1918] 1995) to describe the characteristics of the stage of capitalist development. It is a form of capitalist economy combined with state power, controlled and dominated by the state and represents the control of state power over enterprises and the supervision and regulation of capitalist economic development by the state. Lenin ([1918] 1995) believed that state capitalism as a transition could facilitate the development of socialism. In capitalist countries, state capitalism recognises monopoly and serves the rule of the bourgeoisie. In countries under the dictatorship of the proletariat, the practice of state capitalism in socialist countries first appeared in the Soviet Union. The focus of the practice was on the creation of the inevitable capitalism of the socialist transition. It aimed to make a capitalism subservient to and for the proletarian state. Moreover, this new capitalism distinguishes from the state capitalism of the capitalist state that produces for the benefit of capitalists (Hu Leming et al., 2009, pp. 31–37).

However, it is clear both from the theoretical logic and from historical facts that with the recognition of state capitalism, there are inevitably a capitalist relation of production and a certain degree of exploitation; that is, the benefits will be appropriated by a minority of capitalists, whether this relation is a direct opposition between the proletariat and the bourgeoisie or between workers and state enterprises (which represents state capital). The existence of this exploitation has also been demonstrated in my analysis previously and can be told from the EGC's case. The question mark has been put on whether the workers' sacrifice as a contribution to the state and to the people is still. More directly, from the workers' protests, the direct beneficiaries of the surplus value created by the workers belong to the leaders of the enterprises. In such a circumstance, the question of whether the economy is still socialist in nature needs to be reconsidered.

[17] International Communist Current. 24th Nov, 2007. International Communist Current Declaration. Available on 12th Sep, 2022, *vide*: https://en.internationalism.org/.

State capitalism had emerged in countries that had followed a Soviet-style development path, and in the early stage of P. R. China establishment, unlike the current belief that state capitalism was a stigmatisation of the Chinese socialist system, the concept was acknowledged. Mao Zedong believed that state capitalism was the way for China to transform capitalist industry and commerce and gradually complete the transition to socialism. Same definition as Lenin had defined, this form of capitalism is:

> [An] overwhelmingly capitalist economy under the administration of the people's government, linked in various ways to the state-run socialist economy, and supervised by the workers. This capitalist economy is no longer an ordinary capitalist economy, but a special kind of capitalist economy, i.e., a new kind of state capitalist economy. It does not exist primarily for the profit of the capitalists, but to supply the needs of the people and the state. Yes, workers also produce a part of the profits for the capitalists, but this is only a small part of the total profits, only about a quarter or so, the remaining three quarters are produced for the workers (welfare payments) [,] for the state (income tax) and for the expansion of the production facilities (which contain a small part of the profits produced for the capitalists). This new type of state capitalist economy is heavily socialist in nature and is beneficial to workers and the state. (Mao Zedong, [1953] 1977)[18]

Once the socialist transformation was completed, the basic socialist system with public ownership as the mainstay was established. Once transferred into socialist society, state capitalism as a transitional form of economy would disappear (*Qiushi* Wang, 2018).

[18] Mao Zedong, 9th July 1953. The original Chinese text: *zhongguo xianzai de ziben zhuyi jingji qi jueda bufen shi zai renmin zhengfu guanli zhixia de, yong gezhong xingshi he guoyin shehui zhuyi lianxi zhe de, bing shou gongren jiandu de ziben zhuyi jingji. zhezhong ziben zhuyi jingji yijin bushi putong de ziben zhuyi jingji, er shi yizhong teshu de ziben zhuyi jingji, ji xinshi de guojia ziben zhuyi jingji. ta zhuyao di bushi weile zibenjia de lirun er cunzai, er shi weile gongying renmin he guojia de xuyao er cunzai. bucuo, gongrenmen haiyao wei zibenjia shengchan yibufen lirun, dan zhe zhizhan quanbu lirun zhong de yi xiaobufen, dayue zhizhan sifenzhiyi zuoyou, qiyu de sifenzhisan shi wei gongren (fuli fei) wei guojia (suode shui) ji wei kuoda shengchan shebei (qizhong baohan yixiaobufen shi wei zibenjia shengchan lirun de) er shengchan de. Yinci, zhezhong xinshi guojia ziben zhyi jingji shi daizhe henda de shehui zhuyi xingzhi de, shi dui gongren he guojia youli de*). Available on 12th Sep, 2022, *vide*: https://www.marxists.org/chinese/maozedong/marxist.org-chinese-mao-19530709.htm.

As the socialist transformation of the ownership of the means of production was completed in 1956, China established the public ownership (or the ownership by the whole people, *quanmin suoyou zhi*). Moreover, the Chinese economy was redefined as a "socialist market economy" in 1993. If these arguments hold true, then state capitalism should have ceased to exist. Alternatively, this new type of state capitalism with a socialist nature that still exists is supposed to be good for workers, or at least not detrimental to their interests. However, in my study of workers after SOE reforms, workers do not "own" the enterprise but are instead owned by the SOE. Furthermore, the enterprise has the power to decide whether the workers can continue to be "owned" or not. It is therefore questionable whether it can be claimed that the transition from capitalism to socialism has been completed in China and that state capitalism, the economic form of the transitional phase, has disappeared.

In the afore-mentioned report by China Labour Bulletin (2007, p. 41), SOE reforms have experienced three steps. Undoubtedly, all the time, SOEs have been open to the market economy. But the ownership of SOEs has been steadily and surely moving towards state capitalism. The following chart highlights the changes in the SOE sector for the latter. However, keeping SOEs increasingly open to the market has created a common illusion that Deng Xiaoping's reforms continue in the SOE sector. In reality, in terms of ownership of the SOE sector, we see an increasing tendency towards one destiny which is state capitalism. In other words, SOEs are open but increasingly more and more capitalistic (Fig. 6.7).

This can be confirmed by data: It is known that China's state-owned industry's fixed capital can be accounted for 600 billion Yuan in 1985. Two decades later (2007), the amount became 10 trillion Yuan and then 30 trillion Yuan in 2016.[19] The total increase of the amount invested was 50-fold. The annual gross growth is thus 114%![20] China's inflation rate

[19] Wang Shaoguang. (2019). 70 Years of PRC: Industrialisation and SOEs (*Xin zhongguo 70 nian: gongyehua yu guoqi*). Nov 19th, 2019. Available on 12th Sep, 2022, *vide*: https://www.jingjidaokan.com/icms/null/null/ns:LHQ6LGY6LGM6MmM5Y2QyOTA2ZTcxZmM5YzAxNmU4MjZkOWFlYjAxODgscDosYTosbTo=/show.vsml.

[20] This is with inflation.

from 1985 to 2016 averaged annually 5.7%,[21] which converts to 108.3% annual net growth.[22] There will be little doubt that the SOE sector has experienced exponential growth.

The research of workers reflects the fact that the class contradictions and class relations produced by the existing relations of production are social class contradiction and class relations under a form of capitalism. In other words, that state capitalism still exists as an economic form in a transitional phase and that this existence is an exploitation of workers. When this exploitation has spread to privileged enterprises like SOEs, it means that this exploitation can be inferred in a broader sense. SOEs such as my case, EGC, reflect the control, intervention and even monopoly of the state as the representative of capital in the market in "key", "pillar" and "basic" industries. However, through workers' resistance, my case study well illustrates that even in these industries, workers are not producing for themselves or for the state, but for the capitalists.

So, the so-called new form of state capitalism, whether conceptualised as socialist by Lenin or Mao, is still in its essence the exploitation of the workers as a result of the most naked capitalist relations of production. Moreover, looking at SOE reforms under Xi Jinping's leadership, I see from reviewing the history of the EGC that the enterprise was supported by new investments, such as new projects in nuclear power and aviation, which were related to national security. However, none of the SOE reforms during the 2010s was a fundamental reform of the system, but more like an optimisation of the SOEs that had already been restructured; that is, there was no fundamental change in the relations of production or a major change in the form of the economy. The increased investments in SOEs appear to be a restrengthening or re-emergence of SOEs, but even with such key state investments, workers are still not free from being controlled by capital.

Clearly, the acknowledgement of the exploitation of workers, the identification of the concepts of class and stratum, and the argument for the existence of a form of state capitalism in China are all parts of a clear clarification that the current Chinese social structure is a class society, which

[21] See 1980–2016 China's Annual Inflation Data (*zhongguo linian tonghua pengzhanglv shuju* (1980–2016)). *Hao Jingui Finance*. July 7th, 2016. Available on 12th Sep, 2022, *vide*: http://www.haojingui.com/tonghuopengzhang/1395.html 1985–2016.

[22] Annual Net Growth Rate = Annual Gross Growth Rate - Annual Inflation Rate.

can be well recognised from the reconstruction of the working class as an entry point.

References

Andreas, J. (2019). *Disenfranchised: The Rise and Fall of Industrial Citizenship in China*. Oxford University Press.

Bourdieu, P. (1977). *Outline of a Theory of Practice*. Cambridge University Press.

———. ([1979]1984). *Distinction: A Social Critique of the Judgment of Taste* (*La Distinction: Critique Sociale du Jugement* [1979]). Translated by Nice, R. Harvard University Press.

Castells, M. (1998). *End of Millennium*. Blackwell.

Chan, K., Cheung, T., & Ku, A. (2008). *Chinese Capitalisms*. Brill.

Central Committee of CCP. (1998). *Zhonggong Zhongyang Guanyu Zhiding Guomin Jingji He Shehui Fazhan "Jiuwu" Jihua He 2010 Nian Yuanjin Mubiao De Jianyi* [Proposal on the Formulation of the Ninth Five-Year Plan for National Economic and Social Development and the Visionary Goals for 2010]. Available on 12th September, 2022, *vide*: http://www.gov.cn/test/2008-04/21/content_950407.htm.

China Labour Bulletin. (2007). Reform of SOEs in China. Available on 12th September, 2022, *vide*: https://clb.org.hk/content/reform-state-owned-enterprises-china.

China Merchants Bank. (2019). *Zhaoshang Yinghang Gufen Youxian Gongsi 2018 Niandu Baogao Quanwen* [Annual Report of China Merchants Bank Co., LTD, 2018]. 22nd March 2019, available on 12th September, 2022, *vide*: https://file.cmbimg.com/cmbir/201903/fec83752-d517-4236-a04f-03b97a4cbf15.pdf

Djilas, M. ([1957]1983). *The New Class: An Analysis of the Communist System*. Mariner Books.

Foucault, M. (1999). *Guixun Yu Chengfa* [Discipline and Punish: The Birth of the Prison]. Translated by Liu, B.C. and Yang, Y.Y. Sanlian Books.

Giddens, A. (1973). *The Class Structure of the Advanced Societies*. Hutchinson.

Goodman, D. S. (2014). *Class in Contemporary China*. John Wiley and Sons.

Hao Jinggui Finance. (2016). *Zhongguo Linian Tonghua Pengzhanglv Shuju* (1980–2016) [China's Annual Inflation Data, 1980–2016]. July 7th, 2016. Available on 12th September, 2022, *vide*: http://www.haojingui.com/tonghuopengzhang/1395.html 1985–2016

Hou, X. (2013). *Community Capitalism in China: The State, the Market, and Collectivism*. Cambridge University Press.

Hu, L., Liu, Z., & Zhang, J. (2009). State-capitalism and Chinese mode. *Economy Research, 11*, 31–37.

Huang, Y. S. (2008). *Capitalism with Chinese Characteristics: Entrepreneurship and the State*. Cambridge University Press.

International Communist Current. (2007). International Communist Current Declaration. 24th November, 2007. Available on 12th September, 2022, *vide*: https://en.internationalism.org/.

Kipnis, A. (2006). *Suzhi:* A Keyword Approach. *China Quarterly, 186*, 295–313.

Lenin, V. ([1918]1995). *Lun "Zuopai" Youzhixing He Xiao Zichan Jiejixing* [On the Infantilism and the Petty Bourgeoisie of the "Left"], in *Lenin Xuanji* [*Selected Collections of Lenin*]. Renmin Press.

Li, X. X., Liu, Y. M., & Song, T. (2014). Calculation of the Green Development Index. *Social Science China*, 6, 69–95, and 207–208.

Li, K. Q. (2021). *Li Keqiang Zongli Zuo Zhengfu Gongzuo Baogao* [Premier Li Keqiang's Government Annual Report]. March 10th, 2021. Available on 12th September, 2022, *vide*: http://www.nhc.gov.cn/cms-search/xxgk/getManuscriptXxgk.htm?id=34939d870550475485425ebcbc640893.

Li, Q. (2005). "*Dingzi Xing*" *Shehui Jiegou Yu Jiegou Jinzhang* ["T-shaped" Social Structure and Structural Tension]. *Shehuixue Yanjiu* [*Sociological Research*], *2*, 55–73.

Li, W. (2004). A Comparative Study on Class Consciousness in Societies Between China and South Korea. *Sociology Research, 5*, 80–95.

Li, Z. T. (2016). *Study on Mixed Ownership Economy*. Shanghai Social Science Academy Press.

Liu, X. (2002). Relative Deprivation Status and Class Perceptions. *Sociology Research, 1*, 81–90.

Lu, X. Y. (2002). *Dangdai Zhongguo Shehui Jieceng Yanjiu Baogao* [Contemporary China's Social Class: A Research Report]. Social Science Literature Press.

———. (2003). *Dangdai Zhongguo Shehui Jieceng De Fenhua Yu Liudong* [The Division and Mobility of Social Classes in Contemporary China]. *Jiangsu Shehui Kexue.*, *4*, 1–9.

———. (2006). *Zhongguo Shehui Jiegou De Bianhua Ji Fazhan Qushi* [The Changes and Developmental Trend of China's Social Structure]. *Journal of Yunnan University for Nationalities, Philosophy and Social Sciences Edition, 23*(5), 28–35.

Mann, M. (1973). *Consciousness and Action Among the Western Working Class*. Macmillan.

Mao, Z. D. ([1953]1977). *Guanyu Guojia Ziben Zhuyi* [State capitalism]. 9th July, 1953. Available on 12th September, 2022, *vide*: https://www.marxists.org/chinese/maozedong/marxist.org-chinese-mao-19530709.htm.

Marx, K. ([1844]1932) *1844 Economic and Philosophic Manuscripts*. Available on 12th September, 2022, *vide*: https://www.marxists.org/chinese/marx/marxist.org-chinese-marx-1844.htm. Also Available on 12th September, 2022, *vide* in *Marx Quanji* [*Collection of Works by Marx*]. Translated by Bureau for the Compilation and Translation of the Works of Marx and Engels, Lenin and Stalin, Central Committee of the CCP. People's Press. 2000 Edition.

———. ([1865]1898) *Gongzi, Lirun He Jiage* [Value, Price and Profit]. 25–78, in *Marx Engles Quanji* [*Collection of Works by Marx and Engels*], *Vol. 3 1864–1883*. Translated by Bureau for the Compilation and Translation of the Works of Marx and Engels, Lenin and Stalin, Central Committee of the CCP. People's Press.

Merton, R. K. ([1949]1968). *Social Theory and Social Structure*. Simon and Schuster.

National Bureau of Statistics. (2020). *Zhonghua Renmin Gongheguo 2019 Nian Guomin Jingji He Shehui Fazhan Tongji Gongbao* [PRC 2019 National Economic and Social Development Statistical Bulletin]. February 28th, 2020. Available on 12th September, 2022, *vide*: http://www.stats.gov.cn/tjsj/zxfb/202002/t20200228_1728913.html.

———. (2021). *Zhongguo De Quanmian Xiaokang Baipi Shu Xinwen Fabuhui Da Jizhe Wen* [Q&A at the Press Conference of the White Paper "China's Comprehensive Well-being"]. Available on 12th September, 2022, *vide*: http://www.stats.gov.cn/tjsj/zxfb/202109/t20210929_1822623.html.

Olson, M. ([1982]2008). *The Rise and Decline of Nations*. New Haven: Yale University Press.

Ossowski, S. (1998). *Class Structure in the Social Consciousness*. Taylor & Francis.

Pan, N. (2007). *Dagong Zhe: Jieji De Guilai Huo Chongsheng* [The Wage Earner: The Return or Rebirth of the Class]. *Nanfeng Chuang* [*Southwind Window*], *9*, 35–37.

Pang, S. Q., & Qiu, L. P. (1989). *Woguo Shehui Xianjieduan Jieji Jieceng Jiegou Yanjiu Chutan* [A Preliminary Study of the Class Structure in Contemporary China]. *Shehuixue Yanjiu* [*Sociological Research*], *3*, 63–75.

Qian, C. D., Lei, H. J., & Wang, P. (2004). *Lunti: Yingguo "Gongren Guizu" Yu Gonghui Yndong De Lishi Kaocha* [Thesis: A Historical Examination of the British "Aristocratic Workers" and the Trade Union Movement]. *Lishi Jiaoxue Wenti* [*Issues in History Teaching*], *4*, 38–43.

Qiu, L. P. (2006). *Huidao Marx: Dui Zhongguo Shehui Fenceng Yanjiu De Fansi* [Back to Marx: Reflections on the Study of Chinese Social Stratification]. *Society*, *26*(4), 23–42.

Redding, S. G. & Witt, M. A. (2007). *The Future of Chinese Capitalism: Choices and Chances*. Oxford University Press.

Runciman, W. G. (1966). *Relative Deprivation and Social Justice: A Study of Attitudes to Social Inequality in Twentieth Century*. Routledge.

Sen, A. K. (1983). *Poverty and Famines: An Essay on Entitlement and Deprivation*. Beijing: Commercial Press, 2009 Edition, 38 and/or 2016 Edition,191–192, 202.

Shen, Y. (2006). *Shehui Zhuanxing Yu Gongren Jieji De Zaixingcheng* [Social Transformation and the Re-Formation of the Working Class]. *Sociological Research, 2*, 13–36.

Shi, H. W. (2007). *Reform and Innovation of China's Urban-Rural Dualistic Social Security System*. Jiangsu University.

State Council. (2006). *Guowuyuan Guanyu Yinfa Quanmin Kexue Suzhi Xingdong Jihua Gangyao (2006, 2010, 2020) Nian* [Notice of the State Council on Issuing the Outline of the National Scientific *Suzhi* Action Plan, 2006, 2010, 2020]. Available on 12th September, 2022, *vide*: http://www.gov.cn/zhengce/content/2008-03/28/content_5301.htm.

———. (2016). *Guowuyuan Bangongting Guanyu Yinfa Quanmin Kexue Suzhi Xingdong Jihua Gangyao Shishi Fangan (2016–2020 Nian)* [Notice of the General Office of the State Council on Issuing the Implementation Plan of the National Scientific *Suzhi* Action Plan, 2016–2020]. Available on 12th September, 2022, *vide*: http://www.gov.cn/zhengce/content/2016-03/14/content_5053247.htm.

———. (2021). *Guowuyuan Guanyu Yinfa Quanmin Kexue Suzhi Xingdong Guihua Gangyao (2021–2035 Nian)* [Notice of the State Council on Issuing the Outline of the National Scientific *Suzhi* Action Plan, 2021–2035]. Available on 12th September, 2022, *vide*: http://www.gov.cn/zhengce/content/2021-06/25/content_5620813.htm.

Ten Brink, T. (2019). *China's Capitalism*. University of Pennsylvania Press.

Qiushi Wang. (2018). *Renqing Guojia Ziben Zhuyi Wenti De Zhenxiang* [Getting to the Bottom of the Problem of "State Capitalism"]. Available on 12th September, 2022, *vide*: http://www.qstheory.cn/dukan/qs/2018-09/01/c_1123362691.htm.

Wang, S. G. (2019). *Xin Zhongguo 70 Nian: Gongyehua Yu Guoqi* [70 Years of PRC: Industrialisation and SOEs]. November 19th, 2019, Economic Herald. Available on 12th September, 2022, *vide*: https://www.jingjidaokan.com/icms/null/null/ns:LHQ6LGY6LGM6MmM5Y2QyOTA2ZTcxZmM5YzAxNmU4MjZkOWFlYjAxODgscDosYTosbTo=/show.vsml

Wang, J. W. (1996). *"Zhua Geming Chu Shengchan" De Poxi* [An Analysis of "Grasping the Revolution, Promoting Production"]. *Beijing Dangshi* [*Beijing Party History*], *4*, 11–16.

Wang, L. X. (1989). *Qiantan Dier Guoji Pochan De Shehui Jingji Genyuan* [Socio-Economic Roots of the Bankruptcy of the Second International]. *Shijie Lishi* [*World History*], *4*, 151–152.

Wang, X. Q., & Hu, D. (2016). *"Zhua Geming Chu Shengchan" Mingti De Laolong Qumai Kao-Yi Renmin Ribao De Xiangguan Baodao Wei Yiju*

["Grasping the Revolution, Promoting Production": A Study of The Origin and Context of The Proposition—Based on a Report in *The People's Daily*]. *Dangshi Yanjiu Yu Jiaoxue* [*Party History Research and Teaching*], *3*, 74–80.

Weber, M. ([1922]1978). *Economy and Society: An Outline of Interpretive Sociology (Vol. 1)*. University of California Press.

Wen, J.B. (2007). *Wen Jiabao Qiangdiao: Shenhua Guoqi Gaige Tuijin Longduan Hangye Gaige* [Deepening the Reform of State-Owned Enterprises Promoting The Reform of Monopolistic Industries]. March 5th, 2007. Available on 12th September, 2022, *vide*: http://www.gov.cn/wszb/zhibo20070315/content_541977.htm.

Wright, E. O. (1985). *Classes*. Verso.

———. (Ed.). (1997). *Rethinking, Once Again, The Concept of Class Structure*. Cornell University Press.

Wu, M. S. (1982). *Jindai Yingguo Gongren Guizu De Xingcheng Jiqi Weihai* [The Formation of the Workers' Aristocracy and its Dangers in Modern Britain]. *Lishi Jiaoxue* [*Teaching History*], *4*, 30–34.

———. (1988). *Shijiu Shiji Yingguo De Gongren Guizu (Zhaiyi)* [The Workers' Aristocracy in Nineteenth Century England]. *Dangdai Shijie Yu Shehui Zhuyi* [*Contemporary World and Socialism*], *2*, 236–253.

Wu, M. X., & Sun, C. J. (1994). *Lun Mao Zedong Wannian De "Zhua Geming Chu Shengchan" Sixiang* [On Mao Zedong's Idea of "Grasping Revolution and Promoting Production" in His Later Years]. *Mao Zedong Sixiang Yanjiu* [*Mao Zedong Thought Studies*], *4*, 121–124.

Wu, X. Y. (2018). *History of China's Financial Industry*. Social Science Literature Press.

Yang, Y. H., Hu, A. G., & Zhang, N. (2005). An Alternative to Human Development Index with Principal Component Analysis. *Economic Research Journal, 40*(7), 4–17.

Yeung, H. W. (2004). *Chinese Capitalism in a Global Era: Towards a Hybrid Capitalism*. Routledge.

Yuan, Y. C. (2015). *Jijie Huayu De Bianqian 1950–2010 Yi Renmin Ribao Wei Li* [Changes in Class Discourse: 1950–2010 in *The People's Daily* as An Example]. *Tianfu Xinlun* [*Tianfu* New Theory], *6*, 99–106.

Zhang, M., & Liu, H. Q. (2006). The Social Marginalization of Workers in China's State-Owned Enterprises. *Social Research: An International Quarterly, 73*(1), 159–184.

Zheng, H. S. (2002). *Woguo shehui jieceng jiegou xin bianhua de jige wenti* [Several Issues on The New Changes in The Social Class Structure in China]. *Journal of Central China Normal University: Humanities and Social Sciences Edition, 41*(4), 5–9.

Zheng, Q. (2011). From "Grasp Revolution and Promote Production" To "Grasp Reform and Promote Development." *Zhonggong Dangshi Yanjiu* [Chinese Communist Party Study], *12*, 34–47.

Zhong, D. J. (2002). *Guomin Daiyu Bu Pingdeng Shenshi: Eryuan Jiegou Xia De Zhongguo* [A Review of Inequality in National Treatment: China in A Dualistic Structure]. Workers' Press of China.

Zhou, X. G., Tuma, N., & Moen, P. (2002). *Guojia Shehuizhuyi Zhidu Xia De Shehui Jieceng Dongtai Fenxi: 1949–1993 Nian De Zhongguo Chengshi Zhuangkuang In Shichang Zhuanxing Yu Shehui Fenceng: Meiguo Shehuixuezhe Fenxi Zhongguo* [Dynamic Analysis of Social Classes under the National Socialist System: China's Urban Conditions from 1949 to 1993], in *Market Transition and Social Stratification: An American Sociologist's Analysis of China*. Sanlian Books.

CHAPTER 7

Final Conclusions

Using a sociological perspective on class, I flexibly applied social science research methods such as case study, oral history, interview, etc., to explore social change and class composition through the study of workers in a case study SOE. This research returns to Marx's classic theory to study Chinese society and the working class. The macro issues are explored through a micro methodology. This research has answered my research question and hypothesis and demonstrated that: (1.) The return of the working class to the proletariat and the reconstitution of the *class-for-itself*; and (2.) A redefinition of Chinese society as a society of classes. The decline of class in state discourse does not mean the disappearance of class; on the contrary, economic reforms have led to the replacement of socialist relations of production with capitalist relations of production in the pursuit of efficiency rather than fairness. The restructuring of the proletariat and the confrontations and contradictions between the opposing classes support this judgement of the recreation of a class society.

The economic reforms and reforms on SOEs as triggers for the return of workers to the proletariat proved the failure of SOEs—the constructed socialist enterprises. The reform of the socialist character of SOEs was a return to capitalist relations of production and the quest for competition

S. S. Huang, *The Political Economy of Reforms and the Remaking of the Proletarian Class in China, 1980s–2010s*, Palgrave Studies in Economic History, https://doi.org/10.1007/978-3-031-20455-5_7

and efficiency in the capitalist market, rather than a guarantee of socialist privileges for workers.

It is quite understandable that the management of the non-state sector is representatives of capital, working for it and owning it to varying degrees through the acquisition of shares, etc., so that these highly paid salariats join the ranks of the capitalists and manage those who sell their labour for the means of subsistence instead of capital; ideally, the managers of socialist SOEs should work for the state with the workers, but in reality, after the SOEs reforms, these managers are in no different from those in the non-state sector in terms of their essential economic attributes. As enterprises have transferred closer to the capitalisation and marketisation, managers in SOEs have been more clearly as management in enterprises rather than state cadres, responsible for efficiency, profit and market. Their focus and emphasis are not on socialist equity or on achieving full employment, but on managing the workers in the factories on behalf of state capital. It cannot be denied that under the rules of market economy, these SOEs' managers are personae of state capital.

In the reformed enterprises, SOE workers' privileges as aristocrats of the working class, the care and superior resources that SOEs provided and enjoyed by SOE workers have disappeared. The phenomenon that cadres and workers worked together and shared the same benefits in the same interest group has become history. Even the technicians (white-collar workers in the factories) no longer belonged to the working class. The composition of the so-called working class become purer. The representatives of capital and those who had the right to regulate the labour of the workers were divided from the working class and formed a counterpoint to it, squeezing the surplus labour value from the workers. Workers no longer produced for the people or for the state, but more directly for the managers and for the enterprises. I have discussed these in detailed in Chapter 3, where I presented an overview of my case of SOE and workers, and in Chapter 4, where I compared workers' economic status before and after the economic reforms, as well as with that of cadres and technicians.

Labour-capital relation in the post-reform SOEs was the relation in a capital market. There were no mechanisms to ensure that workers continued to enjoy socialist fairness and equality. Workers have a composite type of nostalgia for the status of working class in the past, especially in Mao's era, driving them to resist in order to fight for the rights that the working class is, or was, entitled to. However, workers' resistance is constrained in China. In such a situation, the reconstructed working class has a clear class consciousness, and it is in the "*class-for-itself*" level. They clarify who are their members and who are excluded, the benefits they want, how to maximise their rights and interests, and how to protest when fighting for entitlements. After, SOE workers' privileges were withdrawn and they were scarified in the pursuit of efficiency in the enterprises, they were more similar to other workers in the working class, and more similar in the rights to be pursued and the means taken to fight for them. I provided a detailed analysis of workers' resistance in Chapter 5.

Marx used the possession of the means of production as a criterion for judging proletarianism, and in his observation the proletariat was exploited in absolute terms; on this basis, this research summarised and deployed sociological theoretical concepts from theorists such as Weber, Bourdieu, Foucault, Olson and Sen, as well as an empirical approach, by exploring the individual at a micro level and discovering that, in addition to the exploitation of workers by the emerging capitalists (cadre managers and technicians in SOEs), workers also perceived relative deprivation including that experienced by historical comparison of their own situation, and the multiple exploitation of other workers by workers with more power and capital (different forms of capital) within the enterprise, transferring the exploitation of themselves by capital and capitalists, onto other workers through personal means. It is worth mentioning that the change in workers' identities brought about by economic reforms and social transition, and the changes in workers' responses to capital-labour relations and labour activism afterward, are similar features observed in other countries that were socialist or still maintain a socialist character, such as Russia and Vietnam (Pringle & Clarke, 2010).

In analysing macro propositions such as a class society and socio-economic formation, I used Marx's theory as a macro guide to explore and define Chinese society. I applied a variety of microscopic theoretical concepts and methodological tools of sociology to demonstrate that Marx's observations and reflections on "class" 200 years ago is still relevant in post-economic reform China. Details can be seen in Chapter 2. I took the working class as the starting point of my analysis and considered class distinctions and antagonisms, contradictions and conflicts, and class struggle as the focuses of my observations. The formation of the proletariat and the existence of capitalist relations of production are used to infer the reconstruction of a class society and the existence of state capitalist economic form.

Orthodox Marxism sees capitalism as a prerequisite, or a necessary stage, for the development of socialism and communism, while one of the completions, or features, of the establishment of socialism is the creation of a classless society. This socialist society, constructed after the establishment of PRC, rapidly skipped the necessary stage of capitalist society. The socialist transformation of ownership did not complete the transition from (state capitalism) capitalism to socialism. It can even be inferred from Deng Xiaoping's reform of the Chinese economy that the construction of a socialist society did not succeed. The capitalist character of the labour-capital relation, the nature of the relation of production, and the reconstruction of a class society all testify to the fact that the state capitalism economic form still exists in China. The economic form of capitalism is the cause of the profound changes in socio-economic development and class structure that have been verified in many Western countries, as well as in countries that have took Soviet-style industrial development pathway, and China is no exception. Meanwhile, as I mentioned in Chapter 6, the socialist transformation in China is not an isolated or creative event. This transition to capital has already taken place in Eastern European societies (Dunn, 2004). This form of capitalism is not socialist in nature but is indistinguishable from the state capitalism that exists in other capitalist countries. The state discourse of socialism with Chinese characteristics, or a market economy with Chinese characteristics, can be understood in a simplified way. In a society, where socialist relations of production have not been developed, social progress can theoretically be classified as progress in the development of state capitalism, rather than to the superiority of the not-yet-established socialist, communist system. My discussion of social formation, from micro level—my case—to a macro level—the society, was presented throughout this book.

In addition, in my discussions of class structure, I disentangled the existing conflation of "class" (*jieji*) and "stratum" (*jieceng*) that has led to a blurring of the understanding of class formation and the reconstruction of a class society. The use of strata or stratification to describe the social structure of China is rejected. Social stratification reflects the diversity of occupational in the post-economic reform society but does not reflect well in the existence of class contradictions in the formed a class society.

Lastly, I want to make speculations about the future. Under the form of state capitalism and the existence of capitalist relations of production, workers will have more explicit protests against the opposing classes in the future. Having shattered the illusion that the socialist state gave workers "the master of the nation" status, workers have a deeper understanding of the labour-capital relations. Chinese workers' demands on the capitalists will increasingly be identified with those of Western workers. Economic reforms or SOE reforms in the post-economic reform China are no longer about changing the system but about optimising it. The transition from state capitalism to socialism will only be possible if the relations of production are transformed. This kind of transformation implies the disappearance of exploitation. In other words, such a transformation is only possible if competition and efficiency in capitalism are met while giving fairness and equality in socialism. I hope that there will be more case studies in the future to prove my observations about Chinese society.

References

Dunn, E. C. (2004). *Privatizing Poland: Baby food, big business, and the remaking of labor*. Cornell University Press.

Pringle, T., & Clarke, S. (2010). *The challenge of transition: Trade unions in Russia, China and Vietnam*. Springer.

Appendix A: The Summary of the Basic Information of Interviewees

See Table A.1.

S. S. Huang, *The Political Economy of Reforms and the Remaking of the Proletarian Class in China, 1980s–2010s*, Palgrave Studies in Economic History, https://doi.org/10.1007/978-3-031-20455-5

Table A.1 The Summary of The Basic Information of Interviewees

Interviewees	*Changes in job occupation*	*Education level*	*Gender*	*Origin from the SOE city*	*Previous working experience*	*Professional occupation*	*Requirements for entering the SOE*	*Self-identity*	*The influence on person of SOE reform*	*The way entered the unit*	*Unit*	*When entered*	*When left*	*Age*
001	N	High School	F	Y	NA	Crane operator	No requirement	Worker	N	Replace parents' SOE identity	Casting	1979	2011	57
002	N	University (Undergraduate)	M	N	NA	Field technique support	Interview	Technican	N	Family relation + employment fair	Subcompany-W	2014	NA	28
003	Y	MBA on the job	F	N	NA	Production planning management	Interview	Employee	N	Uni fair	Heavy machine	2007	NA	32
004	Y	University (Undergraduate)	M	Y	Toy company designer	Purchasing agent	Certificate on machinary	General management cadre	Y	Labor agency	Subcompany-W	2012	NA	31
005	Y	Professional education	M	N	Accountant at another state sector	Accountant	Assigned	Accountant and pioneer	Unassigned	Allocated by supervise unit	Fiance section	1958	1980	89
006	N	University (Undergraduate)	M	N	NA	Engineer	Interview	Technican	Y	Uni fair	Subcompany-W	2007	NA	33

Interviewees	*Changes in job occupation*	*Education level*	*Gender*	*Origin from the SOE city*	*Previous working experience*	*Professional occupation*	*Requirements for entering the SOE*	*Self-identity*	*The influence on person of SOE reform*	*The way entered the unit*	*Unit*	*When entered*	*When left*	*Age*
007	Y	Further education – retired school	F	N	Community officer	Worker	No requirement	Worker	Unassigned	As employee's partner	Military factory	1958	1979	85
008	Y	Further education – night school	F	Y	NA	Analyst	Pass the school graduate examination	Worker	N	Technical school allocation	Electric furnace factory	1981	2009	54
009	Y	Professional education	F	Y	NA	Support staff	Pass the school entrance examination	Worker	N	Natural Attrition (ziran jianyuan)	Forge factory	1986	2014	50
010	Y	MBA on the job	M	Y	NA	Secretary	Pass the school graduate examination	Cadre	N	Technical school allocation	Subcompany-W	1988	NA	50
011	Y	Professional education	M	N	NA	Technican	Interview	Unassigned	N	Uni fair	Second mental work factory	2008	NA	31
012	Y	University (Undergraduate)	M	N	Foreign capital industry	Engineer and secretary of CCP	Interview	Worker	N	Family relation	Petrochemical company	2012	NA	29
013	N	Professional education	M	Y	Pharmaceutical sales	Turner	Certificate on machinary	All are SOE worker	Y	Labor agency	Subcompany-W	2008	NA	36

(continued)

Table A.1 (continued)

Interviewees	*Changes in job occupation*	*Education level*	*Gender*	*Origin from the SOE city*	*Previous working experience*	*Professional occupation*	*Requirements for entering the SOE*	*Self-identity*	*The influence on person of SOE reform*	*The way entered the unit*	*Unit*	*When entered*	*When left*	*Age*
014	Y	Professional education	M	N	NA	Purchasing agent	CV review	Cadre	N	Uni fair	Subcompany-W	2012	NA	30
015	Y	University (Undergraduate)	M	Y	NA	Technic manager	CV review	Unassigned	N	Family relation + Employment fair	Subcompany-H (Avigation)	2013	NA	27
016	N	University (Undergraduate)	M	N	NA	Technican	CV review	Unassigned	N	Uni fair	Subcompany-W (cold working)	2005	NA	34
017	Y	Unassigned	M	Y	Another SOE industry worker	Benchwork	NA	The qualified working class	The influence is negative	Swap from another SOE	Casting	1983	2015	55
018	Y	Professional education	F	N	NA	Electrican	Interview	All are SOE worker	N	Uni fair	Subcompany-W (cold working)	2008	NA	31
019	Y	University (Undergraduate)	M	N	NA	Technic manager	Interview	Unassigned	Y	FAmily relation + Employment fair	Subcompany-W (cold working)	2012	NA	30
020	Y	University (Undergraduate)	M	Y	NA	Secretary	NA	Emprise manager	Y	Allocated by Uni	General factory	1988	NA	51

Interviewees	*Changes in job occupation*	*Education level*	*Gender*	*Origin from the SOE city*	*Previous working experience*	*Professional occupation*	*Requirements for entering the SOE*	*Self-identity*	*The influence on person of SOE reform*	*The way entered the unit*	*Unit*	*When entered*	*When left*	*Age*
021	N	Professional education	F	Y	NA	Electrican	Pass the school graduate examination	Worker	Unassigned	Allocated by Uni	Casting	1994	NA	43
022	Y	Professional education	M	Y	Private company in GZ	Purchasing agent	Unassigned	Unassigned	The influency is negative	Labor agency	Subcompany-	2006	NA	36
023	N	University (Undergraduate)	M	N	NA	Graduate scheme	Interview	SOE employee	Y	Family influence + Employemnt fair	Electric power	2017	NA	23

Appendix B: List of Internal Documents (Chronological Order)[1]

1. 1958–1983 EGC History Book.
2. 1958–1983 EGC Statistics on Economy, Human Resources and International Communication.
3. 1958–2008 The Fifty Years History of EGC.
4. 1963–1990 EGC History of Military Industry.
5. 1984–1988 EGC History Book.
6. 1987 D City Statistical Yearbook.
7. 1989–1997 EGC Diagram of Organisation and Structure.
8. 1989–1997 EGC History Book.
9. 1989–1997 EGC Tables of the Professionals, the Average Pay, the Production Index, the labour Productivity and the Categories of Workers.
10. National Development and Reform Commission's Documents on EGC in 1994.
11. National Development and Reform Commission's Documents on EGC in 1997.
12. 1997 D City Statistical Yearbook.
13. 1998 D City Statistical Yearbook.

[1] For the sake of anonymous purpose, all the website links in this part will not be released in the publication.

S. S. Huang, *The Political Economy of Reforms and the Remaking of the Proletarian Class in China, 1980s–2010s*, Palgrave Studies in Economic History, https://doi.org/10.1007/978-3-031-20455-5

14. 1998–2001 EGC History Book.
15. 2003 D City Statistical Yearbook.
16. EGC Yearbook 2003.
17. 2004 D City Statistical Yearbook.
18. Diagram of EGC Organisation Structure in 2004.
19. EGC Yearbook 2004.
20. 2005 D City Statistical Yearbook.
21. EGC Yearbook 2005.
22. *ST EGC Asset Operation Efficiency Index 2005–2012.
23. Diagram of EGC Organisation Structure in 2005.
24. Table of EGC with other Major heavy equipment listed companies' profitability comparison 2005–2012.
25. Table of EGC with other Major heavy equipment listed companies' fixed assets comparison 2005–2012.
26. 2006 D City Statistical Yearbook.
27. EGC Yearbook 2006.
28. Diagram of EGC Organisation Structure in 2006.
29. *ST EGC Business Structure 2006–2012.
30. 2007 D City Statistical Yearbook.
31. EGC Yearbook 2007.
32. 2008 D City Statistical Yearbook.
33. Diagram of EGC Organisation Structure in 2008.
34. 2009 D City Statistical Yearbook.
35. 2010 D City Statistical Yearbook.
36. 2011 D City Statistical Yearbook.
37. 2012 D City Statistical Yearbook.
38. 2013 D City Statistical Yearbook.
39. Diagram of EGC Organisation Structure in 2013.
40. EGC website, 2013.
41. New Youth- Youth Reviews (*Xin Qingnian- Qingnian Pinglun*). (2013). *Xiri Mingxing *ST EGC Jukui Shi Zenme Zaocheng de* (The large losses of EGC). June 19th, 2013. Jingwei Wang.
42. 2014 D City Statistical Yearbook.
43. EGC 2014 Annual Year Report.
44. New Youth- Youth Reviews (*Xin Qingnian- Qingnian Pinglun*). (2014). *EGC Gongren De Xinsheng (Ruogan Wangyou Tiezi Jihe)* (Voices of EGC Workers (A collection of posts by several netizens)). New Youth.

45. Li, C. (2014). *EGC Huocheng Dierge Changyou: EGC Guanliguang He Gongren Bizhong Dadao 1:1* (The ratio of management posts and workers reached 1:1). September 5th, 2014, Jingji Guancha Bao, quoted from Sina Finance.
46. China Central News Agency. (2014). *EGC Kongcheng Lu Shoujia Pochan Yangqi* (EGC may become the first bankrupt central government managed SOE in Mainland). November 19th, 2014.
47. 2015 D City Statistical Yearbook.
48. New Youth- Youth Reviews (*Xin Qingnian- Qingnian Pinglun).* (2015). *Guanyu EGC Gongren De Zonghe Baodao Xinxi Yiji Baogao* (Comprehensive report information and report on the workers of EGC). New Youth.
49. Xin Jingbao. (2015). **ST EGC Tuishi Yading Guming Qihu Nanxia* (EGC delisting in stock market). 2nd March, 2015.
50. Guo, Y. (2015). *Cong EGC Tuishi Kan Zhongji Hangye Zhe Jinian* (Look at the heavy industry in sight of EGC). March 25th, 2015. Zhongguo Gongye Xinwen Wang.
51. *EGC Jiechu Laodong Hetong Shishi Banfa Shenyi Gao* (EGC Termination of Labour Contracts Implementation Measures (Draft for comments). April 21st, 2015.
52. EGC Tieba. (2015). *Yige EGC Zhigong Jiu 4 Yue 21 Ri Caiyuan Gei D Shiwei Shuji De Gongkaixin* (An open letter from a EGC employee to the Secretary of the D City Municipal Party Committee regarding the layoffs on April 21st). April 27th 2015, quoted from Boxun News.
53. Sichuan D City Stockholders. (2015). *Yige EGC Zhigong Dui EGC Jituan 4 Yue 21 Ri Caiyuan De Kangyi* (A worker's protest against the decruitment of EGC on April 21st). April 27th, 2015, Dongfang Caifu Wang.
54. Boxun News. (2015). *Sichuan D City Yangqi Qiangzhi Caiyuan Ying Shuqian Gongren Bagong Youxing* (Central government managed SOE compulsory redundancies lead thousands of workers on strike to protest in D City, Sichuan). May 11th, 2015.
55. Boxun News. (2015). *D City Yangqi EGC Jijiang Daobi: Shuqianren Kangyi Weiquan Weiquan (40 Tu)* (Thousands of people protest due to Central government managed SOE- EGC in D city- closes to closure (40 Figure)). May 11th, 2015.
56. Jia, H.J. (2015). *EGC Jinqian Zhigong Zai Cangnei Youxing Kangyi Fuli Xuejian* (Nearly 1000 employees of EGC marched

in the factory to protest against welfare cuts). May 13th, 2015, Caixinwang, quoted from China Agriculture News.
57. *EGC Jiechu Laodong Hetong Shishi Banfa Cao'An* (EGC Measures for The Termination of Labour Contracts Draft). June 24th, 2015.
58. *EGC Zhigong Ligang Xiuyang Shishi Banfa Cao'An* (EGC Worker Absences Cultivation Measures for Its Implementation Draft). June 24th, 2015.
59. *EGC Jiechu Laodong Hetong Shishi Banfa* (EGC Measures for The Termination of Labour Contracts). June 30th, 2015.
60. *EGC Zhigong Ligang Xiuyang Shishi Banfa* (EGC Worker Absences Cultivation Measures for Its Implementation). June 30th, 2015.
61. He, G.W. (2015). *EGC Ni Caiyuan Zao Zhigong Kangyi* (EGC workers' protests). May 16th, 2015. Caijing Wang.
62. Boxun News. (2015). *Jiti Tanpan Zai Guoqi De Changshi—Sichuan D City Gongren Jiti Weiquan Jishi Jiqi Fenxi* (An Attempt of Collective Bargaining in SOEs: Records and Analysis of Workers' Collective Rights Protection in D City, Sichuan). July 14th 2015.
63. 2016 D City Statistical Yearbook.
64. 2016 EGC's Recruitment Information.
65. 2017 D City Statistical Yearbook.
66. Sina Finance. (2017). *EGC Chongzu Wu Yili Zhigong Shangfang Susong Shijian* (Official report to summary EGC's status after the 2015 labour activism). 23rd Feb, 2017. Sina Finance.
67. 2018 D City Statistical Yearbook.
68. Data from D City's Bureau of Human Resources and Social Security and Bureau of Finance 2018.
69. SASAC 2018 Report on SINOMACH and EGC.
70. 2019 D City Statistical Yearbook.

Appendix C: Interview Question Guide

EGC Employees Interview Guide (Semi-Structured).

Interviewee Code:
Date of Interview:
Number of Interview with this Interviewee:

A. Basic information

1. Age
2. Gender
3. Original from which place
4. Job position
5. Education level
6. Length of service
7. Current employment situation

B. See Table C.1.

C. From educational perspective

1. The function of EGC's technique school.
2. The further education at EGC—night university and employee university.
3. How does the education degree and the technique certificates help in one's career?

S. S. Huang, *The Political Economy of Reforms and the Remaking of the Proletarian Class in China, 1980s–2010s*, Palgrave Studies in Economic History, https://doi.org/10.1007/978-3-031-20455-5

Table C.1 SOE characteristics in EGC

	People entered the EGC in pre-reform and early reform eras (before 1990s)	*People entered the EGC in late reform era (after 1990s)*
1. Why do you want to work for the EGC?		
2. The comparison of pay and welfares between state sector and non-state sector. (From personal experience)		
3. The criteria for the recruitment		
4. How to get a regular employment at the EGC?		
5. Does the family background and relationship determine your employment?		
6. Does the family background and relationship determine your career development?		
7. Is education act as an important factor when applying for a job at the EGC and for further development?		
8. Is political status an important factor when applying for a job at the EGC and for future development?		
9. Is personal capability an important factor in the EGC environment?		
10. What can the identity of SOE workers can bring you?		
11. The distinction and correlation between the main company and the sub-companies/ among different units		

D. From economic perspective

1. Pay and other business incomes
2. House property and loans
3. The living cost in D city, the commodity price with the comparison of salaries in different companies.
4. The family burdens

E. From social network (relationship) perspective

1. The social network. Does the social network help you in EGC?
2. The family relationship and background.
3. The living society and acquaintances' circle.

F. From political perspective

1. Whether it is important to be a CCP member within the state sector.
2. The benefits and reputations that SOE can bring to the employees.

G. The relations between cadres and workers

1. How do you deal with this relationship?
2. Do you maintain a positive relationship with your leader/subordinate?
3. Does your leader have the power to promote/ punish you?
4. Your attitude toward the cadres.

H. The recognition of SOE reform

1. Did you experience the reform of EGC?
2. What do you think is the key reason for the reform?
3. How many times have you experienced the EGC reform?
4. Did you experience some common event/activity/change before the reform? Is there any indication?
5. The year that you think as the main year of the reform.

I. Attitudes towards SOE reforms and the influence

1. How do you think about the reform?
2. Does your work plant/unit have substantial changes after the reform?
3. Does your and your family life have substantial changes after the reform?

Table C.2 The control of Resources

The control of Resources	*Before 1990s*	*After 1990s*
Economic aspect		
Cultural aspect Social aspect Political aspect		

4. The experiences in a period of good income and in a period of low income. Do you think they are caused by the reform? And which reform?
5. The workers' strike and protests stories at EGC.
6. The employment's situation changed due to the reform if applicable.

J. Questions on self-identity

1. What identity do you address yourself as?
2. Do you think you are part of the SOE workers?
3. Do you think you are part of the working class in China?
4. In your work unit, do you recognize the identity difference among your colleagues?
5. Is there any cliques or small groups in your plant/unit?
6. Do you think your occupation position can indicate your identity or do you have other preference?
7. See Table C.2.

K. See Table C.3.

Table C.3 The career choice

	Why did you (not) Chose SOE	*Why did you (not) Chose EGC*	*Why did you (not) Stay*
People who were in non-state sector before working for the EGC			

(continued)

Table C.3 (continued)

	Why did you (not) Chose SOE	*Why did you (not) Chose EGC*	*Why did you (not) Stay*
People entered non-state sector after leaving the EGC			
People who are thinking about leaving the EGC			
People who insist on working at the EGC			

Appendix D: Memos in NVivo

See Table D.1.

Table D.1 Table of Memos in NVivo

Name	*Contents*
Allocating job role	Allocating a job role when the person enters the enterprise. Before the person comes in, he/she has no idea about the exact job role that he/she would take or at which specific unit. Allocation rule exists due to the whole enterprise working as an entity. Each unit reports its demand at the end of this year, and the supervising unit (human and resource department) allocates people to sub-units. It is interesting that an interviewee mentioned if a leader from a sub-unit has a good relationship with the leader from HR, this unit is more likely to get the number of new employees the coming recruiting season. (Because the EGC is suffering from not being able to recruit enough people or because the supervising unit does not approve of getting more employees). The common procedure for allocating a new employee: HR checks the vacancy or demands, and then allocates. In most cases, the HR does not take the person's major into account and the person does not have the right to choose the job role. It is a one-sided decision. In some very rare cases, interviewees have a clear idea about which sub-unit they want to be in/ will be assigned to.

(continued)

S. S. Huang, *The Political Economy of Reforms and the Remaking of the Proletarian Class in China, 1980s–2010s*, Palgrave Studies in Economic History, https://doi.org/10.1007/978-3-031-20455-5

Table D.1 (continued)

Name	*Contents*
Cadre and worker	It is not a surprise to find that there is a gap between cadre and worker, as these two identities from the state sector system. From the worker side, I collected both the clear and unclear opinions towards cadre: 1. Bad impression about unfair treatment. 2. Doubt on the cadres' capabilities as a leader, assume that most of the leaders are using relationship, flattery, sending gifts to obtain the positions. 3. Admit the cadres' capabilities and notice the gap between him/herself with the cadre. ("Don't ask what the enterprise can give to you/ or why you cannot be the leader, ask what you could provide to the enterprise"). 4. Admit part of the cadres are capable but suspicious of the whole cadre group (From the upper manager to the lower manager, a lot of things changed during the conduction). From the cadre side, quite similar ideas: 1. Very busy with daily work not just "read newspaper, drink tea and get paid". 2. Increased difficulties in managing workers. 3. Lack of understanding from workers. 4. High pressure on pay as they need to meet strict position requirement, and sometimes will have to play the leading role to get less welfare and income to help the enterprise that suffers from a hard time as a role model. 5. As the government sector, SOEs also have a ceiling rule about the "age limitation". There are two stereotypes of cadres, there are two stereotypes of workers. Differing from the cadre/leader, *shifu*, is a unique position that SOEs have. *Shifu* belongs to the workers' group, a *shifu* is an experienced worker (within the rank-and-file workers' group) and will not be promoted as a cadre, nor a technician. *Shifu* is even considered to be a job role among the workers and just like "*lao baixing*" (ordinary people). "Workers complain too much" quoted from a manager who was a worker before; he said "everyone has its sorrow, who can image the manager job position is as biter as this."
Enterprise and state	What is the enterprise's action and what is the state's action? There is a grey area in SOE. About what kind of productions to produce, what reform policies to take and what human resources to assign.

(continued)

Table D.1 (continued)

Name	*Contents*
Enterprise strategy	EGC has its logic when experiencing poor/ rich years and the positive/negative strategies share separately commons. For example, during the rich year, the additional welfare to workers were great: 1. More money award (performance-related pay, completion mission allowance). 2. Monthly subsidy for telephone bills. 3. Annual money (which will contribute to higher pension after retiring). 4. Free travel (overseas or national). The whole unit will do that in batches (official employees, expect the contract worker) no matter what the job position is, rank and file workers, leaders, etc. 5. Extra welfare will be awarded to the model of workers: house, awarded trip, and money award. During the poor year, the common strategy would be: 1. Units shut down. 2. Decreased work shifts to save labour cost. 3. Early retirement policy (employees who are 5–10 years younger than the official retirement age, can take the early retirement pay from the SOE until the official retirement age. The government pays for the pension). 4. "Vacation" Policy (employees are in the valid labour contract but rest and get the minimal monthly salary from the SOE). 5. Buyout. In an SOE, the cost of expelling a person is high; in most cases, if the person does not make a serious mistake, the person can continue the labour contract until the retirement age. However, in every reform, a more aggressive method is taken to save the labour cost i.e., buyout. This means SOEs buy the remaining years in the employee's labour contract, depending on the seniority to provide subsidy. In some interviews, the interviewees mentioned the subsidy is 10000 RMB per year in EGC. Once the buyout occurs, the labour contract with the SOE ends, the person's identity is no longer a state sector employee, and it is hard to return to the SOE.

(continued)

Table D.1 (continued)

Name	*Contents*
Family influence	People get influence from their family background. People who grew up in the SOE environment share a label. They used to the "small society" created by the unit and raised up in EGC's "living areas" as "enterprise's children". It is a factor to differ "we" and "the others". Enterprise children, as the interview describe, are "simpler (innocent), don't think too much and work for basic living requirements". The path for people who grow up in the SOE environment is laid out for them: enterprise kindergarten, primary school, middle school, high school, technical school and then enter the SOE, meet your partner and build a family, give birth to a child and then the child will repeat the process. It's a stable circle with low risk if people follow it, but the next 10 or 20 years' life could be told by looking around or learning from the older generation's experience. Also, as an SOE family child people have more advantages when competing with other people who have the same qualifications but from "the outside".
Female in industry	The gender issue in enterprise. What is a relaxing job role for female workers? What is the promotion pathway?
Institute VS people	Does a large institute cause no-profits, or do the huge amount of people causes no-profits? There are two ways to look at reforms. If the inefficiency was caused by the large institute and system, then the reform on system and institute works. If the inefficiency was caused by high labour cost, then the policy to control the total amount number of workers at 6000 (cited from EGC's news) works. From the workers' point of view, they think the institute is the key reason which causes the inefficiency, so the reform on the system cannot be beneficial.
Lies	Big enterprises will experience this problem. The big gap between the upper and the lower classes. The lies and cheatings about productions, resources and working efficiency could become more when it goes higher (managers).

(continued)

Table D.1 (continued)

Name	*Contents*
Power (relation)	The power discussed in the research is about the right people hold. Whether they have the right to decide or not. The roles of different people (professional position identity) that play in the reform. How it works before entering/within/leaving the SOE and across different units. The work unit in EGC, the leader of the work unit has the power to allocate the "money". The leaders can use their power to gain further promotions. Not only the leader but also the employees have their power to make money from their job positions (for example, the support staff has the right to demand a fee if an outsider wants to use their facility, e.g. bathroom). From statements in the interviews, it is a skill for a person to obtain good relationships among workers and leaders, it requires power/resource to get a promotion. "I only take care the part which concerns in my job responsibility".
Reform	Influence on person; Influence on SOE effectiveness; Influence on Unit; Influence on Management system. Who is going to pay for the reform? (Can the state still have the meaning of security to the workers?) Why do all the SOE employees think that the reform is useless?
SOE cost	"The cost of an SOE produce products are relatively higher because of the machines/human resources/management, etc." "Once a machine is made, it will be used for a long-time. This leads to the problem that SOE's production rate cannot catch up with the updates, but it will be a waste of money if the SOE just abandons the originals and invest in creating a new version."
The importance of obtain the Official Employment	Identity affects how many welfares you could obtain within an SOE. The difference between the contract workers and official workers. The different methods to enter the SOE: agency, university fair and relationship can mean different identities. Why people care about the "official employee"?

(continued)

Table D.1 (continued)

Name	*Contents*
The ways to get into the SOE	The main ways to enter the SOE: 1. Family relations. 2. University employment fair. 3. Labour agencies. 4. Or mix methods to get in: combine family relationship with university employment fair. The difficulties to get into different types of SOEs are different. SOE that could obtain good benefits are still attractive and competitive and could ensure employees' a good level welfare and pay because of these enterprises occupy key roles in the industry. While SOEs that have limited benefits lost privileges and experience more negative influence in the market economy.
Year	There are several years that are used as the milestones by the interviews to mark their experiences.
Welfare	Privileges and power affect welfare right. Decreasing can be observed along with the expanding market economy. Also under this theme, it differentiates interviewees into different groups: 1. Good welfare is the key reason why they choose SOE. 2. It is not important when making a career choice. 3. Having the same pay level, SOE's welfare adds advantages. 4. In some cases, welfare is not the very key reason why they choose EGC but combined with "stability" and other characteristics. This also shows the different key considerations of career selection between the older generation and the younger generation. The gap in "welfare" between private sector and state sector is not that significant before the economy reforms; even in some foreign companies or big private companies, the welfare is better than EGC's. However, in most cases, interviewees mentioned that "Public Servant (PS)" is the perfect job. Both the SOEs and Government Department are "within System"—the state sector, but interviewees regard the PS to be a more stable job and think that is the TRUE "iron rice bowl". Some thoughts on this interesting idea: people hold similar perspectives to investigate jobs at government departments today (similarities shared by pre-reformed SOEs). The key characteristics that they are interested in are: a stable job, relatively high pay and easy work. However, the entrance requirements for PS are much stricter than the SOE, e.g., better degree, younger age and PS is quite competitive in current Chinese society. The concerns on SOE's welfare: whether welfare has a big influence on people's job choices and people's attitudes when comparing SOEs with private sector.

(continued)

Table D.1 (continued)

Name	*Contents*
Unit as a society	People within a big SOE will find their units function as a society in their life. The unit takes care of all living support service, social activities and relationships. All these would be happened within the unit scope. It also means that you know very clearly about what happens to your colleagues, inversely, the colleagues know your family situation very clear. The small society is hard to have personal privacy, even about improper sex relationship, corruption and so on. The detailed knowledge about others' life makes the SOE workers as a clique, and has a special enterprise culture, which is also known as "*jiti*" (a big family and communist education concept). The unit also separates EGC employees' life from others who work in the city/country/non-SOE/other SOEs.
Work pressure	Workload saturation. Different positions, units or even attitudes can lead to various evaluations on workload. The pre and after reform could be a good time point to look into people's descriptions on workload.
Workers' concerns	Workers' common concern is about the salary. They are not interested in the reforms or how the changes in the organisation.

Appendix E: Annotations in NVivo

See Table E.1.

Table E.1 Table of Annotations in NVivo

Interview number	*Annotations item*	*Annotations item*
1	5	1. He is from a SOE family and was born in the D city. A local resident. 2. The interviewee's knowledge about their peers, shows the different choices that people make under the same reform influence, the changes of career plan and the different paths for SOE workers. 3. An unique example which is mentioned only by this interviewee. 4. The concept "*si*" (refer to privacy, relationship, see Fei Xiaotong's "*Xiangtu Zhongguo*"); The environment that people are familiar with versus the environment that people think is not "our" living environment. 5. Several female interviewees mentioned this job position is prefect.

(continued)

S. S. Huang, *The Political Economy of Reforms and the Remaking of the Proletarian Class in China, 1980s–2010s*, Palgrave Studies in Economic History, https://doi.org/10.1007/978-3-031-20455-5

Table E.1 (continued)

Interview number	*Annotations item*	*Annotations item*
2	1	Before entering the SOE, workers with family relationships have advantages if competing with their peers.
3	3	1. Annual salary. 2. Have/ not have the feeling of being proud. 3. The requirements about entering the SOE.
4	5	1. Movement and reform. The significance of the movement. The year numbers of EGC reforms. 2. The meaning of an official employment identity. 3. The difference between contract workers and official workers. 4. Selecting SOE is a choice after deep consideration of personal skills, comparison of different sectors, family situation and so on. 5. The community and small society concept.
5	4	1. The uniform is a way to differ cadre and rank-and-file workers. 2. History of the EGC from the establishment to the culture revolution. 3. *Dingti* (Replacement) system that SOE has. 4. Personal education.
6	1	This interviewee has a strong characteristic which is always improving himself. The attitude towards low income and leader is quite differ from the other workers.
7	2	1. History about the working experience during the establishment period of EGC. 2. The history of the interview's working experience as an early-stage workers at this SOE.
8	1	The professional school (which is especially for employees) could be a way to change one's original job position.

(continued)

Table E.1 (continued)

Interview number	*Annotations item*	*Annotations item*
9	5	1. Details on a gossip about the director of the workshop. 2. In this interview, the interviewee mentioned several different tests about how the grades and education could change a person's career and life. 3. The feeling of security. 4. The different working experience since the year 1997 to the year 2014. 5. Life story of the interviewee to reflect the complicated relationship in her unit.
10	1	The updated detailed information on W Company's operation (a sub-company of EGC).
11	0	NA
12	2	1. About the organisation structure and system in EGC. 2. Since 2012, the benefits for employees had started decreasing year after year. However, 2012 was the year when the workers received the most annual salary. So in pre-reform era, he did not think too much about personal development.
13	3	1. The only one who specifically is a private business owner beyond his job role in EGC. 2. The way to enter EGC as a non-graduate and does not have a family relationship for help. 3. About the work pressure and "the work is only for making money".
14	1	The changes of units influenced a person's job; however, most of the workers don't think the reform really brings any benefits.
15	2	1. Interesting comments on the differences between cadres and workers. 2. The gap between different sectors!
16	1	This interviewee took working experience as a key factor to explain why he chose to stay in EGC rather than a private company, regardless of the low income.

(continued)

Table E.1 (continued)

Interview number	*Annotations item*	*Annotations item*
17	3	1. "*lai zai guoqi*" (stay in SOE) is an interesting description. People thought they do not have the skills to find a job in a private enterprise. 2. Xi Jinping raised up the concept: "the national craftsman". Then SOEs put focuses on the workers who have techniques. 3. How the political factor influences on EGC's operation.
18	1	About female workers' welfare in EGC. The maternity policy.
19	3	1. The concept of "*si*" (privacy). 2. In the same SOE, different subcompanies have different benefits. 3. Had been mentioned several times by different interviewees that they regard officials at government departments are better jobs than working in an SOE, though both are state sectors.
20	0	NA
21	1	A common sense on the ideally relaxed jobs for female workers.
22	0	NA
23	1	He was born in 1995. The new generation's idea about employment choice and attitude towards SOEs. The whole picture in different SOEs is almost the same.

Appendix F: Photos Collected from Fieldwork Research

On the left – Photos of EGC factories

On the right- Banners in EGC factories, from top to bottom:

Party Culture and Socialist Core Values- from state, society to citizen level.

Roll up your sleeves and work hard, happiness is a struggle.

Fight the heat, be brave and work hard in the Third Quarter.

S. S. Huang, *The Political Economy of Reforms and the Remaking of the Proletarian Class in China, 1980s–2010s*, Palgrave Studies in Economic History, https://doi.org/10.1007/978-3-031-20455-5

Photos of some office buildings in EGC for management and technicians.

Data Source The author's original work.

Index

S. S. Huang, *The Political Economy of Reforms and the Remaking of the Proletarian Class in China, 1980s–2010s*, Palgrave Studies in Economic History, https://doi.org/10.1007/978-3-031-20455-5

Kolibri 360 GmbH
Ferdinand-Jühlke-Straße 7
99095 Erfurt, Deutschland
produktsicherheit@kolibri360.de